KEEPING THE
BARBARIANS AT BAY

KEEPING THE BARBARIANS AT BAY

THE LAST YEARS OF KENNETH ALLSOP

GREEN PIONEER

DAVID WILKINSON

SIGNAL BOOKS

OXFORD

First published in 2013 by
Signal Books Limited
36 Minster Road
Oxford OX4 1LY
www.signalbooks.co.uk

A catalogue record for this book is available from the British Library

ISBN 978-1-908493-84-2 Paper

Cover Design: Tora Kelly
Typesetting: Tora Kelly
Cover Images: © Colin Varndell; Courtesy Allsop Estate
Printed in India

CONTENTS

FOREWORD
By Richard Mabey

KENNETH ALLSOP WAS POLYMATHIC as a communicator: jazz commentator, novelist, dinner-party wit, distinguished television journalist, crusading environmental elder. But it was as a literary critic that I first came across him, when I was a student in the 1960s. His book, *The Angry Decade*, was a waspish, acute appraisal of the cultural revolt of Britain's young writers in the 1950s, and marked out the contours - if not the future content - of his own idiosyncratic radicalism.

When, a few years later he began using the same sharp, sceptical, and often luminously original language in writings about nature and the countryside, it was, for me, a kind of revelation, a recognisable greeting from the wilderness. I was struggling to find my own voice as a nature writer, and coming (as Ken had) from a suburban middle-class background, found no resonance whatever with the mannered, proprietorial, conservative, 'way we do things here' school of contemporary country writing. Ken's deeply personal prose-style seemed to have been melded out of staccato US contemporary fiction and Thomas Hardy lyricism, and his attitude to nature and land inspired by the Diggers more than *Country Life*. Here at last was a modern country writer, ecologically literate, politically fearless, and speaking to the growing constituency of urban nature lovers. His remarkable 1969 essay for *The Sunday Times* on the wildlife of London challenged every cosy preconception about what nature 'needs' and who it 'belonged' to.

I was working as an editor for Penguin Books education division at the time, and asked him to contribute a 'topic book' on nature conservation and land-use for secondary school leavers. It wasn't an entirely professional invitation. As an apprentice writer I was in thrall to this urbane cultural hero, at that time one of the best-known faces on television, and wanted to touch his hem.

He agreed. The short book, *Fit to Live In? The Future of Britain's Countryside* (the only title he was ever to publish on conservation), came out in 1970, and we became friends, of a kind. Two years later, when my own first book *Food for Free* was published, Ken returned the compliment, and wrote a feature on the book for *The Sunday Times*. I was treated to a weekend at the idyllic mill-house he had recently moved to in West Dorset, an area of England he loved above all others, and which he hoped might balance some of his compulsive metropolitan edginess. We took a long walk over the great whaleback of Eggardon Hill, the *axis mundi* of his personal landscape. It was a journey I shall never forget, because it made me aware of the full extent of Ken's *pain*, not just the visibly physical, jaw-tightening ache of his stump as he climbed the strip-lynchets (he had had an artificial leg fitted after a war-time amputation) but the extent to which it also embraced the travails of the landscape itself, as if he and they were part of the same body. Not long before, he had learned of the Forestry Commission's plans to destroy the core of the ancient oak forest of Powerstock Common, which lay below Eggardon; and of Berkley Petroleums' closet prospecting for oil in the region, supposedly protected as an Area of Outstanding Natural Beauty. These two developments represented not just an attack on what was now his home country, but seemed to Ken symbolic of the erosion of all that was sacred about rural England, and they turned him from a passionate naturalist into a crusading environmentalist.

The story of his battles over the next three years, before his death in 1973, is the subject of David Wilkinson's revelatory book. It is both inspiring and shaming. For all our world-weariness and cynicism about modern political sleaze, it is somehow especially shocking to see it alive and malignant forty years ago: the corporate lobbying, the biddable councillors, the suppression of information, the contempt for community feeling. Ken, in the face of this, became a force of nature. For three years he turned his incandescent anger and immense powers of rhetoric into what in the end was a kind of kamikaze attack on all environmental wreckers.

Some of what he did is hard to credit. Imagine a major front-man in BBC current affairs today, at the climax of the now legendary mock funeral for West Dorset, standing on the tor of Welcome Hill like a modern King Arthur and, watched by millions of television viewers, castigate an entire cast of planners, placemen and corporate wheeler-dealers: 'what is happening here is a warning of what the next ten years could bring throughout Britain...' Or the few glorious weeks in which he was able to turn his new environmental magazine programme, *Down to Earth*, into what was in essence an on-air pressure group. The programme lambasted agribusiness, industrial polluters, government connivance and complacency. Astonishingly it got away with it for a while. The turning point came when the programme's special award for 'environmental idiocy' - the Plastic Banana - was given to Peter Walker, Secretary of State for the Environment, for the creation of Spaghetti Junction. The BBC's management were outraged. The programme had broken the Corporation's rules about impartiality. Allsop was additionally reprimanded for taking part in televised protests in Dorset. *Down to Earth* was emasculated, then taken off the air, and in the higher echelons of the BBC Ken became increasingly regarded as a loose cannon.

For a while he was able to channel his fury in a column in *The Sunday Times*, where there was no requirement for impartiality. Again he made frontal assaults on the new 'barbarians'. His tract - there is no other word for it - on the activities and questionable ethics of the mining giant Rio Tinto Zinc in December 1972 is widely regarded as one of the most powerful and eloquent environmental polemics of the post-war years. But RTZ sent in their lawyers, and after months of wrangling, *The Sunday Times* issued an apology. Then they began to censor Ken's pieces.

Allsop, 53 years old and a depressive by nature, was now facing a double despair, experiencing not only the destruction of all he loved but the silencing of his public responses. At the end of May 1973, he was due to face, on two successive days, interviews with the deputy editor of *The Sunday Times* and the Controller of BBC2. He was convinced that he was about to be sacked by both institutions, and on 23 May, in an untypically calm mood, he took his own life.

Ken's story was heroic, but also tragic, because of the inevitable failure of his crusades. Diplomacy was a process entirely foreign to his temperament. It is tantalising to ponder on what he might have achieved, with his charisma and extraordinary rhetorical power, if he had been prepared to compromise, or perhaps retire to Oxford (he loved his brief Fellowship at Merton College) and write the big book on the environmental crisis he had often dreamed of. But such moderated engagements with the world were simply not his style. It would be easy but insulting to make a clinical rationalisation for his sheer bloody intransigence: focusing one's despair on external 'enemies' is a well-known survival tactic for depressives. Ken simply did not believe in compromise, which he saw as part of the reason for the degradation of nature he saw all about him.

But he left two great legacies. Many, like me, discovered in his unique prose voice a celebration of the energy and resilience of *wild* nature, and of a new *terroir* beyond the tidy, sanitised world of agribusiness. And, for the brief time he blazed comet-like across the sky, as the most high-profile campaigner in Britain, he helped energise the nascent environmental movement, into a state where it began to be able to make the difference Ken was not able to achieve by himself.

ACKNOWLEDGEMENTS

MANY PEOPLE AND VARIOUS sources of information have together made possible the publication of this book, but two of them require special mention. The first is the archive of Kenneth Allsop's papers - a comprehensive and amazingly well-ordered collection of his diaries, letters and memoranda; the drafts of his books and short stories; his scripts and newspaper articles, press cuttings and photographs. The second is Kenneth's eldest son, Tristan, who has allowed me unrestricted access to this cornucopia. Without his generosity, enthusiasm and practical help the book would not have turned out as it has. My thanks, too, to him and his wife Rosie for the hospitality and friendship extended to me and my wife on our visits to Dorset.

I am grateful to several of Kenneth Allsop's friends, colleagues and admirers for sharing their memories of him, and of what Britain's environment movement was like in the early 1970s. They include Richard Mabey, Sue Clifford, Angela King, Brian Jackman, Tom Burke, Ann Hudson and Dr Roger Highfield. Particular thanks are due to David Baldock, Director of the Institute for European Environmental Policy, for putting me in touch with his former colleagues at Friends of the Earth. And a special mention is due to Ian Breach, Allsop's colleague on *Edition* and the BBC's former Environment Correspondent. His colourful stories of life at the BBC in the early 1970s were recounted with humour and enthusiasm - but sadly he died before the book was completed.

I should like to thank the staff of the Bodleian Library, Oxford, and especially the Vere Harmsworth Library; the Bursar and Fellows of Merton College, Oxford; the British Newspaper Library, Colindale; the BBC Written Archives, Caversham; and the Dorset History Centre in Dorchester.

Several people gave their time to read a number of chapters in draft, including Tristan Allsop, Sue Clifford, Kathryn Wilkinson, and Dr Sarah Burton. I am very grateful for their comments, factual and editorial corrections, and above all their encouragement. However, the opinions expressed in the book, and any errors, remain my responsibility alone.

Finally, I should like to thank my wife Kathryn for her continued support and good humour (most of the time), despite being obliged to share with 'Ken' what should have been the leisurely first two years of my retirement.

INTRODUCTION

THREE DAYS IN THE LIFE OF KENNETH ALLSOP

These days you have to pay attention to Nova.

Nova was one of the many publications to which Allsop contributed. As 'the intelligent woman's pin-up', his monthly personal column proved a big attraction for its female readers. (Author's collection)

Thursday 6 April 1972

The bright Easter sunshine sparkled off the burnished paintwork of the sleek Jaguar parked in the station car park. The top-of-the-range, 4.2 litre E-Type coupé, finished in British racing green, contrasted starkly with the run-down dinginess of Bridport's railway station, condemned ten years earlier by Dr Beeching, and now forlornly awaiting the fall of the axe.

Most passers-by would have recognised the figure seated at the wheel, not just from his nightly television appearances on the BBC's *24 Hours* news programme, but also as the irascible local environmental campaigner who had rallied opposition to plans to drill for oil and gas in the surrounding West Dorset hills. His straight, steel-grey hair and sideburns of fashionable length made him look younger than his 52 years. One poll had voted him the fifth most handsome man in the world.

He glanced at the clock on the Jaguar's dashboard. 12.15 pm - five minutes to go before he was due to meet Simon Millar from the London train. Simon was a young New Zealander, a geologist from the embryonic pressure group Friends of the Earth, launched in Britain only eighteen months before. It was already in the headlines for dumping lorry-loads of non-returnable bottles outside Schweppes' London headquarters, and for challenging the multinational giant, Rio Tinto Zinc, over the legality of its mining operations in Snowdonia National Park. FoE's 25- year-old Executive Director, Graham Searle, was due to arrive separately by car from a holiday on the Scilly Isles.

Allsop knew he needed their help. While he waited, he leafed through the agenda of the meeting they were to attend together that evening. As President and founder member of the Defenders of West Dorset (DWD), he had called a meeting at his nearby mill house to decide tactics for opposing the Canadian oil company's planning application for exploratory drilling.

Allsop walked across the platform as Simon Millar got down from the train. Simon noticed that his host had a slight limp. He was to find out later what few television viewers appreciated: that Allsop had an artificial right leg, fitted after a training accident during his wartime RAF service. Simon observed that the brake and clutch pedals on the E-Type could both be operated by his left foot only, and that the accelerator had an extra strong spring to support the dead weight of a tin leg. He wondered whether it was this that contributed to the speed with which Allsop accelerated out of the car park.

They soon exchanged the slightly shabby Georgian streets of Bridport for the beautiful, sunlit, crumpled landscape of West Dorset - formally designated by the government as an Area of Outstanding Natural Beauty.

2

As they were leaving the town, a blue Triumph Spitfire sports car appeared in the rear view mirror. 'It's Graham!' Simon shouted. Good timing. Allsop's plan was to give both his guests a conducted tour of the proposed drilling site on Welcome Hill, and the downs and hidden coombes surrounding it.

They turned off the main Dorchester road towards Spyway and climbed 800 feet to the Iron Age hill fort on Eggardon Hill. The panorama from the summit took in the sparkle of Lyme Bay to the south; the ancient scrub oak woodland of Powerstock Common to the north; and to the west, the folded hills, valleys and hidden lanes of the landscape around Allsop's own home in West Milton. 'There is nowhere like it,' he had explained a few months earlier to readers of his Saturday *Daily Mail* column 'In the Country':

> This one hundred square miles bounded on one side by the Great Heath - Hardy's 'haggard waste of Egdon' - and on the other by the Great Marsh. Crushed between are terminating rock seams from east and north, colliding in a mad pile-up. There is a tumbled anarchy of hills, contracted Pyrenees: long hogbacks of chalk, sheer limestone scarps, billows of down, knaps and knolls and batches, and high conelets of sandstone like emerald plum puddings... Old green-roads and droveways and tangled tracks wind into mysterious furzy coombs where on a summer afternoon you hear nothing but the bees and the wail of a soaring buzzard, and in winter perhaps the bubbling trill of curlews flighting down to the estuary saltings.

His guests couldn't fail to be impressed. They descended the steep rutted track to Powerstock for a lunch of cheese and Palmer's bitter in The Three Horseshoes, then proceeded in convoy to Welcome Hill so that Graham and Simon could see for themselves the geological, engineering and planning questions the oil company needed to answer. Half a mile further on, they stopped below Bell Hill at an old bakery to watch four buzzards thermalling over the down. At a nearby ruined kiln (a favourite birdwatching spot), Allsop noted that 'on cue the barn owl wafted out of the shed, blearily swerving and yawing in the sun across the hedges, almost as if being blown like a dandelion clock.'

Searle smiled. 'I'm afraid it doesn't beat the Snowy Owl I saw on the Scillies last week.' Highly unlikely though this was, Allsop was prepared to believe him.

He then led the way along the narrow lane alongside Round Knoll to his home at Milton Mill. They came across it suddenly, for the seventeenth-century Mill - with its eight acres and an adjoining cottage - was completely enfolded by the surrounding hills and invisible from the public road. It was exactly two years since he and his wife Betty had moved in.

After settling into the cottage, the FoE visitors joined Allsop, Betty and leading DWD committee members for an early supper, before the rest of the committee arrived. Top of the agenda was to ensure that the Defenders were properly represented at the forthcoming Welcome Hill site visit, and the subsequent public meeting in Beaminster Town Hall. The President of Berkley Petroleums (UK), Mr Lawton Clark, had felt obliged to fly in from Canada to answer the local and national press campaign that Allsop and the DWD had orchestrated against his company. It was agreed that Graham Searle should be their expert witness.

Discussion then turned to the list of the many eminent public figures who had expressed support for their cause. Allsop pointed out that they ranged from the Archbishop of Canterbury to Count Dracula (in the forms, respectively, of Michael Ramsay and Christopher Lee).

Friday 7 April 1972

Allsop's friends had departed for London before the telephone call came from the Dorset County Planning Officer, Mr Alan Swindall. He and the Chair of the Planning Committee had decided that the Defenders should be excluded from the Welcome Hill meeting. After all, said Swindall, this was a meeting intended for local councillors and oil company representatives only, and if the DWD was to be invited, then all other local and national pressure groups would have to attend too.

Allsop put down the phone. The call was enough to tip him over the precipice into one of his periodic, black depressions. For the rest of the day, his frozen misery prevented him from attacking the long list of work tasks he had set himself. Everything was 'in slow motion like a cranked-down camera, with a circumference of deep shadow all around me,' he wrote in his diary. He couldn't fight through the sense of deep despair that everything he valued was vanishing, and 'the forces that want to drive drills into Eggardon, and the forces which acquiesce, are unconquerable.'

That evening he was due to be in Southampton at 8.30 pm to record an interview for a forthcoming TV series, *Conversations*. His guest was Professor Asa Briggs, Vice-Chancellor of the new University of Sussex, and a distinguished social and media historian. Like many of his journalist colleagues, Allsop had never attended university as a student, but still he and Briggs had much in common. They were both Yorkshiremen, of a similar age, with a mutual commitment to broadcasting. And three years before, Allsop had enjoyed a term in Oxford as a visiting research fellow, and had recently completed a stint as Rector of Edinburgh University, championing the interests of the students.

His mental incapacitation meant that it was late in the day before he began to revise the script, and it was 7.20 pm before he eventually set off on the seventy-mile journey to the studio. There followed a 'terrible nightmare drive through the raining blackness', with the E-type touching 90 mph along the ill-lit single carriageways. In the event, he was just half an hour late, but afterwards everyone seemed pleased with the way the talk went.

His day was not finished yet. Having to be in London early the next morning, he set off from Southampton at high speed northwards up the A30. By the time he reached Staines, he had almost run out of petrol, and after a frantic search for a late night garage, it was 1.00 am before he arrived at the Kensington flat. Betty and their eldest son Tristan had been waiting for some hours, and had already eaten dinner. 'I had no food,' he wrote, disconsolately.

Saturday 8 April 1972

A day out at the Grand National lifted Allsop's spirits. His 'very enjoyable, peculiar day' was hosted by Geoffrey Keating, the head of public relations for British Petroleum (BP). He had hired an entire train for a party of journalists and politicians to go from London to the Grand National at Aintree, in the belief that the company's lavish entertainment would boost the image of the oil industry amongst key opinion formers. Predictably, Allsop's invitation came just a week after the BBC had announced that he was shortly to leave *24 Hours* to host Britain's first-ever TV environmentalist series, *Down to Earth*.

The mobile party started promptly at 9.00 am with champagne, and never stopped all day. The eminent guest list included such BBC household names as Alan Whicker (Allsop's former colleague on *Tonight*); Peter Dimmock (former head of BBC outside broadcasts and now head of BBC Enterprises); his wife Polly Elwes (former BBC announcer and *Tonight* journalist); Australian actor Ray Barrett (from the oil-industry TV series *The Troubleshooters*); and Christopher Tugenhadt (a Tory MP and a future European Commissioner).

Allsop was the target of some smoothly expert lobbying by his hosts. 'The BP people were an extremely pleasant and agreeable crowd of brain-washers,' he recorded. But in a neat reversal of roles, he buttonholed two BP executives and suggested they should do something about the 'shabby eyesore' of their oil rig at Kimmeridge Bay in Dorset - much vaunted as an environmental success story, but probably never actually seen by the executives themselves.

The train reached Liverpool in good time for the start of the National - Allsop's first race meeting. But to him, 'the brief spasm of spangled excitement seemed disproportionately brief for the elaborate organisation and preparation'. The race was won by Well to Do, one of only nine of the 42 entries that managed to cross the finishing line. Even so, Betty won money on the runners-up. 'The name of mine was never uttered,' he remarked ruefully, revealing without a hint of irony (which was unusual for him) that his horse was called L'Escargot (the Snail).

Back in London, the train pulled into Euston at 10.00 pm, and with others Allsop and Betty were chauffeured back to Alan Whicker's Regent's Park 'palace'. At his flat the following morning Allsop got up late and drank tomato juice to relieve his throbbing hangover.

1

THE MAN

A frank 1968 interview with nature writer Henry Williamson, Allsop's 'personal *Maharishi*' during his teens. Subsequently, Williamson's fascist sympathies made theirs a rocky friendship. (Courtesy BBC)

THE YEAR 2013 MARKS the fortieth anniversary of Kenneth Allsop's death, but most people in Britain over the age of 55 still remember him. For twelve years from 1960 to 1972 he appeared almost nightly on BBC television, making more than two thousand appearances, first as a reporter on *Tonight*, and then as an anchorman on the late night news programme *24 Hours*. He became one of Britain's first 'television personalities'.

He was fastidious in his use of English, sharply witty and polite - but with a keen nose for the bogus and a quick ear for cant. For many viewers, particularly women, his celebrity status probably owed as much to his physical appearance as to his interviewing style. As he neared fifty, he grew his straight, iron grey hair and sideburns, for a time sported a Zapata moustache and started a trend in the Corporation with his striped American button-down shirts and bright kipper ties. The magazine *TV Times* shortlisted him for an award as 'best dressed TV man'. The Oxford magazine *Isis* in 1968 conducted a poll in which he was voted the world's fifth most handsome man, beating Omar Sharif, Paul Newman and Tony Curtis. When asked if he was disappointed at only coming fifth, he replied sardonically that he was more than satisfied to be at the same level that Brigitte Bardot had attained in the women's poll.

Allsop enjoyed the London high life of expensive restaurants, celebrity parties and cool jazz; in his *Who's Who* entry he listed his club as Ronnie Scott's. He also loved fast cars, especially Jaguars - an XK 140 followed by an XK 150 and then two E-types, with just a brief flirtation with an Aston Martin DB5. But the E-type was his favourite, described by one motoring journalist as that 'slinky 150 mph vision of the future: instantly you were a Lothario, you were a film star. You were so glamorous, you ached.'[1]

But despite the trappings, he hated being pigeonholed as a 'personality'. In a letter to *The Times*, he wondered why it was only television that should produce 'personalities', and not other professions. 'Could it not, with equal relevance be used in, say, a "House of Commons personality" (an MP); a "pulpit personality" (the Archbishop of Canterbury); or Chi Chi the panda as "the zoo animality"?'[2] The answer of course was that from the mid-1950s growing television ownership had brought the faces and voices of a small band of presenters and performers into the living rooms of most of the nation, so that they became part of everybody's family. And for him, there was a positive aspect to his celebrity status. This was the influence it gave him, both through access to government ministers, captains of industry or cultural icons, and the platforms he was given to reach out to millions of people across the nation.

Allsop's main objection to the term, however, was that it obscured and devalued other areas of his life and work that he considered to be more substantial. For example, on radio in the 1950s and 1960s he presented serious programmes on books, jazz and wildlife. A random selection of his interviewees would include Robert Graves, Julian Huxley, Raymond Chandler, Norman Mailer, Tennessee Williams, Evelyn Waugh, the Duke of Edinburgh and John Lennon.

As a freelance newspaper journalist for over 25 years he contributed either as a reporter, feature writer or columnist to *The Sunday Express*, *Picture Post*, the *Evening Standard*, *Nova*, the *Daily Mail* and *The Sunday Times*, as well as heavyweight periodicals like the *Spectator*, *Encounter* and *The Listener*. In 1965 he calculated that he had interviewed a thousand people; reviewed two thousand books; visited forty-odd countries, several of them many times; and written (apart from books) a million-and-a-half words - almost twice as many as in the Bible. 'Let me speedily add that I bring in the Bible merely as an instant picture of bulk,' he wrote, 'not from any illusions of comparative holiness.'[3] His reputation as a highly respected critic among the *literati* was such that he was frequently invited to chair the prestigious Foyles Literary Luncheons.

But he was happiest when he was writing. He told Michael Parkinson on the BBC's *Parkinson* show that what gave him most satisfaction was 'crouching in solitude late at night over a typewriter putting words down. This is where the greatest satisfaction is. Writing is a misery, a solitary occupation. It's not a pleasurable thing to do, but I like producing things from myself, particularly images, and trying to illuminate things that have struck me...'[4]

He was the author of fourteen books and several more unpublished novels, short stories and snatches of autobiography. In his teens and twenties he aspired to be a novelist, and his first published novel *Adventure Lit Their Star* was awarded the John Llewellyn Rhys Memorial Prize for the best work of literature by a young British or Commonwealth author. The book described the struggle of a bird new to Britain - the little ringed plover - to establish itself as a breeding species in the post-war edgelands of west London.[5] But this early flash of success was not repeated, and in later life he accepted that it was better to stick with the facts rather than fiction.

According to the nature writer Richard Mabey, Allsop's writing showed 'an eclectic mixing of styles, that unique brew of Romanticism, condensed journalese, scientific argot and Raymond Chandler that was to become his trademark.'[6] 'His virtuosity as a wordsmith was always an inspiration,' his friend and colleague Brian Jackman recalled. 'I loved the freshness of his metaphors and the way his copy fizzed with adjectives.'[7] Some critics, however, thought he overdid it, with one of his former editors encouraging him to 'go easy with the Roget's'.

Allsop also wrote a detailed diary continuously from the age of 14, filling a foolscap page late each night with meticulous details of meetings and conversations, the clothes and records he had bought, the birds he had seen and the weather he had enjoyed or (more often) endured. This was in addition to long memos he would write for himself organising the research and interviews in preparation for forthcoming major newspaper articles.

Alongside writing, his major passion was the natural world - especially birds - and most of his early contributions to BBC radio and several of his books concerned aspects of Britain's wildlife and man's relationship with it. *Adventure Lit Their Star* was partly autobiographical, for it was Allsop himself who on 31 May 1947 had first discovered the nest and eggs of the rare visitor. He was a founder member of the Middle Thames Natural History Society and was considered a sufficiently accomplished ornithologist to be a principal contributor to the authoritative *Report of the Oxford Ornithological Society* for 1947. Through the Society, he successfully persuaded Slough Borough Council to designate as a bird sanctuary Slough sewage farm and the surrounding farmland. This helped put a stop to trespassing youths killing and maiming birds with shotguns and slings, and robbing their nests.[8]

Allsop's introduction to wildlife during his boyhood came from these same outskirts of London, 'the messy limbo that is neither town nor country, where suburban buildings, factories, petrol stations and trunk roads sprawl and blight.'[9] He was actually born in Yorkshire in 1920, the only child of parents John and Mary. He was still a small baby when his father's work dictated a move south to Hounslow. His father was a chartered surveyor who worked on the Co-operative Society's housing developments, later becoming a self-employed property developer.

So for most of his childhood, young Kenneth lived with his parents in a newly-built detached house fronting the recently-constructed Great West Road. It was an area of new light industries, airfields and gravel pits gouged from the landscape to feed the building industry in a rapidly expanding London. But nearby Osterley Park - not yet scythed through by the M4 - was his green oasis. Many years later, he recalled: 'Some of the most magical memories of boyhood are centred around a particular lake where I (illicitly) swam, and searched the reed beds for reed warblers', great crested grebes' and dabchicks' nests, and where I saw two otters one winter's night - all within ten miles of London.'

He was only technically a Yorkshireman, and had no hint of a Yorkshire accent. Indeed, as an adult he spoke with perfect 'received' pronunciation, indistinguishable from that of BBC colleagues like Robin Day or Ludovic Kennedy - although his upbringing was far more modest than theirs. Even so, his parents could afford to send him, from the age of six, to a local preparatory school, and then as a fourteen-year-old to Pitman's Private School, where he excelled at English and performed competently at the inevitable Pitman's shorthand.

As an only child, the young Allsop often had to make his own entertainment, and reading - particularly nature books - became a favourite pastime. He would spend hours in the public libraries of Hounslow and Ealing, devouring the works of naturalists like Richard Jefferies, W. H. Hudson, Gilbert White and especially Henry Williamson, best known for his 1927 children's novel *Tarka the Otter*. But it was another of Williamson's books, *The Lone Swallows*, that had the greatest impact on him. He recalled being overcome by 'a cloud of wonder that that there was actually another person living who felt as I did about birds and the countryside, and who could express in words the agonising, poignant, inexplicable yearnings I felt.' Determined to meet his hero, Allsop wrote to Williamson asking if he might visit him at his home in north Devon. He received no reply, so during his summer holidays in 1935 Allsop cycled the 200 miles, alone, all the way to Williamson's long, low thatched house at Shallowford, near South Molton. On arrival he had to be satisfied with a guided tour of the estate by Williamson's nine-year-old son 'Windles', and on this occasion was not able to speak to Henry personally. But this was just the beginning of an up-and-down relationship with the author that was to last a lifetime.

In later life, Allsop maintained that he had wanted to be a journalist from the age of twelve. His parents would have preferred a more stable and secure occupation like bookkeeping or publishing, but, after 25 fruitless applications to newspapers around the south-east, in 1937, at the age of seventeen, Allsop secured a part-time position on the *Slough Observer*, the largest circulation weekly newspaper in Middlesex. For a fee of twelve shillings and sixpence (63p), he was to write a Friday column, 'Country Log', of 250 words on local birds and the countryside. In the following year, he was promoted and given a full-time job and a salary increase as a junior reporter. His pieces stuck largely to the traditional country column formula, with descriptions of the 'Fullness of Summer', 'Summer Nights' and 'A Nesting Expedition'. It was not yet the time nor the place for environmentalist articles, although hints of what was to come were revealed in a piece he wrote when he was nineteen, entitled 'Is there a good reason for hunting wild animals?' He wrote: 'I have met a number of hunting people: the typical male has, probably, plenty of room to spare in his head, for his brains do not occupy much space; the female has, in all likelihood, a packet of nails where her heart should be.'

Throughout his journalistic career he believed in 'spilling the beans, not selling the beans.'[10] Politically, he veered towards the left but had no firm party affiliation, partly because the environment was an issue that cut across the left-right divide, and partly because in those pre-Thatcher years the centrist post-war consensus muted party differences. He felt quite detached about the Conservative victory in the June 1970 general election. 'Main emotions: some pleasure that Wilson won't inflate euphonically even more, also interest in seeing just what the Tories will do.' Two years later he was equally sceptical about the new environmentalist Movement for Survival launched by Edward Goldsmith, the millionaire proprietor of *The Ecologist* magazine, and by the eccentric casino and zoo owner John Aspinall. Both held sinister right-wing views alongside their greenery. The Movement was the precursor of the People Party (later the Ecology, and then the Green, Party). Allsop's early scepticism about the philosophical and organisational underpinnings of the People Party was to be vindicated when in the February 1974 general election it managed to contest only six seats and attract just 4,500 votes.

He was not a 'joiner'. 'That's what I've always felt to be, on the edge, but preferring it there to the safe centre,' he wrote later. 'After all, it's a better observation point than being part of that mass in the middle - precarious, but where you can hold on to some identity.'

He had a deep suspicion of the intentions and competence of all governments and big business, and the bureaucracies which served them. This even included established environmental organisations - as witnessed by the portrait in his 1958 novel *Rare Bird* of Bartlett Brown, the arrogant, self-serving Director of SCAB, the Society for the Co-ordination of Animals and Birds.[11] If the concept of an Anarchist Party had not been a logical impossibility, he might just have joined it.

Like most newspaper journalists of his generation, he did not go to university, despite having the undoubted intelligence and ability to do so. He always regretted this, and took a vicarious pleasure in the success of his two eldest children, Tristan and Amanda, in gaining places during the mid-1960s at the Universities of Kent and East Anglia respectively. (Fabian, his youngest son, attended art college some time later). Allsop had a great respect for learning and academic attainment, and was delighted when he was offered a Visiting Research Fellowship at Merton College in Oxford for the summer term of 1969. He was actually entitled to stay at Merton for a full three years, and sometimes toyed with the possibility of becoming a visiting professor in an American university, but the need to earn the money to support his expensive lifestyle drove him from the quadrangles back to the corridors of the BBC. The previous year he had been elected to the part-time post of Rector of Edinburgh University, and during his three-year term of office championed student demands for greater participation in University affairs. He worked alongside the President of the Students Union, the 22-year-old Gordon Brown, who was to succeed Allsop as Rector in 1972, and then move on to greater things.

Allsop's early career as a journalist was interrupted after only eighteen months when in 1940 he was called up for national service in the Royal Air Force. He was to return briefly to the *Slough Observer* after the war - but by then two major events had changed his life completely.

When Allsop eventually became a regular television presenter in the 1960s, few viewers realised that the sedentary, head-and-shoulders picture of him on their screens concealed the fact that, lower down and out of shot, he had an artificial leg. It had been amputated in July 1945 above the right knee as a result of a condition called sarcoidosis, a form of tuberculosis which had flared up following what at the time appeared to be a minor injury sustained in 1943 during an RAF assault course. For two years during the war he was in constant pain and confined to various military hospitals. After ten separate operations, he insisted that the offending limb should be removed. This, however, did not get rid of the pain, which in one form or another he had to endure for the rest of his life.

In 1968 in a personal column in the *Spectator*, Allsop explained what this had meant.

> Since I was twenty-three, on morphia and the danger list with a smashed and gangrenous knee, I don't think there has been a waking hour when I have not consciously been in discomfort at best, or agony at worst. This derives from wearing an artificial leg.
>
> First, there were two years of futile attempts, including ten operations, to get the knee joint repaired, followed by amputation, after which came nine months on crutches... Then I received my grotesquely ill-matched tin leg. For years I hobbled and clanked about on this, while the socket, loose as a curtain ring, produced a ridge of abscessed callouses... One inwardly sweated and outwardly smiled - the corny requirement of putting as good a face as possible on it while performing one's active journalistic life.
>
> Then there are the nerve pains. This is the famous 'invisible limb' phenomenon, the vibrations running the length of where the leg was. This can be no more disturbing than mild tremors extending like inflamed antennae from the end of the stump. Or it can flare into attacks of horrible violence, when electric shocks stab through the stump as if live, high-voltage wires were being jabbed at the tip in some esoteric Bond-ish torture, neuralgic spasms that convulse the body and stretch one's sanity like a fraying rubber-band...[12]

Apart from the pain, and the consequent inability to enjoy periods of quiet, peaceful contemplation, the most obvious consequence of losing a leg was to put an end to the day-long walks and cycle rides in the countryside that he had so enjoyed in his teens and early twenties. But it had an important psychological effect also:

> Possibly to offset both the physical limitations and the personal knowledge of how much effort and ingenuity are needed to negotiate such routine tasks as climbing stairs, enduring long walks and standing half-drunk at cocktail parties, one drives oneself so much harder, and makes unwise and unreasonable demands on the remaining portions of one's body - with other consequences and pain of a different kind, in a different place: at least life brings variety.

As if all this wasn't enough, in his late forties a major kidney complaint associated with the tuberculosis kept him in hospital for a month, and thereafter flared up from time to time. 'I have always seen myself as a fit and energetic person,' he wrote subsequently, 'quite tough and strong, capable of enjoying and surviving both the killing rigours of Fleet Street pubs and the axe-swinging and spade bashing of country weekends. Yet recently it was reluctantly borne upon me that really I have never enjoyed good health during all my adult life...'[13] Not least because these physical frailties tended to compound episodes of deep depression that frequently laid him low.

In a bid to manage the pain, throughout his adult life he took a cocktail of drugs, which were often washed down with large quantities of whisky. Before going on air to present an episode of *24 Hours*, he would drink precisely two-and-one-third glasses of whisky and water - any more, and he couldn't perform, and any less, he couldn't control his nerves. The combination of drink and drugs probably contributed to his impatience and outbursts of temper, and almost certainly to feelings of indisposition the morning after.

The second major event during the war - and one that helped him to cope with the first - was Allsop's marriage to his wife Betty. He first met Betty Creak on New Year's Eve 1941 at an RAF dance in High Wycombe, and ten weeks later they were married. She was small, dark- haired, well-organised, attractive and a socialist - a combination which Allsop couldn't resist. In 1943 Betty became an agent for the recently-formed Common Wealth Party, which preached common ownership of wealth and a moral re-birth of British politics based on co-operation rather than greed and competition. Its leader, Sir Richard Acland, practised what he preached when during the war he gave the thousands of acres of his two estates in Devon and Somerset to the nation, via the National Trust. His party opposed the wartime truce between Labour and Conservatives and won a number of by-elections, but was eclipsed by the Labour landslide in 1945.

It was Betty's moral and practical support that got Allsop through his two years in hospital, the amputation of his leg and the dark, post-war days of convalescence and poverty. She looked after the cooking, cleaning, household finances and later the children's upbringing, and like most women of her generation put her own interests second. Later in her husband's career, she provided secretarial and practical back-up to the campaign against drilling for oil in Dorset while he was away working in London or abroad.

During the 1960s and 1970s at the BBC there was a culture of sexism and sexual exploitation that many television 'personalities' took advantage of, and, as the fifth most handsome man in the world, Allsop was no exception. Betty was aware of, and hurt by, the one-night stands and the more serious affairs, but reluctantly felt she had to put up with them. Looking back, she revealed that there was only one occasion when he left her, 'but he was back later that day, home by six in the evening. Somehow he always saw a reason why we shouldn't split up at that particular moment. It was not an easy marriage, but life was never dull.'[14]

It became even less dull when in April 1970 Kenneth and Betty at last left the orbit of London and moved into a seventeenth-century water mill in West Dorset.

✳

1. Quentin Wilson on BBC Radio 4 *Today*, 8 October 2012
2. *The Times*, 21 November 1968, p.11
3. Allsop, K., *Scan*, Hodder & Stoughton, 1965, p.5
4. *Parkinson*, BBC1, 21 October 1972
5. Allsop, K., *Adventure Lit Their Star*, Latimer House, 1949
6. Allsop, K., *One and All: Two Years in the Chilterns*, Introduction by Richard Mabey, Alan Sutton Publishing. 1991, p.ix
7. Introduction by Brian Jackman in Allsop, K., *In the Country*, Little Toller Books, 2012, p.10
8. The Middle Thames Naturalist, *Annual Reports of the Slough Natural History Society 1947-48*, with Introduction by James Fisher, 1949; *Report of the Oxford Ornithological Society on the Birds of Oxon, Berks and Bucks for 1947* (1948)
9. *Adventure Lit their Star*, op. cit., p.vi
10. *Parkinson*, op. cit.
11. Allsop, K., *Rare Bird*, Jarrolds Publishers, 1958, p.59
12. Allsop, K., 'On Living with Pain', *The Spectator*, 13 September 1968, p.356
13. *The Spectator*, op. cit.
14. *Daily Express*, 2 June 1973

2

IN THE COUNTRY

Allsop in favourite countryman's attire outside the Mill – 'half gnawingly worried about the bills, half consumedly happy...' (Courtesy Allsop Estate)

THE LONGED-FOR RURAL refuge was Milton Mill in West Milton, a few miles north of Bridport in Dorset. After a year of searching, Kenneth and Betty finally moved into the house in April 1970. '(I am) fortunate enough to live in what I maintain is beyond contestation the loveliest part of the United Kingdom,' he wrote later. 'The last place left, I think, and the one I love most…'

Although he had been born just two miles from the centre of Leeds, in Holbeck, for most of his first fifty years he lived within commuting distance of central London, and sometimes in the heart of the capital itself. For a short time he worked in Wiltshire on the *Swindon Advertiser*, just like his hero, the nineteenth-century nature writer Richard Jefferies. But Swindon depressed him, particularly in the frozen winter of 1947: 'As I dragged through the bitter, iron, snow-blinded days of that awful January,' he wrote, 'I became more and more rawly exposed to the spirit that had killed the visionary farmer's son [i.e Jefferies], the spirit of this town which was a monument to nineteenth century industrialism, a town of railways and smoke and wastes of black slums. I did not stay long.'

Allsop longed to move to real countryside, but during the late 1940s a succession of hack journalism jobs imprisoned him within London's reach. After a spell living in a dingy flat in Highgate, north London (east of the A1, rather than the much leafier west), he and Betty moved to Langley in Middlesex. But he still regarded their *urbs in rure* existence as an unsatisfactory compromise.

Allsop was twenty-eight when at last an opportunity to escape arose. He, Betty and their two-year-old son Tristan were invited to join a commune in a large Queen Anne manor house standing 700 feet up in thirty acres of pasture and woodland on Hertfordshire's north-west border with Bedfordshire. Barwythe Hall was to be the home of eight families of professional, middle-class people, mostly socialists and/or adherents of the Common Wealth Party. They proposed to create separate flats from the generous accommodation, while sharing the costs and the physical effort of buying, renovating and managing the house and estate.

'We went on the Sunday,' wrote Allsop of their first site visit. 'The train from Euston thrust northwards through the embroiled squalor of Outer London. It was not easy to be sure where a bomb had dropped. The rubbly gaps harmonised so well with the universality of desolation - the brief interruption of the Green Belt and then the semi-detached eczema of Watford and Abbots Langley…'[1]

The landscape improved as they were driven from Boxmoor station northwards through the Hertfordshire countryside.

We began climbing up and up a narrow crooked lane, and through the funnel I could see exhilarating limbs of hill-land striding up to a sun-patched sky. I saw a magpie rippling across the lane and a flock of greenfinches flurried up from the low thorn hedge like a burst pillow, with bright flashes of yellow from the cocks...

The wind-blown February sunshine lit the estate in an erratic, ragged way that may have either harmonised with or propagated my moods. Slatey skeins of clouds swished like wild geese across the sun, making the woods and bare gardens wintry stark, and then it all seemed hopeless, unattainable. Then the geese-clouds passed and the sun propelled down, hot and brilliant, bringing an instant transportation of spring brightness to the country and me. Of course it was possible! Determination and imaginative financial juggling could make it possible...!

We straggled through the stable yard, peeping into the silent cobwebby buildings, past the kitchen wing, and the small square lawn where I saw a nuthatch in the walnut tree beside the badminton hall, through the orchard of crooked worn-out trees, and along the side of the wood. From there one's gaze went skimming like a partridge down the full-breasted bulge of park-like meadow, across a deep wooded gulley, and then on over a succession of high-hedged fields across the Gade Valley to the distant rising mass of Ashridge Park... My leg began to ache sorely but I didn't care. This was an exploration into new country to be colonised![2]

It was real countryside, a mild foretaste of the Dorset hill-country where years later he and Betty would settle. Although he was required regularly to commute to newspaper offices in London, the two years at Barwythe provided Allsop with his first experience of living in the country. But the experiment soon came to an end for the usual reasons - personality clashes, the reluctance of some of the residents to share joint household tasks, and mounting financial strains. A meeting on the future of the community was followed by a vote, which produced a majority, including the Allsops, to wind up the experiment. He was disdainful of some of those who wanted to carry on: 'Those who supported the proposal that the community should continue were the very people who all along had shown least enthusiasm for communal activity; who, in fact, had fairly well succeeded in transforming [Barwythe] from a community into a block of flats...'

The Allsops chose to remain in Hertfordshire, and in February 1950 they moved to a seventeenth-century whitewashed cottage in Digswell Water to the north of Welwyn Garden City. Alder Cottage was closer to London than

Barwythe, but at least commuting to Fleet Street was easier. The next step up the property ladder was a move to a farmhouse - Gurneys - outside the village of Holwell, near Hitchen. This was followed by Fleece House, nearer still to London, in the pretty village of Braughing, north of Hertford.

By the late 1960s, the Hertfordshire countryside had indeed been 'colonised', but not quite in the way that Allsop had hoped for, twenty years before. The bursting sprawl of London had jumped the Green Belt and coagulated in the expanding new towns of Hemel Hempstead, Hatfield, Stevenage and Welwyn Garden City. The growth in population, material living standards and mobility had turned the stream of cars and lorries outside the front door of Fleece House into a thundering torrent. Motorways linking London with the Midlands and the North now cut through the county, while London's proposed third airport threatened yet more concrete and noise. In May 1967 Harold Wilson's Labour government had identified Stansted - just ten miles east of Braughing - as its preferred location. So fierce was the outcry from local Essex residents that a Commission of Enquiry chaired by Mr Justice Roskill was set up to investigate alternative locations. A shortlist of four was published in March 1969. Stansted was not among them (although this was still unofficially the government's preference), but of the four new options, one - Nuthampstead - was still too close for comfort, just ten miles north from the Allsops' home.

In April 1969 Allsop took a three-month sabbatical and moved to Merton College, Oxford as a Visiting Research Fellow. Sponsored by Churchill's official biographer, Martin Gilbert, he intended to use the time to research the links between the growth of the nature and open air movements in Europe, and the rise of fascism. But it also provided him with some respite from his life of remorseless deadlines, traffic and commuting - a haven from which he might consider his future.

From the wide south-facing windows of his rooms in the early seventeenth-century Fellows' Quad, Allsop looked out on a bucolic scene of Longhorn cattle and deer grazing in the quiet tranquillity of Christ Church Meadow, fifty acres of peaceful countryside right in the heart of busy Oxford. As a fellow of Merton, he had privileged access to the meadow during late summer evenings when the public were excluded. Early in May he described what was to become his favourite after-dinner walk:

> ...round the perimeter of Christ Church Meadow, down to the
> Thames where crews were at practice, and back along coiling
> Cherwell, chill and damp but in a thick lucent green light through
> groves of elms, blackbirds prinking, duck flighting over the rushy
> swamp. Young people punting. The towers and spires of Merton

and Corpus and Christ Church calm, grey, enchanting, as was every
bend of the river through the green arcade…

It might well have been on one of these walks that he resolved finally to move
away from near London. Already Rector of Edinburgh University, he found that
the Merton term instilled in him an attraction to the conviviality and flexibility
of a more academic existence: on more than one occasion around high table he
discussed the possibility of reducing his television and newspaper commitments
and taking up well-paid temporary Visiting Professorships in the United States.
And his children were now at university or college, and, for the moment his
income was healthy. Now was the time to make a move.

Mill Race

Any plans he may have had to join the international lecture circuit were put on
hold, for Allsop had set his heart on living in an English water mill. He yearned
for somewhere quieter and more rural, a place set apart from village life yet near
enough to enjoy its amenities. He wanted larger, more spacious accommodation
and perhaps some land. Doubtless his weeks in Oxford, surrounded by the
dampness of tangled rivers, streams and ditches, had reminded him of the
attractions of watery landscapes and the birds and wildlife they hosted. Rooted
in antiquity, water mills also represented stolid continuity in an age of rapid
change - most of it, to him, undesirable.

During the last six months of 1969, Allsop quartered the counties south
and west of London in his dark green Aston Martin DB5, usually with Betty but
sometimes alone. First, he explored Oxfordshire and the northern extremities
of Hertfordshire, but then turned his attention further west to Wiltshire, East
Devon and Dorset to escape the spreading influence of London's commuter belt.

There was something wrong with all the mills he was shown. In Oxfordshire,
the mill at Stanford in the Vale was in 'a horrid position', while the one at nearby
Hardwick, although 'attractive and full of possibilities' was too expensive. On
the border of Hertfordshire and Cambridgeshire, the mill house at Ashwell was
'pretty derelict' and opposite an abandoned brewery which was 'not very pretty'.
Further afield, at Littleton Pannell on the edge of Salisbury Plain, he was shown
a property that was 'sweet, but too dinky'. And he asked: 'Why go to Devizes to
live in what is indistinguishable from a Watford suburb?'

By mid-summer, a note of desperation begins to creep into his diary. From
Fleece House, he complains of the 'howling traffic - like being under shellfire',
with 'cars hurtling past the house almost incessantly until 1 a.m. (the heaviest
traffic ever, according to reports - 10 million cars on the road)'. And he was

beginning to doubt that they would be able to sell the house at all, until a decision was taken on the third London airport.

But in the last week of October a glimmer of hope pierced the late autumn gloom. 'We are much exercised by a delightful (sounding) mill house near Bridport,' he wrote. 'We shall view it. But with what shall we buy it…?' So on the following Monday, 3 November 1969, on a grey and blustery day, Allsop loaded the bags into the Aston Martin, and with Betty drove westwards. The cold, uncomfortable night they spent at The Bull in Bridport (then without any central heating) reinforced his feeling of depression and pessimism. During the journey he had noted 'the overall pollution of towns, villages and the countryside in between, by cheap, nasty building. Really, the country where we already are is less botched up. There probably simply isn't anywhere to escape to…'

Next morning the weather had turned very cold, grey and threatening, but the Allsops' spirits lifted when they arrived at West Milton Mill - a 'very attractive' large house with almost eight acres and a separate cottage. The mill was at the end of a long drive, separate from the village, yet 'close to it in atmosphere'. Later, he was to write appreciatively of 'the plain lines, the grey stone and slates, the rich brilliance of the orange lichens and the mini-forests of hart's tongue ferns'. Birds were everywhere. 'How long is it since I saw this sort of wildlife?' he asked. 'It could be delightful, but needs much attention,' he concluded. 'Yet it is such a lovely house which deserves putting back into order, and indeed, making the most of.'

Allsop's eyes were also opened to the 'ravishingly lovely' deep, soft hills of the surrounding countryside. After a lunch of bread and cheese in The Red Lion in West Milton (which in 1969 was still trading), they drove through Powerstock and 'up the long precipitous climb to Eggardon Hill through a gated track, where one runs along a rubble ledge along the most magnificent of panoramas, across a vastness of country under huge skies.' Along one-car lanes through Forestry Commission land they circled into Beaminster, 'a small pretty town' where the shops had 'bow windows, curved doors and fanciful little fanlights'. Then to Bridport: 'a nice town with wide handsome streets, good 18th century buildings (also supermarkets and washeterias)' and to West Bay ('a shantytown').

Back in Braughing the next day, the Allsops concluded that West Milton was the only possibility, but they were daunted by the price, £25,000, and probably almost as much again for major refurbishments. Negotiations over the following weeks secured a deal of £21,200, but Fleece House still had to be sold. Just before Christmas, one potential buyer 'seemed to flinch from the stunning roar of the lorries passing by', so at subsequent viewings Allsop played Beethoven loudly on his stereo system in the hope that the ear-splitting cars and thundering lorries would be drowned out. 'I fervently want to get shot of this place,' he wrote in late January. 'Already, spiritually feel transferred to Dorset...'

The conviction that his life had now reached a watershed was heightened on Thursday 29 January 1970, his 50th birthday. 'How unspeakably gloomy: 50! It seems partly obscene, partly preposterous - half a century of fairly futile occupation of this planet. Also the increasingly melancholy sense of fewer years left than have already been consumed...'

But there were compensations. Work commitments meant that his real birthday celebration with the family was held over until the Saturday - 'my "Queen's Birthday"' - and it was an occasion when he could re-discover his sense of fun. One of Betty's presents to him was a set of four water pistols 'only one of which worked with a strong jet - which I bagged and the boys and I had a hilarious, desperate gunbattle in and around the house...'

Fleece House was eventually sold; and contracts on the purchase of the Mill were exchanged on 13 March. Allsop had been reassured by the reply from his friend and solicitor Edward Moeran to his letter a few weeks earlier stressing that he (Moeran) should be especially 'attentive to any plans for M-roads, New Towns, supersonic airports etc' in the course of his local searches. In the light of future developments, Moeran's reply was particularly significant. He pointed out that the Mill was in an Area of Outstanding Natural Beauty (AONB) under the 1949 National Parks and Access to the Countryside Act, and underlined an important assurance from Dorset County Council: 'Such designation of an area confers upon it national significance, and local authorities when exercising their powers under the Town and Country Planning Acts will exercise them with greater regard for the preservation of an area which is so designated.'

Saturday, 4 April 1970, was a day of cold, but brilliant weather. Daffodils were out in hosts along the river bank at Milton Mill, amid primroses, violets, celandines and dandelions. 'The lushness of this valley constantly impresses itself,' Allsop noted, despite the constant bustle of removal men and builders.

> The grey-beard lichens hang from the old apple trees like Spanish moss in the Everglades; the ferns and moss are an undergrowth; the stone walls are tufted with green creeper and piebald with gaudy orange lichens. It is such a beautiful *plain* house, in such beautiful country, that I am repeatedly brought up to a halt while plodding to and from the barns trying to reassemble our household, and stand staring. The problem will be forcing myself to concentrate on the typewriter and ignore the seductiveness of it all, and do enough work to make it financially possible to stay here. I feel deeply schizophrenic - half gnawingly worried about the bills, half consumedly happy.

A month later, as the dust was just beginning to settle, Allsop reflected on his new life.

> I awake every morning and cannot believe my good fortune to be among such beauty. It is quite literally out of this world - an England of perhaps 40 years ago. I feel to have been returned to the countryside as I saw it and responded to it in the New Forest... or North Devon in the mid-30's, when peregrines still bred on Baggy (Point). There is in our part of Dorset the same teemingness of wild life, a (quite illusory) sense of eternal richness and beauty. Ferns, butterflies, birds are more numerous, more beautiful...

The move to West Dorset and the Mill was a turning point in Allsop's life, in a number of ways. Financially, the costs of buying and refurbishing the new house were substantial, and considerably inflated by his insistence on top quality materials - for example, York stone paving rather than cheaper alternatives. 'I have most of the time the sensation of treading water at frantic speed and gradually sinking,' he wrote. 'I simply don't know how we can stay solvent with taxes and prices at the levels they are...' It meant that from now on he had to accept as many commissions from newspapers, journals and publishers as he could get, and at the same time turn down television work that was less well paid - although in other ways more congenial - than his regular contract with *24 Hours*. This was one of the reasons why he was unable to make a bigger commitment to the BBC's Natural History Unit in Bristol (see p.115).

The move also had a profound influence on Allsop's development as an environmental campaigner. In early August 1970, in a bid to allay his financial anxieties, he invited the editor of the *Daily Mail* Arthur Brittenden to lunch, and offered to contribute a regular country column based on his new life in deepest Dorset. Brittenden was receptive, and they talked about a Saturday piece of around 500 words, to appear either fortnightly or monthly. Three pilot pieces were subsequently received 'ecstatically', and in September 1970 Allsop was offered a one-year contract for what had now been decided would be a weekly column. In the event, 'In the Country' appeared from late September 1970 until the end of August 1972, managing to survive the appointment in April 1971 of David English as the *Mail*'s new and reforming editor.

With a few minor exceptions, 'In the Country' stuck closely to the traditional country column formula: descriptions of wildlife, the Dorset landscape, countryside festivals and customs, the allergic reaction to buttercups of Allsop's pet donkey and so on. It proved to be hugely popular, and he received hundreds of letters, mostly from urban dwellers, thanking him for bringing them closer to the daily rhythms of rural life. But at this time, his articles were rarely political. The nearest he came to highlighting examples of local damage to the environment were a few mild references to the pollution of streams through churn washing by upstream farmers, or the ploughing of downland, encouraged since the early 1950s by government grants. Nevertheless, 'In the Country' provided a platform from which he was later to be offered the lead role in the BBC's thoroughly environmentalist series *Down to Earth*.

But more than this, he now had a very personal stake in defending 'the loveliest part of the United Kingdom' from the threats posed to it by industry and government departments, which began to mount alarmingly as the 1970s unfolded.

1. Allsop, K., *One and All: Two Years in the Chilterns*, Alan Sutton Publishing, 1992, p.10
2. *One and All*, pp.11-12

3

PARADISE LOST?

Powerstock church and village sheltering amid West Dorest's 'tumbled anarchy of hills and coombs', just a few hundred yards from the exploratory drills of Berkley Petroleums' (UK) search for oil and gas. (Author's collection)

THE FIRST EIGHTEEN MONTHS at the Mill brought Allsop the closest he had ever come to happiness. 'But for the financial anxieties, this would be a near perfect time of my life,' he wrote. 'I have never, anywhere, been so consciously enhanced and ever anew replenished by the beauty and "organicness" of the house and all its buildings and trees.'

Much of his time as a Dorset countryman was spent, with Betty, managing the extensive restoration of the Mill and its overgrown gardens, and exploring his new territory. By the end of 1970, he could list 54 species of birds seen or heard around the Mill, including several of his favourites: buzzards, kestrels, a peregrine, sparrowhawks and barn and tawny owls. Alongside the house, the leat or millstream hosted dippers, kingfishers, grey wagtails, moorhens and even a common sandpiper. When he was not outdoors, his days (and much of the nights) were spent in his study or on the balcony writing his regular book column for the London *Evening Standard*, or contributions to *The Spectator*, *Punch* and *Nova*, or his *Daily Mail* articles.

But the rural idyll occupied only part of his life. For one and sometimes two weeks in every month he stayed in London, hosting BBC1's late night *24 Hours* news programme, or preparing and recording contributions to other television and radio series. He was also obliged to spend three days every month attending to his duties as Rector of Edinburgh University.

The contrasts between his two existences, rural and urban, were often bizarre. During a heat wave in early June 1970, immediately after a weekend of writing and sunbathing in bucolic tranquillity at the Mill, he found himself pitched into the throbbing heart of swinging London:

> at a quite extraordinary party, like an Antonioni film... with a cross-cut through the worlds of high aristocracy, rich fashionable and hippy swingers - dress ranged from verdigrised DJ's of older gentry and ruffles of younger, to Eastern robes and sweaty Mick Jagger T-shirts. The host, Quentin Crewe, had invited a galaxy of personalities from the media and the arts, ranging from John Betjeman to Sandy Shaw, through Robin Day and George Melly... Kenneth Tynan, his eyes rolling Proustianly was waiting for someone to insult or sock him, while Lord X was camping outrageously - I find the flagrancy staggering...

That night, Allsop returned to his flat in St John's Wood at 2.30 am and awoke at 8.30, once again feeling the effects of too much champagne and too little sleep.

But his life in London was not all glamour. In late September 1971 he was obliged to vacate his St John's Wood *pied-à-terre* and move to a small studio flat on the fifth floor of a block in Colville Gardens, Notting Hill. In those pre-Hugh Grant days, Notting Hill was what Allsop described as 'a very scrofulous district'. Crime was rife: 'Police cars three days ago were here in herds looking for the attempted assassins of the Jordanian ambassador. I think we may have the whole Black September gang here in Trident House.' Often the lift was out of order, which, given his artificial leg, affected him more than most of the other residents. And it was some weeks before he could get a telephone and entry intercom installed. He felt 'utterly isolated, though on the rooftop of rotting London'.

He might have felt a little better had he known that, just a few hundred yards north of Colville Gardens was St Luke's Road, where one of Britain's most distinguished field naturalists and writers had lived for much of his life. No. 40, 'Tower House', had been the home of W. H. Hudson until he died in 1922, when Allsop was just eighteen months old. Following Hudson's migration to England from Argentina in 1874, most of the twenty-three books he wrote described the natural history and countryside of the counties of southern England through which he rambled. Dozens more pamphlets and articles campaigned against the slaughter of millions of birds for the fashion industry, and for the establishment of the Royal Society for the Protection of Birds. Allsop had much in common with Hudson, including their shared opinion of 'loathsome London', but it would appear that he remained ignorant of this remarkable coincidence.

Fittingly, most of his 'In the Country' columns were written in Dorset rather than London. Even so, Allsop continually felt obliged to censor his real views on what was happening to the environment around him. His dissimulation was mainly a response to the conservative orientation of the *Mail* and its readers - and the fact that the column appeared at the weekend, when the newspaper tried to assume a lighter tone. In addition, he was concerned about the impact of what he wrote on his relations with his new local neighbours. After the first column appeared, he had 'gone to sleep worrying about how I would do it (the column) without offending everyone and appearing to send (West Dorset) up and being ostracised… (of course I may be ostracised anyway).'

Elsewhere - and only a month after he began his column in the *Mail* - he felt able to pen darker thoughts, a little less publicly, in an introduction to *The Environmental Handbook*. This had been written by John Barr, one of the founders of the then-fledgling environmental pressure group, Friends of the Earth (FoE). Barr issued a call to action to combat what he described as a 'Them and Us' situation. Allsop paraphrased the argument thus: '"They" are governments, industrial complexes, corporations public and private, monolithic officialdom and orthodox "hardened" authority in its modern, central, executive form,' he wrote. '"We" are greater in number and finer in spirit. Given the energy and determination the meek shall thwart the caparisoned brutes and yet inherit a sweeter earth.'

But Allsop wearily drew attention to the power of the opposition. He pointed to the then-Governor of California, Ronald Reagan, who when challenged about the clear-felling of ancient forests, had famously observed: 'If you've seen one redwood tree, you've seen 'em all'. And to the President of the giant US Steel Corporation, who did not believe in clean water 'for its own sake'.

> Loutishly flippant or barbarously stupid, such remarks come from de-natured men, and it would be a mistake to underestimate their numbers or to fail to weigh that this is the uttered outlook of the vast bulk of the population who are conditioned to a tree-less neon-lit, profit-geared environment - indeed to whom that environment is more 'natural' than that which conservationists take as their criterion...
>
> Our generation of campaigners feels anguish that the countryside and its marvellous multiplicity of life is under siege and succumbing; our aesthetic is that of the greenwood and birdsong and space and solitude. I think we must recognise that we may be on to a loser and that the enemy's ingenuity may be able to dispense with that archaic and romantic traditional idyll, and not necessarily perish as a result...[1]

He had not always been quite so pessimistic. Four years before, in October 1967, he had highlighted the pressures from development and tourism that had brought irreversible changes to the countryside. 'The change is resented by no-one more keenly than by me - an out-of-time, thwarted eighteenth century parson-botanist, reared to the idea of there being a Selborne life awaiting all who care to seek it,' he wrote. But all was not lost. What was needed was effective planning and management 'to safeguard areas within this great industrial complex that can be justified as lungs for an urban population.'[2] Similarly, a long article in 1969 on *The Wildlife of London* was also fundamentally optimistic. Despite the fact that humans had turned the city into a 'pig-sty', many species of birds, animals and plants had proved themselves to be resilient and had survived, and in some cases even thrived in the most unpromising of habitats.[3]

Allsop's environmentalism was turned a deeper shade of green by his gathering awareness of the global 'environmental revolution' overshadowing the dawn of the new decade. The phrase was coined in 1970 by the first Director of

Britain's Nature Conservancy, Max Nicholson, who explained:

> The environmental revolution, amid which we live, has a double face. It can be seen as a man-made change, sudden and worldwide, in our natural environment. It can equally be regarded in the light of a transformation in our attitude to that environment. By going as far as he now has towards taking over the earth from nature man has made it inevitable, not only that he should manage nature, but also that he should henceforth learn to manage himself as a part of nature... continuing to live on this planet with our present utter disregard for the limitations and requirements which nature sets for us is simply not a course which can be pursued much longer without disastrous consequences.[4]

In the late 1960s, a number of (mainly American) academics and journalists had sought to highlight the huge challenges that population growth and rapidly expanding global resource consumption were posing for the future of the planet. These so-called 'New Jeremiahs' included the US biologist Garret Hardin, who in 1967 expounded the theory of the 'Tragedy of the Commons'; Paul Erlich, who the following year published *The Population Bomb*; and Barry Commoner, who in 1971 wrote about *The Closing Circle*. By 1972, the message had spread to Europe. Barbara Ward and Rene Dubois published *Only One Earth*, while a group of European economists called the Club of Rome issued their influential report *The Limits to Growth*. In Britain in the same year, the *Ecologist* magazine published its radical environmentalist manifesto *Blueprint for Survival*.

But such green radicalism was to have little impact on British politics and government. The thirty-page Conservative manifesto for the June 1970 general election included just three paragraphs on green issues, while Labour's managed just seven lines in fifty-one pages.[5] Two months before he became Prime Minister, Edward Heath had set out his views on how the Conservatives would approach environmental policy. With unemployment at a post-war peak of 600,000, and mounting daily, it was no surprise that jobs and economic growth, rather than the environment, were his priorities.

> If our pollution problem has become acute in these last few years, it is precisely because our rate of economic growth has been so low. Inadequate economic growth robs us of choice; it condemns us to the shoddy and second rate... I also reject the approach which defines a policy for the environment in terms of authoritarian measures imposed from Whitehall on unwilling private industry and unwilling individuals... The scope for voluntary effort, both at local and national level, is very great indeed.

Rather than resort to government regulation and the 'polluter pays' principle, Heath asked:

> Are people prepared to pay extra for freedom from fumes, dirt and ugliness of every description? Are we, for example, willing as members of the community to pay the extra cost required to site the third London airport where it will cause least damage to the quality of life of our fellow citizens? The Government should not prejudice such questions.[6]

A robust response to what many regarded as the Conservative government's complacency came in the first report of the Royal Commission on Environmental Pollution (RCEP) in February 1971.[7] The Royal Commission had been set up by the Wilson government exactly one year before, as an independent watchdog to monitor the quality of the environment and government responses to it. Its chair, Sir Eric Ashby, didn't pull his punches:

> [The UK's] record of action gives no ground for complacency. Avoidable pollution of air, land and water still goes on. Legislation often fails in its purpose not on account of inadequate laws, nor through lack of technical knowledge, but because the laws are not being enforced, sometimes through indifference, but usually because those responsible are unable (or unwilling) to meet the costs of controlling pollution. Some anti-pollution measures have been brought in only as a response to public anxiety over grave dangers (such as the London smog in 1952) rather than as a comprehensive policy for protecting the environment. Some kinds of pollution are likely to overtake the present measures of control. The nation's resources for reducing pollution are limited; difficult choices will have to be made in their deployment...

But mounting pollution was not Ashby's only concern:

> If recent trends were to continue the gross national product would roughly double by the year 2000. Apart from any increase in population, this would mean more industry, buildings, roads, airports and reservoirs. These in themselves are not 'pollutants' but, without adequate planning, their overall effect could be a grave deterioration in the quality of the environment which would outweigh the benefits of efficient anti-pollution measures. Nothing less than a comprehensive policy for the environment will suffice.

The protection of the countryside was not part of the Royal Commission's terms of reference, otherwise Ashby might well have included among the legislation that 'often fails in its purpose' the National Parks and Access to the Countryside Act passed by the Labour government in 1949. This established machinery for creating and administering National Parks, defined as extensive tracts of countryside that were notable for their natural beauty and the opportunities they provided for open-air recreation. By 1971, ten National Parks had been established in England and Wales, mainly in upland country, starting with the Peaks and the Lake District.

The ownership of the land in Britain's National Parks - unlike those in the US - remained with existing landowners, so that the protection of the landscape had to be achieved through land-use planning controls that were intended to be more stringent than elsewhere. However, lobbying by farmers and landowners during the passage of the Act meant that in most cases planning decisions within the parks were in effect given to the relevant local authorities, despite the *national* importance of the landscapes within their jurisdiction. This meant that jobs and local economic development - no matter how brutal the visual impact - almost invariably took precedence over the preservation of natural beauty.

Allsop's home in West Dorset was not in a National Park, even though the county's coasts and heaths had been put on the shortlist.[8] It was, however, in an Area of Outstanding Natural Beauty (AONB), the second largest in the country, covering no less than 1100 square kilometres (425 square miles) of Dorset and Somerset. AONBs differed from National Parks in that they tended to be located in more lowland, cultivated areas and were therefore less suitable for some forms of outdoor recreation. However, the 1949 Act confirmed that AONBs were, by definition, 'of such outstanding natural beauty that it is desirable that the provisions of this Act relating to [National Parks] should apply thereto.' So AONBs were in effect second-tier National Parks that should be managed accordingly, particularly since they were potentially eligible for promotion to the first division. However, planning decisions in relation to AONBs remained even more firmly in the hands of local planning authorities than in the case of the National Parks, for they were given no special planning machinery to ensure they were adequately protected.

In the Country was published as a book by Hamish Hamilton in December 1972, after Allsop had left the *Mail*. In collecting and editing the articles for publication, Allsop took the opportunity to expand and revise them, this time injecting a more hard-hitting, environmentalist edge. In early June 1972 he had been offered a contract by *The Sunday Times* to write a regular campaigning column on the environment. Thereafter, some of his remaining *Mail* articles became noticeably more political, including a piece that appeared on 1 July highlighting the damage inflicted on the West Dorset AONB by oil and gas exploration (see Chapter 5). He asked:

> How then can the murder of such places be got away with? Because central government - Labour and Tory - flouts the law for a cut in the commercial gain and has encouraged the wrecking of our National Parks. Because local authorities betray the trust vested in them. Because landowners agree to it. Money talks. Beauty is voiceless... this is Britain's loss, not just ours, and the names of the politicians - professional and amateur - who had a hand in it should be remembered by the larger public they serve.

Of the book's first print run of 3,000, 1,700 copies were sold on the first day. A second and third impression appeared in January and March 1973, and in 1974 it was issued as a Coronet paperback. In 2011 it was re-published by a small Dorset publishing house, Little Toller Books.[9]

Despite its popularity, Allsop knew that the 'larger public' could often be indifferent to the environment. 'There could be a real change of values. People could begin to say, "Well, we rather like an element of danger in the streets; we like traffic noise, it is somehow involved with the excitement of city life; we do not at all object to the squalor and untidiness."' And he concluded: 'Implicit in most ecological arguments is the assumption that common to most people is an attachment to, and a longing for, the idealised countryside of Constable and Cobbett. That may be shaky ground.'[10]

Shaky Ground

It was Saturday morning, 16 October 1971, and the Mill was unusually quiet. Twenty-one-year-old Fabian had taken advantage of his parents' absence shopping in Bridport, and he was enjoying a lie-in. At around 10.30 am, he stumbled downstairs to make tea for himself and his girlfriend, who was still sleeping. Quite suddenly, the quiet peacefulness of the morning was shattered by a loud subterranean explosion. Vibrations, like an underground train rumbling beneath the bar of a London pub, came up through the floor under his bare feet. The sash windows rattled; on the Welsh dresser the crockery chattered; and concentric ripples ruffled the surface of the tea he had just poured. Upstairs, Fabian's girlfriend cowered beneath the blankets, convinced that the house was being blown up. By lunchtime, four more of these underground shocks had rocked the house, and a three-foot crack appeared in the plaster of the hall ceiling.

Earlier that week, Betty had found the drive to the Mill blocked by a large tanker siphoning water from their private stream that ran through the garden. After making local enquiries, she had driven to the nearby Askers Hotel where a team from Seismograph Service (England) Ltd had set up their headquarters. A Major Hellings explained that the company was undertaking a seismic survey on behalf of Berkley Petroleums (UK) Ltd to search for underground oil and natural gas reserves. This involved drilling holes and inserting a 'small' explosive charge, the sound waves from which could indicate the form and depth of the rock strata, and hence the likely presence of hydrocarbons. The Major subsequently sent the Allsops a letter with a map showing the line of the proposed 'geophones': it came within a few yards of Milton Mill and nearby St Mary Magdalene, the historic village church. One drilling point in Larcombe Lane was less than 150 yards from the house. The Major revealed that operations had begun in Dorset on 4 October, and it was proposed to survey an area within a fifteen-mile radius of their headquarters at the hotel.

Allsop was, of course, furious. After just eighteen months, the sanctity of his rural retreat had been violated. He quickly did some research and discovered from the vicar of Powerstock Church that work had been undertaken clandestinely as early as a year previously, in a remote area of the county around Kingston Russell. They were using 'Mayhew rigs' which could drill to a depth of 1,000 feet, posing a potential threat to the water table through damage to the rock strata. Already his mill stream, for hundreds of years fed from underground springs, was running at a lower level.

Allsop's immediate thought was to take legal action against Seismograph Service for its 'high-handed and deceitful' actions including trespass, failure to seek from landowners permission to drill and possible damage to the foundations of his house. But in a letter to his solicitor he stressed that the matter went much further than this, for future exploitation of oil or gas would have huge consequences for an area supposedly protected under the 1949 National Parks and Access to the Countryside Act. 'I feel strongly that we should exploit to the utmost every chink in their armour we can find, starting by making maximum legal trouble for them.'

In a reply two days later, his solicitor Nicholas Bohm proposed a two-pronged approach: 'a political approach to the planning authorities, preferably on behalf of a body of local residents... combined with a moderate level of harassment from us, is the right approach for the present.' And despite his doubts about the effectiveness of John Barr's 'call to action', Allsop had no choice now but to become an activist himself.

1. Barr, John (ed.), *The Environmental Handbook: Action Guide for the UK*, Ballantine/Friends of the Earth, Pan Books, 1971
2. *The Listener*, 16 October 1967

3. Allsop, K., 'The Wildlife of London', *Sunday Times Magazine*, 23 March 1969
4. Nicholson, M., *The Environmental Revolution*, Penguin, 1970, p.21
5. Johnson, Stanley, *The Politics of the Environment: The British Experience*, Tom Stacey Ltd, 1973
6. Heath, Edward, 'A Policy for the Environment', *The Spectator*, 11 April 1970
7. Royal Commission on Environmental Pollution: First Report, Cmnd 4585
8. Ministry of Town and Country Planning, *National Parks in England and Wales: Report by John Dower*, Cmnd 6628, HMSO, May 1945
9. Allsop, K., *In the Country*, Little Toller Books, 2011
10. Barr, John, op. cit., p.xv

4

SAVING POWERSTOCK COMMON

Allsop demonstrates 'a touch of the sherpa spirit' among the tangled ancient oaks of Powerstock Common, threatened by the Forestry Commission's chainsaws. (Courtesy Allsop Estate)

BEYOND [EGGARDON HILL], LAPPING the farm pasture, is a summer surf of leaves, a choppy green tide of foliage cascading into troughs and piling into high breakers on the pleated ridges. From Eggardon's 900 foot summit you look upon a miniaturised inland ocean of fronds, rippling with shadow waves under the cloud fleets sailing through the immensity of sky, wheeled over by buzzards and where ravens sometimes fly along the rocky bluffs below Barrowland Down. The oak spread looks as remote and pagan as Merlin's greenwood, an orient dream of deep glades, cool and mysterious. It is massy yet unsubstantial, and tantalisingly out of reach. [Powerstock Common] is not much traversed by observers… it needs a touch of the sherpa spirit to get on intimate terms with that interior.

This explanation is borne upon you more penetratingly if you do thread and shoulder and slide your way into the mazy ravines and hollows beneath. The oaks, you discover, are not big. They are squat, gnarled trees, twisty as those in a fairy story picture of a witch's haunt. Writhing boughs are festooned with mosses and feathery lichens, and ferns hang green tongues from their crevices, licking the fungi and velvet sphagnum of the clayey ooze. The oaks are dwarfed like Japanese cultures, for they grow on a mattress of spongy soil, and rushes and orchids cluster richly in the squelchy dells.

Then suddenly you have clambered through a flush of mature alder, sallow, willow and thornbrake, and are swimming up out of the aquarium greenness into brushy, sun-dappled thickets of hazel with a nightingale pealing close by.[1]

Allsop 'combined the poet's eye with the journalist's pen,' according to the novelist John Fowles, a friend and neighbour from nearby Lyme Regis. Nowhere was this more clearly confirmed than in this description of Powerstock Common - the last ancient oak forest left in Dorset, and barely two miles east of Allsop's home at Milton Mill.

But close as it was, it was not until early August 1971 - well over a year after moving to Dorset - that he ventured into this botanical treasure house, accompanied and guided by his Powerstock friend, Brian Jackman. Jackman was a young travel writer in his early thirties who had recently joined *The Sunday Times*, after a period with the British Tourist Board and two successful years playing banjo with The Eden Street Skiffle Group on the BBC and at the Royal

Festival Hall. He first made contact with Allsop in October 1970 in response to one of his *Daily Mail* pieces about the forest, and they became firm friends.

Allsop's eyes were opened to the ornithological richness of the Common in May 1971, when he and Jackman sat on the limestone cliff edge of Eggardon Hill and watched the buzzards, hobbies and a rare Montagu's Harrier gliding along the ridge towards their nests in the forest below. Later, he learned that at least 113 separate species of plants (including three orchids and nine sedges and reeds) had been identified on the Common. Forty of Britain's 67 species of butterfly had been observed within a one-mile radius of the centre - as many as at the Nature Conservancy's own Monks Wood National Nature Reserve in Cambridgeshire. Local naturalist Mr Michael Murless wrote to Allsop emphasising that 'the importance of Powerstock entomologically cannot be stressed enough.' He said that the checklist of butterflies included the Adonis blue (otherwise virtually confined to Kent, Surrey and Sussex); the Duke of Burgundy fritillary; the painted lady and the silver washed fritillary. This was indeed a 'biological and entomological wonderland'.

Not surprisingly, in 1952 the Nature Conservancy had declared both Powerstock Common and Eggardon Hill to be protected Sites of Special Scientific Interest (SSSIs) under the 1949 National Parks and Access to the Countryside Act. The Nature Conservancy explained that the designation was not so much to safeguard ultra-rare species, but was a reflection of the 'great variety of soils, moisture and aspects', which together supported such a rich diversity of plant, bird and animal habitats.

The SSI covered 217 acres of Powerstock Common, south of the then railway line between Maiden Newton and Bridport. Two-thirds of it - 141 acres - fell within a larger area leased to another government agency, the Forestry Commission, Britain's largest landowner which, nationally, owned almost three million acres of land.

The very existence of the Forestry Commission had come under the spotlight in December 1970, when the Conservative government elected six months before announced a fundamental review of the UK's forestry policy, including the financial return it was making on its expenditure of public money. The government had decided that other forms of public investment should show a minimum rate of return in real terms of ten per cent. However, even taking account of the non-commercial, social benefits of state afforestation, such as combating depopulation in Britain's remote rural areas, the Forestry Commission's rate of return was still only between three and four per cent. And in 1970-71 it had gone ever deeper into the red, with a trading loss of £2.4 million, half a million more than the previous year.[2] The axe was poised, and there were just two ways in which the Commission could secure a reprieve.

It could either significantly increase its timber sales through an accelerated programme of planting and felling coniferous woodland; or it could persuade the government that it had greatly underestimated the non-commercial, social and environmental benefits of its activities. Or it could try to do both, despite the fundamental tensions between the two objectives, particularly as regards the environment. In 1970-71, over 97 per cent of the 13,500 acres planted by the Commission in England contained conifers, and less than three per cent consisted of biodiversity-rich broadleaved species.[3]

During his August exploration of Powerstock Common, Allsop noted that almost all of the relict oak woodland in the northern third, nearest the railway line, had already been felled and replaced by conifers. Jackman explained that the best of the oak in this area had actually been cut down some forty years earlier by a previous lessor, but the Forestry Commission were now clearing the remaining scrub timber and undergrowth, and steadily replanting with softwood species.

Some other parts of the SSSI had, for now, escaped the Commission's chainsaws. The southern third below Eggardon had been leased back to the freeholders of the Common - the Tindall-Lister family from Luccas Farm - and appeared to Jackman to be sensitively managed and conserved. Meanwhile, after six years of negotiations, an area of scrubland along the railway line had been given by the Forestry Commission to the Dorset Naturalists' Trust (DNT) to manage as a nature reserve, but this amounted to just three and a half acres.

What was most at threat from the Commission's drive to boost timber production was the heartland, the bog-oak wildland in the central third of the Common. Allsop was appalled to come upon a new, high-banked metalled road which had recently been driven deep through the heathland towards this crucial virgin stretch in the marsh bottom. 'What had held back the hunters and defied the firewood collectors since early times was now easy pickings for modern machinery and hydraulic power,' he wrote later. Returning in the autumn on another casual visit, he realised that the Forestry Commission was purposefully extending its domain. 'They were not only filling the gaps - they were creating new ones. The glades where a few months earlier we had wandered on the outer fringes of the heartland - those jungly depths over the swell - were now churned earth, scattered with razed oaks which had spread marquees of green light through which jays flashed, squawking. A power saw was whining and a sub-contractor was piling up the logs for carting off.'[4]

Peter Lewis was the Forestry Commission's head forester on Powerstock Common. He had a local reputation for being a conscientious naturalist, and indeed Allsop had noted that the replanting in the northern section of the Common had included some landscaping with beech belts on the more visible rises, and the seeding of special deer lawns to encourage the animals to stay inside the woods. Even so, when he telephoned Lewis on 15 December he was fully prepared for a verbal confrontation.

'Mr Allsop, as a private individual I am bound to agree with you that felling ancient oaks is a terrible crime,' came the disarming reply. 'But I'm at the bottom of the ladder and limited in what I can do by my terms of reference, so we've had to do the best we can. No-one would be happier than us if our terms of reference could be enlarged,' Lewis observed ruefully. He added that during the current winter they were planning to plant 34 acres of conifers on Powerstock Common, starting from the north-east. There would be several more years cutting and planting after that.

Immediately, Allsop rang the Forestry Commission's London headquarters to demand more information. The head of information, a Colonel David Rooke, was not available, and in his absence a hapless subordinate had to take the flak. Allsop warned him that he intended to give the razing of Powerstock Common as much local and national publicity as possible.

'If we were replanting with hardwoods, would that satisfy your objection?'

'No. That wouldn't even begin to meet the cost of destroying such an old and absolutely unique forest,' was Allsop's terse reply.

Two days later, a letter arrived from Colonel Rooke. The message could not have been clearer: during the next four years, the Forestry Commission intended to clear and re-plant some areas of 'scrubby woodland' as follows:

    1972 35 acres (14 ha.)
    1973 32 acres (13 ha.)
    1974 30 acres (12 ha.)
    1975 42 acres (17 ha.)

The first phase of this four-year programme was to begin in September 1972 - and would target the Common's sensitive, secret heartland.

Summit Meeting

Gingerly, Allsop edged the highly-polished, dark green E-type Jaguar over the rough stone chippings of the Forestry Commission track. He was trying not to stall the powerful V8 engine at such unaccustomedly low revs, but was also anxious to avoid going faster and chipping the Jaguar's paintwork, still as immaculate as when he had taken possession of it just three weeks before. After about half a mile, the metalled road gave way to a rutted muddy bridleway, where a group of five men stood around a Forestry Commission Land Rover examining a large-scale Ordnance Survey map spread over the bonnet.

Allsop pulled in, and with some physical and mental effort lifted himself out of the warmth of the car. Immediately, he regretted not having dressed more appropriately. It was Friday, 31 December 1971, New Year's Eve, a cloudy, icily-cutting day of cold winds and scoured countryside. Today, his normal weekend countryman's wear - a battered leather jacket, needle-cord shirt, green checked neckerchief, jumper and jeans - was not going to be up to the job.

One of the group, a tall moustached man of military bearing dressed in a sheepskin coat and flat cap, briskly walked over and shook hands: 'Good to see you, Mr Allsop. David Rooke.' Allsop had not expected the Forestry Commission's head of information to come all the way from London to look at what, from the Commission's perspective, was only a local problem. 'Let me introduce my colleagues,' he said, leading Allsop towards the Land Rover.

Geoffrey Rouse, the Forestry Commission's Conservator for the South West and responsible for the region's felling programme, was a squat, stocky man, with a long upper lip and a brusque manner. He had driven from Bristol that morning, and it was plain that he felt he had better things to do on a New Year's Eve. Peter Lewis, the head forester, was by contrast relaxed and appeared to be enjoying himself. Neither he nor Allsop gave any indication that they had already spoken to one another.

Before Allsop had arrived, the three Forestry Commission men had walked along the Eggardon ridge to get a bird's eye view of the whole of Powerstock Forest. Colonel Rooke had impressed upon his colleagues the importance of reaching some accommodation with Allsop. In two weeks' time the Commission was intending to launch a public relations offensive emphasising its 'unique role' in meeting the public's rapidly increasing demand for countryside recreation - a move aimed at justifying the Commission's continued existence, despite its mounting trading losses. Nothing would torpedo this carefully-planned initiative more effectively than a press campaign now, from someone as prominent and popular as Allsop.

The rest of the party back down in the valley comprised Rodney Legg, editor of *Dorset The County Magazine,* and Michael Shepherd, the Forestry and Woodlands Officer in the Environment Department of Dorset County Council. Legg looked tense and uncomfortable. A few months earlier, following a guided tour by Forestry Commission officials, he had written a eulogistic article which proclaimed: 'The Forestry Commission has designed a plan for the future of Powerstock Common that will leave it looking more like a nature reserve than a state forest. It is a plan that can have few parallels in both its enlightened approach and determined bias towards conservation.' He was still angry that he had been taken in, and felt a little humiliated that Allsop had managed to extract the Commission's real intentions, where he had failed.[5]

Michael Shepherd had been invited to join the party both as a County Council planner, and in his personal capacity as an accomplished ornithologist. Allsop had spoken to him a week before, when Shepherd revealed that he was investigating the use of powers under the 1968 Countryside Act enabling councils to step in and manage sensitive areas as countryside parks, using a 75 per cent grant from central government. 'I like the sound of him,' Allsop had written afterwards.

They climbed up the boggy track through the wizened trees and scrub to the ridge where a beech hedgerow separated the wood from the fields of Barrowland Park, sloping down towards the east. Allsop winced silently as every footfall on the uneven ground twisted and jarred his artificial right leg. On the tumulus at the high point, the roar of the wind was now strong enough to drown out the sound of the contractors' sawing and chopping below. From there, the group looked down across the bracken slopes to the beginning of the heartland of the old forest, half of which the Commission intended to clear and replant in the autumn.

Eventually, as they descended, Allsop showed them where the harriers had nested. Lewis said that there were redstarts and breeding barn owls there, and Shepherd related the story of how he had stumbled across a pair of ravens a few months before. 'Botanically, the central part of the Common is of key importance,' Allsop explained. 'It's the replenishing well from which so much of the entire valley's biodiversity is renewed and revitalised.'

Later, Rooke drew him to one side, and said quietly: 'You know, Kenneth, this doesn't seem to me to be as much of a problem as we had feared, because we're only talking about thirty-odd acres. I am sure we can find a satisfactory solution.'

They returned to the cars and drove in convoy the short mile to The Three Horseshoes, perched on a hill looking west over the village of Powerstock. The log fire in the back bar reddened their faces as they hurriedly retreated out of the icy wind. Soup and ploughman's lunches were accompanied by pints of Palmer's bitter, and, in Allsop's case, whiskies. Several whiskies. It was after all New Year's Eve, and he didn't have far to drive home.

Hard drinking led to hard talking. 'Well, gentlemen,' said Allsop at last. 'I hope what you've seen this morning has convinced you of the wisdom of revising your plans, at least for the central wilderness heartland. Even government agencies have a duty to respect what is a legally protected site of special scientific interest, and in the case of the Forestry Commission, this would seem to chime in particularly well with the new emphasis on providing public amenity.'

Rouse had remained very quiet during the walk through the forest, but now, sitting in the corner, the beer had loosened his tongue. His face turned a deeper shade of red as he said, testily: 'Mr Allsop, I'm responsible for the management of over 100,000 acres of forests, and as far as I'm concerned my primary duty - and the reason the government pays me - is to raise timber. I can't shelve my entire forestry programme every time some busybody - a would-be Bruce Campbell agitating about a white-tailed redstart - makes a complaint. I can't make any exceptions.'

Allsop moved closer and looked him in straight in the eye. 'Well, you seem to know as much about birds as you do about the Forestry Commission's wider responsibilities to the public. Why didn't you consult the experts who know about these things - or even the county planners - before charging in and razing this irreplaceable, ancient woodland?'

Rouse was getting angry, but felt at a distinct disadvantage sitting down while Allsop stood over him. 'I consider that my duty has been carried out sufficiently by consulting such bodies as the Nature Conservancy and the Dorset Naturalists' Trust...'

Allsop sneered, moved his face closer to Rouse's and spoke slowly and distinctly. 'Just because they're "bodies" doesn't mean that the feeble compromises they are willing to make are necessarily the right ones.' The whisky had released his underlying anger and contempt for officialdom. 'You may think that I'm a busybody, Mr Rouse, but I think you are nothing but a wooden-headed timber merchant who can't see the wood for the trees. You know the price of matchwood, but the value of absolutely nothing...'

By now the room had fallen silent. Rouse, pinned in his seat in the corner, had lost his colour and looked as though he was about to cry. 'You really hate me, don't you?' he whimpered.

Victorious, Allsop turned his back and returned to the bar.

Keeping up the Pressure

Back in London, the launch of the Forestry Commission's New Year PR offensive was planned for 19 January 1972. The Chairman, Lord Taylor of Gryfe, called a press conference to showcase the new emphasis on making greater provision for public recreation in the management of its forests. His statement declared:

> Public demand for countryside recreation is increasingly rapidly. The Forestry Commission is in a unique position to help meet this demand since it is responsible for almost three million acres of land in Great Britain, distributed widely throughout the country. Further, forest and woodland have a greater capacity for absorbing people in the countryside without impairing the environment than other forms of land use...

Greater emphasis should be given to maintaining the woodland character of the countryside, particularly in the south of England. [The Commissioners] have recognised that to this end in certain of their woodlands the maintenance of hardwoods, where silviculturally this is possible, is an essential part of landscape. The objective of the Commissioners is to perpetuate by active management the living character of the woodland landscape for future generations to enjoy.

He promised that a series of regional Recreation Plans would be drawn up in consultation with local planning authorities and other interested bodies, including the Nature Conservancy and the three Countryside Councils for, respectively, England, Wales and Scotland. Alongside the statement, the Commission also published a glossy, heavily illustrated booklet *Wildlife Conservation in Woodlands*, which it had commissioned especially from the Nature Conservancy. The Commission's Director-General, Mr J. A. Dickson, declared in the Foreword: 'I commend it as a practical guide illustrating how our woodlands' rich store of plant and animal life can be maintained for all to enjoy.'[6]

Unfortunately for Lord Taylor, three days before his press conference, *The Sunday Times* had printed a long article by Brian Jackman spotlighting what was actually happening on his doorstep on Powerstock Common. Under the headline 'Requiem for a Forest', Jackman drew attention to the Forestry Commission's 'senseless environmental blitzkrieg' which was 'dismembering this irreplaceable fragment of medieval English woodland and scattering its treasure trove of wild creatures... How sad it is that men who grow trees for a living can be so unfeeling for the living landscape entrusted to their safe keeping.'[7]

Incandescent with rage that his PR campaign was crumbling before his eyes, Lord Taylor dispatched two letters to *The Sunday Times'* editor, Harold Evans. In the first of these, which was published on 30 January, Colonel Rooke, the Commission's head of information, was mercilessly hung out to dry. Taylor wrote:

> I regret that in previous correspondence which we had with Mr Jackman we got our wires crossed, and consequently the five year (felling) plan to which Mr Jackman referred relates not to Powerstock Common, but to the whole of our Powerstock Forest, which covers about 2,700 acres in Dorset and Somerset. As far as the Common is concerned, we have virtually finished the treatment of the 157 acres of woodlands under our control... What we have done at Powerstock Common is in no way in conflict with the statement I recently made on the emphasis we are giving to maintaining the woodland character of the countryside in managing our hardwood

forests.

Somewhat ironically, Lord Taylor's letter appeared alongside lengthy correspondence from readers praising Antony Jay's *Householder's Guide to Community Defence Against Bureaucratic Aggression*, which had appeared in *The Sunday Times Magazine* just the week before (see pp.55-6). Amusing though this was, for Allsop and Jackman, Lord Taylor's assertion that they were misinformed could not have been more serious. If true, it meant that their campaign over the past few months had simply been tilting at windmills, a humiliating waste of energy.

However, several factors cast doubt on Lord Taylor's 'crossed wires' explanation:

- His assertion that the felling and planting programme on Powerstock Common, as outlined to Allsop and Jackman by Colonel Rooke, in fact referred to the far wider Powerstock Forest area was undermined by figures in the Forestry Commission's own Annual Report for 1970-71. Rooke had provided figures for four years, from 1972 to 1975, which showed that 139 acres of the Common were to be felled and replanted with conifers over this period. If the 34 acres felled in the winter of 1971 are added to the total (as reported by Peter Lewis, the head forester), then the 'five year plan' would involve 173 acres. Yet, under the heading 'Poorstock, Dorset and Somerset' (the wider Powerstock Forest) the Annual Report indicated that from a total area of 2,736 acres, 291 acres were to be planted - that is, two-thirds more than Rooke had reported. This discrepancy is so large that the two sets of figures must refer to two different areas - Rooke's to Powerstock Common, and those in the Annual Report to Powerstock (or 'Poorstock') Forest.
- It also stretches credulity to believe that the Forestry Commission's own information chief would have confused figures in a letter written to Allsop on the very same day (16 December 1971) that the Commission published the Annual Report referred to above.
- During lengthy discussions with Peter Lewis, and subsequently with Geoffrey Rouse and Colonel Rooke on New Year's Eve, at no time were the figures contested, nor the area to which they applied.
- And if the Forestry Commission had 'virtually finished the treatment' of Powerstock Common, why then had the new 'woodland motorway' been scythed into the heartland of the forest?

The evidence suggests that the Chairman's letter was a hurriedly concocted piece of 'spin' from a man desperate to salvage the Forestry Commission's image, and dig it out of the hole that its own bulldozers had excavated.

Lord Taylor's letter went on to report that 'neither the Nature Conservancy nor the Dorset Naturalists' Trust, whom we consulted before we acted at all, has objected to what we have done on the Common, whose conservation we have all along had very much in mind,' and he concluded: 'We are considering a sub-lease of the remaining 30 acres to the Dorset Naturalists' Trust.'

Allsop was both depressed and irritated when Brian Jackman telephoned from his office at *The Sunday Times* and read over the letter. Depressed, because earlier that morning he had spoken to Rooke, who had confidently declared: 'I think we've succeeded. It looks like we're going to offer Powerstock Common to the Dorset Naturalists' Trust'. Yet Lord Taylor's commitment only to 'consider' the option was far more general and ambiguous. And irritated, because he understood the reference to the acquiescence of the Trust and the Nature Conservancy in a sense completely opposite to that which Taylor had intended.

And even if it was the case that the Commission was now prepared to hand over the Common, Allsop feared that it would still not be in safe hands. The practical achievements of the DNT in safeguarding the Common were less than impressive - just three and a half acres, in fact - and he had been told that a member of the Trust's council had said privately that 'Powerstock Common isn't worth saving' because it was too wild and difficult of access.

Lord Taylor must have been uncomfortably aware that Jackman and Allsop could, without too much difficulty, counter his version of events. So in the second, private letter to Harold Evans, Taylor demanded that Jackman should be sacked for besmirching the Commission's reputation. 'Harry called me up, and asked if I had my facts right,' Jackman recalls. 'I said yes, and presented him with the evidence. He said, basically, "Good man - I love it when we stir up the establishment."'[8]

So there was no let-up in the campaign. Two days after *The Sunday Times* had received Lord Taylor's letters, an unrepentant Brian Jackman wrote a second article on the Forestry Commission's new, 'sensitive' approach to conservation. Under the headline 'Death of the Oaks', he wrote: 'Lord Taylor's words have a strangely hollow ring. Certainly it is hard to reconcile this statement with what is happening on Powerstock Common, where the Commission have been felling West Dorset's sole surviving primeval oak forest and re-planting with alien species in which a conifer mix predominates.' Jackman also drew attention to a strongly-worded statement from the Ramblers' Association pointing out how few broadleaved trees the Commission was actually planting, and demanding a public inquiry on the future of the Forestry Commission, which was 'now more than ever dependent on subsidies from the taxpayer.'[9]

For most of January, Allsop had been away filming in South America, and so it had fallen to Brian Jackman to take the campaign forward. However, following his return, Allsop gave an interview to the *Western Daily Press* in which he confirmed that he continued to be 'involved in a struggle with the Forestry Commission over West Dorset's historic Powerstock Forest'.[10] He remained unconvinced of the Commission's sincerity, despite a letter from Colonel Rooke pledging that the Commission 'will not go back on its word in this matter, for this decision will be written into the management plans for years to come.'

However, by the end of February, Allsop was feeling more optimistic. The relationship he had built up with Mike Shepherd from the County Council's planning department, and the pressure he had put on Geoffrey Rouse, seemed to be bearing fruit at last. After the summit meeting on New Year's Eve, Shepherd had persuaded the County Planning Officer, Alan Swindall, together with Helen Brotherton from the DNT, to walk the Common and discuss what needed to be done. 'The Planning Officer was more impressed than I expected, and he agreed that action must be taken to save the Common,' Shepherd told Allsop. 'Then we got Rouse over. He was a changed man, and leaned over backwards to be co-operative and helpful. As a result, the Commission will hand over in perpetuity more than a hundred acres of the Common to the Trust - all seventy acres of the sensitive central section, plus a further thirty acres at the northern end. Despite its earlier reservations, the Trust was apparently delighted to have it, and was already investigating how much fencing it would need.

'I am 99 per cent certain that the danger is past,' Shepherd declared. 'There will be no more felling there.'

Allsop ended his written record of the conversation on a triumphalist note: 'Altogether marvellous news - we acted only just in time!'

With Friends Like These...

But the question of who should get the credit for saving Powerstock Common involved Allsop in a very public wrangle with the DNT, which lasted through most of 1972. The Trust was only ten years old when Allsop took up the cudgels to save the Powerstock oaks, and was still relatively small with fewer than 2,500 members. Most of these lived in the east of the county rather than the poorer west. The Honorary Secretary, Miss Helen Brotherton OBE, JP, lived in Parkstone, overlooking Brownsea Island and Poole Harbour, where much of the accessible richness of Dorset's biodiversity was to be found.

In 1964 the freeholders of Powerstock Common - the Tindall-Lister family - had discussed with the DNT the possibility of renegotiating the Forestry Commission's long lease over the land to enable the management of the whole of the central area to be handed over to the Trust, in addition to the dramatic northern flank of Eggardon Hill (which they also owned). But the Trust turned down the offer, mainly on financial grounds; the Common would need a warden, which the Trust at that time could not afford, but also because there was uncertainty about the ecological attraction of such a remote and relatively unexplored area. One DNT Committee member, also from Parkstone in Poole, admitted to Allsop that he had 'no personal knowledge of the position at Powerstock or its value in relation to the many other parts of Dorset. Time and money are never unlimited.'[11]

Subsequently, desultory discussions between the DNT and the Forestry Commission produced a number of promises but very little concrete action, apart from the donation to the Trust of the three acres of more accessible scrubland adjacent to the railway line to the north of the Common. Nevertheless, the Chair of the Trust, Mr David Le Cren, insisted that there was 'never any doubt' that since 1964 there had been in existence a commitment on the part of the Forestry Commission that at least forty acres would be preserved (plus the three acres already donated), 'the only uncertainties being exactly where this area would be, and how much more the Trust might get'. Then, in 1970 the Commission had indicated that it would 'favourably view' a request from the Trust for specific areas, up to a limit of 25 per cent of the total area of the Common.[12] A year later, three-way discussions between the Commission, the Trust and the Nature Conservancy appeared at last to have nailed down a firm commitment that around one quarter of the Commission's leased land would remain unplanted in its semi-natural state, including the more outstanding biological areas. But this meant that the remaining three-quarters, including significant parts of the SSSI, would not enjoy any such protection.

'Thus, while keeping a close watch, we thought it best to bide our time knowing that official policy in the Commission was gradually becoming more favourable to conservation,' wrote Le Cren. 'There was a distinct danger that the negotiations could be set at risk by too firm a pressure or interference on our part, and by unwarranted publicity…'[13] This was a scarcely veiled attack on Allsop and Jackman. Many members of the DNT's Board resented the intervention of well-connected incomers from London, especially because they chose to act independently rather than through the Trust, which could well have done with their financial and practical support from the inside.

In early February 1972, these tensions became public. Lord Taylor's attack on Brian Jackman's *Sunday Times* article attracted some support in the local *Bridport News*. 'Why all the fuss?' asked a Mr Charles Waterfall. 'There is in fact very close co-operation between the Dorset Naturalists' Trust and the Commission with regard to the preservation and future well-being of all types of wildlife on the Common. The Head of the Forestry Commission in this area, Mr Peter Lewis, is a keen naturalist and I am sure the future of this lovely piece of Dorset country is in very capable hands.'

From the tone of the letter, the last sentence might well have ended: 'thank you very much.' Jackman's ire was raised:

> Moving though Mr Waterfall's faith is in Powerstock Common's immutable safety in the joint hands of the Forestry Commission and the Dorset Naturalists' Trust, it is sadly unfounded. After six years' negotiations, the Dorset Naturalists' Trust was fobbed off with (and seems touchingly grateful for) three and a half acres of scrub beside the railway line, a perfectly nice plot but with no relevance to the oak forest...
>
> What was imminently at risk was the heartland, the central third comprising 70 acres of bog-oak wildland, the bulk of which was scheduled for clear felling starting next autumn and replacement with conifers, and for the preservation of which the Dorset Naturalists' Trust had taken no action whatsoever. Fortunately, another freelance group intervened, and direct consultation with the Forestry Commission now gives reason for some optimism that cutting will be halted... If there had not been some (people) a little more sceptical and vigilant than Mr Waterfall, two-thirds of this irreplaceable forest would have been razed.[14]

The Chair of the DNT, Mr Le Cren, soon escalated the argument in the March edition of the Trust's newsletter. While welcoming the imminent acquisition of much of the Common, he described press reports of how the Powerstock oaks were saved as 'misleading', and indeed sought to downplay their importance. The history of Powerstock Common was 'still to be unravelled', he wrote. The forest was not ancient, for most of the oaks had been planted, with the best of them subsequently felled for timber during the past century, while other trees were used for charcoal. 'Even though the remaining trees may not be primeval, they are attractive, gnarled and excellent habitats for mosses, insects and birds,' he conceded, with just a hint of condescension.

Allsop now entered the fray. In a letter to Miss Brotherton, he wrote that he 'neither expected, nor especially wanted, acknowledgement from your Committee of the part one was able to play... just before the heartland was due to be felled. But the version presented by Mr Le Cren is almost amusingly shameless in its use of the word "misleading". Charitably, one must of course assume that he is sadly ignorant of the true course of events...'[15] He then expanded his case in a long article printed in *Dorset The County Magazine,* under the headline 'Why did the official conservers take no action when Dorset's primeval forest got the chop?' The attitude of both the Trust and the Nature Conservancy to the Commission's plans for clear-felling was, he wrote:

> ...dismayingly indifferent: the whole situation seemed blanketed in a disastrous complacency. Could it really be true that one of the executive officers of the Trust had expressed disinterest in pressing for its acquisition because it was 'too wild' and had declared that 'it wasn't worth saving'? That didn't seem all that far-fetched after conversations on the telephone with two of the officials. One thought that they had held on to a 'splendid amount' - three acres! - after having 'so much trouble' about this place; the other considered they had got possession of 'the part which matters most', and seemed not actually to have seen the precious wilderness booked for imminent demolition. A powerful impression was conveyed that interference of this kind was not welcome.

The moral of the story, concluded Allsop, was that with mounting pressures on the countryside 'it is not enough to assume that all action can safely be left to the appointed custodians - because, not infrequently, it may be discovered too late that there has been no action. The individual's vigilance has never been so vitally important.'[16]

The Nature Conservancy (NC) was the government-appointed custodian of Britain's biodiversity, and, according to the Forestry Commission, it had been fully consulted about the planned felling of the Powerstock oaks. So a few days after his New Year's Eve confrontation with Rouse in The Three Horseshoes, Allsop telephoned the Conservancy's headquarters in London's Belgrave Square to try to establish exactly what it had agreed to. Nobody seemed to know the details of the case, and he was transferred from one official to the other, eventually being referred to the Regional Officer for Dorset, based in Wareham. But it was not until the end of January that he received a letter from the Assistant Regional Officer explaining the extent of the Conservancy's involvement in the management of the Common. Allsop had to read the final paragraph several times: 'In 1971... our recommendations to safeguard the nature conservation interests were accepted by the (Forestry) Commission,' wrote the Assistant Regional Officer. 'In effect this meant that approximately 25% of the leased land would remain unplanted in its semi-natural state, including the more outstanding biological areas.'[17]

'A quarter left unplanted!' Allsop spluttered in disbelief. 'So three-quarters of the SSSI under Forestry Commission management would be razed to the ground - but it's all OK because it has the formal blessing of the Government's official, so-called nature conservation watchdog!'

He picked up the phone and dialled the Conservancy's HQ. Trying hard to control himself, he demanded to speak to the Director, Dr Duncan Poore, whose own background, he had just discovered, had also been in forestry. Could this be a conspiracy, he wondered? Inevitably Dr Poore was not available that afternoon.

A week later, Allsop was in London on BBC duty. With only a couple of hours until he had to be in the studio, he drove at high speed from Lime Grove to Belgrave Square. He pulled up outside No. 19, a cream, four-storey Regency terrace, but finding no free parking space, he drove on to the wide pavement, wincing as he heard the scrape of Jaguar's hub caps as he mounted the high kerb.

He stormed up the steps to the marble-tiled, porticoed lobby, and pushing through the heavy, black carved doors, demanded to see the Director - immediately. 'You know who I am. I don't need an appointment.' The startled receptionist disappeared for a few minutes, then returned and escorted him to the lift.

Duncan Poore was slightly younger than Allsop, a balding, quietly spoken Scotsman, with an academic air. 'Well, Mr Allsop,' he said, rising from his chair and extending his hand, 'this is a somewhat unconventional meeting, but now you are here, let's talk about how we might help each other.'

Allsop had come prepared for a flaming row, and this was not the reception he had expected.

'Let me say first of all that I admire what you're doing in relation to Powerstock Common, and I agree with you that the Nature Conservancy is not fulfilling the duties it was given in 1949,' said Dr Poore. 'But let me tell you why.' Allsop sat down, suddenly feeling disadvantaged and uncomfortable, like an unprepared undergraduate receiving a one-to-one tutorial from his professor.

'The powers we have been given are very limited. The designation by us of a Site of Special Scientific Interest means only that public bodies like the Forestry Commission must consult us about planned activities that threaten damage - but they don't have to do as we advise. It ends up as a process of negotiation. Then, the human and financial resources we need to undertake surveys of species and habitats, to monitor trends and manage national nature reserves, have been progressively cut in recent years. For the past six years, my colleague Derek Ratcliffe has been drawing up a new list of sites that should be NNRs. He's identified around 400 of them. There are only 130 now, and it would cost over £10 million to create and manage all 400. Meanwhile, Lord Rothschild's review of government research and development is proposing to strip us of our independent research functions - so it will be left to the Ministry of Agriculture, for example, to determine what research it should commission, say, on the impact on species of crop spraying.'

Allsop intervened: 'I sympathise with the situation you're in, but the fact is that at this very moment an irreplaceable, ancient oak forest in Powerstock is about to be destroyed - and you must do something to stop it!'.

Poore looked out of the French windows across the road to the leafless lime and maple trees in the square, becoming indistinct in the grey, fading February light. 'I know Lord Taylor well from my forestry days, and rest assured I'll have a strong word with him. But you have to realise that Powerstock is only one of a hundred such threatened sites. This is just firefighting, and what we need is a complete re-think of how we approach nature conservation in the future, and the powers of the agencies charged with managing it.' He then proceeded to outline the need for strategic assessments to help plan the management of all natural resources - land, water, wildlife— and for a review of the way decisions were made about how we use them. Two years later, he was to set out these ideas in a more considered way in a paper to the Royal Society:

> Although such strategic assessments can reduce potential conflict, their effectiveness is greatly reduced because at present there is imperfect correspondence between value, and the degree of statutory protection… If conservation of natural heritage in the countryside is to be taken seriously, great weight should be given, in my opinion, to loss of potential - to irreversible change or irrevocable loss… Money can accomplish much in an affluent society; more scientific knowledge can extend our powers. But neither can re-create a species once extinct; nor can human wit recreate the complexity of many natural ecosystems. Completely undisturbed ecosystems are irreplaceable; a way of life, once disrupted, can never be recovered. It is these characteristics that should weigh heavily in the scales against change that will destroy.
>
> A searching intellectual debate is needed to examine whether the premises on which we make decisions on the use of resources are sound; whether the results are either what we intend or what we really want. To be productive, this debate must draw together men and women of wisdom and understanding in religion and philosophy, together with natural scientists, economists and sociologists. For the problem is one of ends as well as of means.[18]

'What we need is a kind of independent British Environment Institute to take all this thinking forward. That's something I think you could help with, Mr Allsop,' concluded Dr Poore, ushering him towards the door.

While Allsop may have reached some level of understanding with the Nature Conservancy, back in Dorset relations with the Dorset Naturalists' Trust remained tense. Most of the local newspapers were to splash Allsop's article. It was too good a story to miss - 'local celebrity takes on County nature establishment' - but the publicity prompted the officials of the Trust to mount an autumn offensive against him to salvage their reputations. On 1 September 1972 a letter from Miss Brotherton appeared in all the local press pleading that no formal agreement could have been drawn up with the Forestry Commission any earlier because of delays by the Tindall-Listers in formally leasing all the land over to the Commission. Moreover, she argued, it was only very recently that the Commission's brief had been extended to include conservation.

Local allies of the Trust were brought in to reinforce the press campaign. The Hon. Secretary of the West Dorset Naturalists' Association confirmed that lengthy surveys had to be undertaken before a reserve could be declared, while a representative of the British Herpetological Society declared that 'we have been greatly impressed with Dorset for their outstanding, immediate and progressive action, especially in achieving site protection… Constructive criticism is helpful, but this attack must be regretted as being both misleading and misguided.'[19]

By now, Allsop had had enough. After all, Powerstock Common now appeared to be safe, and anyway in his new role at *The Sunday Times* he needed to shift his attention to national environmental issues. So on 15 September, in the *Bridport News* and other local papers, he gallantly offered a metaphorical bouquet of red roses to Miss Brotherton. 'May I, a trifle timidly, add my voice to the hosannas of praise which have been reverberating through the press of southern England for Miss Brotherton and the Dorset Naturalists' Trust?' he wrote.

But he could not resist adding one last thorn: 'The sympathy has managed to drown one rather crucial fact: that, but for the outside intervention which took place, the Forestry Commission would this very month be busy starting on their scheduled task of razing the central oak forest of Powerstock Common.'[20]

It was his last public word on the matter. The following month he wrote privately to Colin Graham at *Dorset The County Magazine*: 'I hate all this bickering, and don't want to have any part in keeping it festering away in public, so it would please me most if I could evaporate away into the background shadows of the whole affair.'[21]

Forty years later, in 2012, Powerstock Common Nature Reserve covered no less than 284 acres, and the (re-named) Dorset Wildlife Trust managed a further 41 reserves with the support of its 26,000 members and 55 staff.

*

1. Allsop, K., 'Why did the official conservers take no action when Dorset's primeval forest got the chop?' in *Dorset The County Magazine*, No. 26, 1972, pp.12-21

2. Pringle, Douglas, *The Forestry Commission - The First 75 Years*, Forestry Commission, 1994, p.65

3. Forestry Commission: *Fifty-first Annual Report and Accounts 1970-71*, HMSO, 16 December 1971

4. Allsop, K., in *Dorset The County Magazine*, op. cit

5. Legg, Rodney, 'Saving the Countryside', in *Dorset The County Magazine*, No. 20, 1971

6. Steele, R. C., *Wildlife Conservation in Woodlands Forestry*, Commission Booklet No. 29, HMSO, 1972

7. Jackman, Brian, 'Requiem for a Forest', *Sunday Times,* 16 January 1972

8. Personal communication with author

9. *Sunday Times*, 23 January 1972

10. *Western Daily Press*, 4 February 1972

11. Letter from A. F. Dean, 28 August 1972

12. Letter from Mr E. D. Le Cren to Allsop, September 1972

13. Letter from Le Cren, op. cit

14. Letter from Brian Jackman to the *Bridport News,* 7 February 1972

15. Letter from Allsop to Helen Brotherton, 27 May 1972

16. *Dorset The County Magazine*, No. 26, 1972, pp.12-21

17. Letter to Allsop from M. E. Dennis, Nature Conservancy's Assistant Regional Officer (Dorset), 26 January 1972

18. M. E. D. Poore 'A Conservation Viewpoint' in Proceedings of the Royal Society of London, Series A, Vol. 339, 1974, pp.395-410

19. Letter from K. F. Corbett, *Bournemouth Times and Poole and Dorset Herald*, 9 September 1972

20. Letter from Allsop to *Bridport News* and others, 15 September 1972

21. Letter from Allsop to Colin Graham, 27 October 1972

5

DEFENDING WEST DORSET (1)

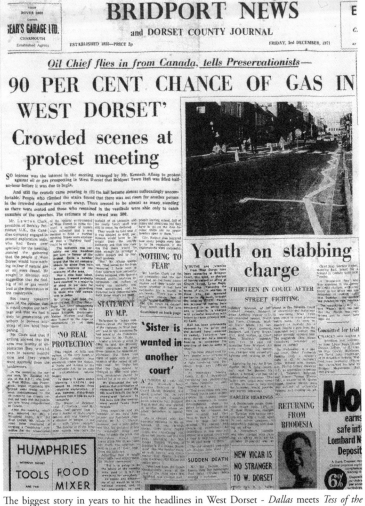

The biggest story in years to hit the headlines in West Dorset - *Dallas* meets *Tess of the D'Urbervilles* as oil company President Lawton Clark faces a mixed reception from the locals at Allsop's 1971 protest meeting in Bridport Town Hall. (Courtesy Tristan Allsop)

HIDDEN DEEP AMONG THE piles of Allsop's letters, scripts and memos is a yellowing twelve-page extract from *The Sunday Times Magazine* of 23 January 1972. Headlined 'If they want to build a motorway through your garden here's how to stop them', it is a summary of a book that was to be published later that year entitled *The Householder's Guide to Community Defence Against Bureaucratic Aggression*, by Antony Jay.

Jay is best known for the satirical comedies *Yes Minister* and *Yes Prime Minister*, which he co-wrote with Jonathan Lynn in the 1980s. Allsop knew him well, for in the early 1960s Jay had worked for the BBC, first as a writer for *That Was the Week That Was*, then editor of *Tonight* and subsequently as Head of TV Talk Features. Jay's article could have been written specifically as a blueprint for Allsop's campaign against oil drilling: he might have obtained an early draft directly from Jay himself, or from a sympathetic *Sunday Times* journalist, of whom there were several.

In his book Jay cautioned against being intimidated by official government policy proposals. He explained these were not the product of 'evidence-based policy making' (to use the current jargon), but rather of 'policy-based evidence making':

> [The proposal] started as a quick decision by a busy man several years ago. All work thereafter has been directed at making that early decision stand up. All the statistical analysis, the surveys, the expenditure forecasting, the projected growth of demand - these did not lead to the choice at all: they were initiated and selected in order to bolster it up afterwards.

Antony Jay's step-by-step guide to counter 'bureaucratic aggression' proceeded as follows:

- Start early if you can, before anything firm is announced
- Hold a public meeting - mainly to demonstrate the size of the public's opposition, but also to gather names and addresses of sympathisers, and to authorise the establishment of an Action Committee
- Set up six 'guerrilla bands' or cells, to organise
  - Grass root support at street or area level
  - Funding
  - Legal advice
  - Technical experts - 'the storm troops' of the attack on the proposal, on its own terms

- Publicity and background briefing for journalists
- Lobbying (overseen by a respected and influential chairperson)
- Bombard the media with your message
- Open up the 'paper barrage' - writing letters to key officials, councillors and MPs
- Hold a further public meeting to challenge the proponent at a detailed level
- Prepare the counter attack through shock tactics - demonstrations, pageants, petitions, press events etc.

Over the next twelve months, it provided Allsop and his supporters with the 'to do' list for the campaign to defend West Dorset.

Rallying local support

On 5 November 1971 Allsop made the front page of the local weekly *Bridport News*. The lead story was prompted by his letter attacking Seismograph Services for the damage caused by the drilling and explosions, and asking as many citizens as possible for their support in what was likely to be a 'tough fight'. The enemy were bureaucrats in both central and local government, he wrote. Nationally, the Department of Trade and Industry (DTI) had issued licences for exploratory drilling, which Allsop declared were 'for the intended disembowelling of a zone which falls within the County Authority's description as "an area of great landscape value", and upon which an order was made under the 1949 National Parks and Access to the Countryside Act, and which is thus designated for preservation.' This 'pussyfooting' permission for prospecting had also been endorsed by the county and local councils 'without public consideration'. Hence he demanded a public meeting where people could air their views, and invited readers to let him know if they would lend their support.

Despite his celebrity and his ability to open doors in high places, Allsop needed local help. At the end of October, he enlisted the support of his GP, Dr Michael Hudson, a Londoner who seven years earlier had moved to Beaminster. Hudson had a special interest in ecology and the local environment, declaring that he could now live nowhere else. As well as a keen naturalist, he was a film buff, and a member of the local branch of the Council for the Protection of Rural England (CPRE). Allsop suggested to him that although they should try to enrol as large a number of local people as possible, they should 'concentrate action in the hands of half a dozen activists - 'Nader's Raiders' formula'. (This was a reference to the campaigning tactics of an American environmental activist against the US automobile industry). Hudson dispatched a letter in similar terms to Allsop's to another Dorset newspaper, the *Western Gazette*, and wrote to West

Dorset's Conservative MP, Simon Wingfield Digby, to elicit his support.

Brian Jackman was to join Michael Hudson on the dedication page of *In the Country* as one of Allsop's two 'Wessex Companions'. Although he was often absent in London, like Hudson, he wrote to Wingfield Digby, sent supporting letters to the *Bridport News* and promised to try to generate national publicity in *The Sunday Times*.

Another young local journalist, Rodney Legg, described himself as one of Allsop's 'acolytes to be mobilised to produce the grassroots pressure'. In fact, his role was far more significant than that, for at the age of 24, he was already the founder and editor of *Dorset The County Magazine*, whose columns he often used to establish a second front in the campaign.

Christopher Geering was to become secretary to the action group. In early October 1971 he had written to Allsop from his Beaminster home asking for help in securing a public enquiry into the proposed demolition by Bridport town council of a Georgian mansion, Wykes Court, and an adjacent rope works, just to make way for a municipal car park. Allsop sent a sympathetic reply, but used the opportunity to suggest that Geering might widen his field of action to include the oil prospecting. Geering agreed - but in the expectation that Allsop would at some point reciprocate and lend his support to other local causes.

Allsop also made contact with Lord Hinchingbrooke, the owner of Mapperton House, an Elizabethan manor two miles north of Allsop's home. As Victor Montagu, 'Hinch' had for twenty years until 1962 been the MP for South Dorset, and had a wide network of influential friends and contacts, both locally and in Westminster and Whitehall. He replied revealing that he had refused access to the Seismograph Services' drilling team and 'threatened to set his beaters on to them if they persisted in trespassing'.

The Conservative member for Dorset West, the 61-year-old Simon Wingfield Digby MP, was a local Tory grandee who owned not only the seventeenth-century Sherborne Castle and its 14,000 acres, but also two other estates in Oxfordshire and Scotland – 55,000 acres in all. He had represented West Dorset for thirty years, and tended to put the interests of his constituents above those of his party. After wartime service in the Royal Artillery, he had become a junior Navy minister, but when Harold Macmillan became Prime Minister in 1957 his reputation as a maverick robbed him of a government post, and so he returned to the backbenches. He was to prove invaluable in tabling questions in the House of Commons on local and national mineral extraction policy, and lobbying ministers and civil servants behind the scenes.

The front page story in the *Bridport News* had generated many letters and telephone calls of support. One of these was from the Mayor of Bridport himself, Alderman P. C. Norfolk, offering Allsop a venue and date for a public meeting:

Friday 26 November, in Bridport Town Hall.

Allsop had to be in London on BBC duty in the run-up to the event, so much of the task of organising the meeting fell to Betty. She was responsible for a myriad of jobs, including dropping off leaflets to distributors around West Dorset. One night she was still up at 2.00 am counting out handbills for distribution the next day. She kept a meticulous record of her activities during that week beginning 15 November, including the following telephone calls to:

Newspaper journalists (12)
TV and radio journalists (6)
Leaflet distributors and newsagents (17)
Various supporters (11)
Advertisers (5)
Local government officials (5)

On his return from London, Allsop gratefully, and rightly, described her as 'a one person committee'.

Berkley Petroleums (UK) Ltd

Back at the Mill, Allsop had begun to piece together a picture of his adversary, Berkley Petroleums (UK). Research by friends and colleagues on *The Sunday Times,* the *London Evening Standard* and in Parliament established that the company was a subsidiary of a Canadian corporation, Berkley Oil and Gas, based in Calgary. The British offshoot had been set up two years previously, specifically in order to obtain licences to prospect for oil and gas in the UK. Its two nominee British directors, Peter Morley Jacob and Nicholas Wilson, were both solicitors in a big City law firm, Slaughter and May. The President of Berkley Petroleums (UK), Mr Lawton Clark, although based in Calgary, was in fact an American, a Texas oil millionaire from Amarillo.

Allsop discovered that the British government, in the form of the Department of Trade and Industry (DTI), had been issuing licences to American, Canadian and British oil companies allowing them to prospect for oil and gas, right across the UK. Berkley's licence covered no less than 461 square kilometres (178 square miles) of Dorset and Somerset, at an annual cost to the company of only 50p per square kilometre for the first three years - that is, a total of just £230 per annum. He could barely believe that the government was almost giving away the licence to prospect across a swathe of Thomas Hardy country and a designated Area of Outstanding Natural Beauty, with minimal conditions attached.

Allsop reached for the phone and dialled the DTI official in charge, a Mr H. L. Maggs. He introduced himself, but dispensed with the polite preliminaries:

Mr Maggs, don't you think that your department operates in an oddly blinkered way, perfectly oblivious of current thinking that planning should be integrated so that we can leave at least some decent landscape behind for future generations? Would it not be sensible if there was some consultation at least with the Department of the Environment?'

Rather taken aback by Allsop's full frontal approach, Mr Maggs tried to stay calm. 'As far as we are concerned, for a financial consideration you can search for and get whatever is there. We don't as a Department give any consideration to the kind of country we are granting licences for. If someone wanted consent to search for oil under Ben Nevis - even if it couldn't be got at - we would grant a licence'.

Allsop riposted: 'So theoretically, Mr Maggs, I suppose you would grant a licence to search for oil under Buckingham Palace?'

There was a long pause. 'Well, yes. I suppose we would.'

'Thank you, Mr Maggs'. Allsop's jaw tightened, and he replaced the receiver. He stood up, looked out over the garden through the window and paused for thought. After a minute or so, he turned and looked along the rows of books and pamphlets arranged neatly on the floor-to-ceiling book shelves that covered the four walls of his study. He reached up and took down a dog-eared and faded blue government publication, dated May 1945, entitled *National Parks in England and Wales: A Report by John Dower*.[1] Ruefully, Allsop recalled that during those dark days of the war, the Ministry of Town and Country Planning had given Dower the enviable task of surveying the most beautiful parts of Britain to assess their suitability for future National Park status. This was during 1943, when Allsop was confined for months in an American field hospital in Oxford, while extensive tests were undertaken on his painful right knee.

Dismissing such thoughts of life's unfairness, he turned to page 9, to a section headed 'Division B: Reserves for possible future National Parks'. This was a list of geographical areas of England and Wales, which - although not wild countryside as in the Lake District or Snowdonia - were nevertheless sufficiently beautiful to be treated as reserves for possible future National Parks. Dower had noted that these areas 'should be generally safeguarded by the co-operative action of central and local planning authorities... Within this reserve no substantial development other than for agriculture and forestry should be permitted unless shown to be desirable in the public interest...' Most of these areas were subsequently designated as Areas of Outstanding Natural Beauty (AONBs) under the provisions of the 1949 National Parks and Access to the Countryside Act. Third down Dower's list of these twelve regions were 'The Dorset Coast and

Heaths'. Almost half of the county of Dorset was declared an AONB in 1959.

Folded in the back of Allsop's copy of the Dower Report was a faded extract from the *Hansard* report of House of Commons debates, dated 31 March 1949. He took it towards the window to get more light. It was a report of a speech by Lewis Silkin, the then Minister of Town and Country Planning, during the second reading of the National Parks Bill. The Minister was explaining that he could give no permanent guarantee that mineral extraction would never be allowed in any National Park or potential National Park. But if it were to be permitted, this would only be under the strictest of conditions:

> The first condition is that it must be demonstrated quite clearly that the exploitation of those minerals is absolutely necessary in the public interest. It must be clear beyond all doubt that there is no possible alternative source of supply, and if those two conditions are satisfied then the permission must be subject to the condition that restoration takes place at the earliest possible opportunity.

Allsop underscored this paragraph with a thick, felt tipped pen, folded the page and put it in his jacket pocket.

On the following Monday morning, Allsop was back in his study trying to put together his speech for the Bridport meeting, now only four days away. Over the weekend he had noticed with some alarm that despite the recent exceptionally heavy rain, the flow down the spillway of the mill stream had been reduced to the merest dribble - probably, he concluded, a consequence of damage to the aquifer caused by the underground explosions. But his anxious thoughts were abruptly broken by the ringing of the telephone on his desk: 'My friend Maggs again,' he sighed with some irritation.

'Mr Allsop?' The Texan drawl took him by surprise. 'Lawton Clark here. I'm in London for a few days, being briefed by my colleagues on the situation down there in Dorset. I must say it's a very beautiful part of the world - I was there myself last April - and I can understand why you don't want our company altering it. You know, I'm a paid up member of the Sierra Club myself, and I'm deeply concerned with conservation.'

Allsop had gained his composure and answered with a polite but cool formality. 'Mr Clark, our stand is that scheduled country like this should not be subject to the kind of industrial intrusion you are proposing. I'm afraid to say that I have experience of the professed interest in the countryside of oil and mining companies, but when it comes down to it, our two interests are fundamentally incompatible.'

'Well, if we did find something worthwhile, the chances are it would be gas rather than oil, and I guarantee that we will put everything back as we find it.'

On the notepad in front of him, Allsop's doodle in red ballpoint of a towering, gushing oil rig became ever more elaborate. 'A sprinkling of grass seed can't replace ancient heathland, Mr Clark. And besides, the activities of your Seismograph Services contractors - trespassing and misleading people about rights of entry they don't possess - don't give much reassurance about the conduct of a bigger operation.' Lawson Clark paused, and then, with a hint of diffidence, asked: 'Would it be OK if I were to come to your meeting? I rather hoped I could show a few slides.'

Allsop replied that, as a believer in democracy, he could see no reason why he should not attend, but contributions from the floor would be limited to a few minutes each. 'And I'm not putting this on as the occasion for a Berkley Petroleums' PR show,' he declared firmly.

'Well, Kenneth, I shall make the meeting if I am not stoned in the streets.'

'I can assure you I don't see you as the villain,' Allsop replied, 'but as a result of our government's policy you are in pursuit of an objective which I shall do my best to prevent you reaching. So I'll see you on Friday.'

The Public Meeting

The large Victorian clock at the back of the hall showed two minutes to eight. Seated on the platform, Allsop adjusted his tie and shirt cuffs, slightly nervous at the unaccustomed engagement with a live audience - over 350 people, a sea of tweed, denim, Barbour jackets, anoraks and Afghan coats, all crammed together and uncomfortably warm in the stuffy hall. Above the murmur, he could hear outside several protesting voices from the latecomers - around 150 of them - turned away because of lack of space. Below him, on the front row, was Lawton Clark, looking younger than Allsop expected, and wearing a pair of black-framed spectacles. Flanked either side of him were an assortment of Berkley Petroleums' executives, geologists and PR professionals. A journalist remarked that with their smart suits and short haircuts, they looked like characters from the television series *The Troubleshooters*, who had wandered by mistake into a scene from *Tess of the D'Urbervilles*. Also at the front, wearing his official gold chain, sat the mayor, Alderman Norfolk, and positioned on both sides of the hall were reporters and photographers from both the local and national press, including Nicholas Tomalin, another of Allsop's friends from *The Sunday Times*.

The clock struck eight. Programmed to be punctual, Allsop noisily pushed back his chair, stood up, cleared his throat and tapped the microphone. 'Good evening, ladies and gentlemen, and thank you all for coming to this important meeting.' The room fell silent.

'First of all I want to introduce those of us at this end of the hall - I'm deliberately avoiding saying "platform" because we're here not to preside, but to join in.' In turn, he introduced the panel of four sitting next to him. They had been carefully selected to reflect the geographical and social breadth of the support the campaign had already attracted: Miss Betty Brierley, a naturalist who had lived in Dorset for thirty years; Mrs Judy Miller, a farmer's wife from Askerswell; the local Conservative MP Simon Wingfield-Digby; and Dr Michael Hudson.

After the introductions, Allsop welcomed Mr Clark, explaining that he had 'flatteringly' flown all the way from Canada to be with them. 'He said he would like to attend "if he wasn't stoned on the streets". On the contrary, I said, my impression was that there are those down here who might well strew his path with flowers. But I added that I put my faith in the democratic process and that he was welcome to come and make himself heard.'

Before giving the floor to the speakers, Allsop explained that an important purpose of the meeting was to seek nominations and volunteers for what he described as a 'Watchdog Committee' to monitor closely the local activities of the oilmen, and also to set up a fighting fund in case there was eventually a public enquiry. 'I've seen at close quarters how industrial giants, equipped with Queen's Counsel and public relations departments and coffers of money can, with dismaying abruptness, confront unorganised and bewildered local residents who don't know what's hit them.' Later, he was to regret using these words, which lent weight to accusations from his opponents that the locals were being patronised as if they were 'a lot of country yokels with straw in our mouths'.

When he was invited to speak, a slightly bewildered Lawton Clark made the same mistake. 'Believe me, no-one respects the concern felt by the natives - I mean locals - about your beautiful British countryside more than I do,' he said. Otherwise, he was courteous and sought to be reassuring. The results of the exploratory drilling had so far been inconclusive, he said, and would not be known for several weeks. In any event, there was a ninety per cent chance that gas rather than oil would be found. This would mean that no pipes would be laid above ground. The final well, if there was one, would only be a small, eight-foot-square concrete pad with a standing pipe about as tall as a man, which could easily be screened by trees. In reply to a questioner, he conceded that the effect on local employment in the event of discovery would not be great: 'only around fifteen people'.

This information was not enough to quieten the loud and persistent cries from a large section of the audience for the company to be given full rein in the interests of the local economy - a classic example of a conflict between jobs and the environment. The letters page of that day's *Bridport News* had included a contribution from Bridport Town Councillor L. A. J. Radnor, who hoped that Berkley Petroleums would 'strike it rich'. 'The working population of Bridport cannot live on fresh air and beauty alone,' he wrote. 'I would be quite happy to see a few oil wells in the area. They would bring prosperity to Bridport and provide many excellent jobs for the working population... But of course, the preservationists are already opposing the idea. They have always opposed change in the past and no doubt some are sincere, but the majority will oppose for purely selfish reasons, and because they have vested interests.'

His colleague on the council, Mr John Stickland, told the meeting that the whole of the country, including West Dorset, should be systematically re-surveyed to find out was beneath the land. Even the chair of Powerstock District Council, Mr J. C. Shoobridge, was in favour of exploratory drilling, for 'if there was a war, we would need to be more self-sufficient in oil and petrol,' he declared. 'The people who have got the petrol at the moment are connected with Russia.'

Allsop had stressed at the opening of the meeting that the debate should not be acrimonious, with opposing views exchanged 'rationally and with good will'. But after two hours, the tone of his summing up had become tetchier. 'I have to say that I was horrified by the blithe ruthlessness of one lady (who didn't come to the meeting) who owns a certain amount of land and property in the district, who said: "What a lot of fuss! We can make enough money and move out." It's almost too sad to be horrifying - that the attitude of use-up-and-throw-away, consuming land like Kleenex for soiling, screwing up and destroying, should still exist when... most people today recognise the crisis of population and pollution which is so near.' He pointed out that, in fact, no royalties would be payable to the landowner, since the oil or gas belonged to the Crown, and the most they could expect would be a one-off payment of between £100 and £200 for permission to drill. There was 'no dazzling prospect of dollars-from-heaven, of riding about in Cadillacs in Texan ten-gallon hats,' Allsop declared.

Winding up the debate, Allsop inadvertently handed more ammunition to his detractors by stressing that, for him, the question of oil and gas exploration was a moral rather than an economic one, and national rather than merely local.

> There can be a variety of reasons why one is for or against this proposal. I personally am against it mainly on conservationist grounds. I think that the most *telling* case against Berkley Petroleums getting their claws on this area is the factual, economic one; but I believe that fundamentally we should take a stand against our uniquely beautiful hill country being turned into an oil or gas field, for the reason that it is uniquely beautiful. It is our heritage. And we are its trustees. We don't own it; it is, for our time, in our care. We owe it as patriots, not

just to Britain, but to the human race, to see that there is something worthwhile and enduring to pass on to the generations to come - not just exhausted wells, derelict machinery and a network of roads...

[And] I want to stress that although I, like so many here, care passionately that our part of Dorset should keep its particular character and beauty, this is not merely a local issue. It is national. Britain is crawling with prospectors, up to 100, here or heading this way. Everywhere our remaining stretches of wild and open country are being invaded and eroded, and I believe that everywhere the British people are rising in alarm and wrath.

We at this meeting can help... by preventing West Dorset being turned into an oil or gas field, but also making our aim a longer one. Ultimately, the only solution is to give, by Parliamentary legislation, the National Parks and other designated areas *real and inviolable* protection...

At the end of the meeting, around fifty people queued up to offer Michael Hudson their practical support to the campaign. Outside, the crowd gradually dispersed through the dark, quiet streets of Bridport. Back at the Mill, in the early hours of Saturday morning, Allsop confided to his diary his mixed feelings about how the meeting went. 'As far as one can judge, it was a success: possibly 150 turned away and 350 packed in, and on the whole a deeply concerned atmosphere. Lawton Clark and his gang of oil men didn't really put up much of a case. But of course this is merely the start of what may be a long, hard - and unsuccessful - fight.'

Bombarding the Media

Having rallied at least a significant level of local support, Allsop moved to a new stage in Antony Jay's campaigning roadmap: bombarding the media. But it was the national rather than the local press that was the focus of his attention. Allsop had repeatedly emphasised that the violation of a protected area could only be solved at a national level by reforming Whitehall procedures. As he explained later: 'We have deliberately been trying to get through, stage by stage, to the highest quarters the case for legislative changes, if already designated countryside is to be secure from being turned into an oil field or, say, a tank training ground.'

Immediately after the weekend, on 29 November, he drafted and despatched identical letters to the *Guardian* and the *Daily Telegraph*, both of which appeared later that week. After explaining the campaign in West Dorset, he stressed its national implications. 'Up and down Britain are hundreds of groups of citizens watching with agony similar erosion and destruction. Although various bodies are charged with care of the countryside, we feel that there is urgent need for an action movement, not in competition with those bodies, but which could co-ordinate efforts to press for parliamentary revisions. May we hear from those willing to join in?'

Allsop's bid for national attention and support was given a major boost by a sympathetic 1,300-word report of the Bridport public meeting written by Nicolas Tomalin in *The Sunday Times* of 28 November.[2] 'The basic point revealed by the Bridport protest meeting,' wrote Tomalin, 'was the bureaucratic muddle and lack of co-operation between the Department of Trade and Industry and the Department of the Environment. Surely, as Allsop explained, this is a national problem. Surely it is ridiculous to issue licences encouraging indiscriminate oil drilling. Surely no prospecting should be allowed, for instance, in National Parks or in Areas of Outstanding Natural Beauty. It is entirely unfair both to the Dorset residents and to Mr Clark to encourage prospecting and then - perhaps - veto it at a later stage.'

During the next week, Tomalin's report was followed up by supportive leading articles in both *The Sunday Times* and *The Guardian*.[3] *The Sunday Times* pointed out that the Mineral Exploration Bill, then before Parliament, would offer a £50 million inducement to mining companies to explore for mineral deposits anywhere in Britain, because the government deemed it to be in the 'national interest' to reduce Britain's annual £2 billion bill for imported minerals by an insignificant £100 million:

> Against it, however, there stands no countervailing force. The Department of the Environment's involvement is apparently limited to planning and local government matters. Although a large portion of unmined minerals happen to lie in national parks, the parks stand virtually undefended...
>
> Exploration itself can be a gross invasion of the peace, as was shown in our report last week about the 'exploratory' explosions of oil-prospectors in Dorset. Planning permission is often not needed at this stage. Moreover, it is disingenuous to pretend that the exploration process itself, if successful, is not capable of creating irresistible pressures.

'Against the influence of vast financial empires,' *The Sunday Times* concluded, 'the muddy boots and good intentions of conservationists are dismally inadequate. Only the government can stand effectively against them. Rio Tinto Zinc can look after itself, but the environment cannot.'

Allsop was overjoyed, and straightaway sent a note to the paper's editor, Harold Evans. 'After Nick's super report, today's leader was a magnificent follow-up. It actually increased to the point of optimism my deliberately tempered hope that it may be possible to build up enough pressure to get the necessary changes in Whitehall… Very, very many thanks for the marvellous support on this.'

But not everyone was so pleased at all the national attention. A Mr K. Macksey from Beaminster wrote to the local *Western Gazette* accusing the West Dorset 'preservationists' of shifting their sights to the national media because the Bridport 'mass meeting' had shown that a large section of the local populace - 'not just recent arrivals' - were positively in favour of prospecting being continued. 'Thereby they have invited a much greater danger, the danger of polluting Dorset with every professional protester, misguided enthusiast and trouble lover in the country.'

And a number of existing environmental pressure groups were also very unhappy that Allsop's grassroots initiative had bypassed them. In a veiled attack, the Chairman of the Council for the Protection of Rural England (CPRE), Lord Kennet, wrote to *The Times* on 22 December 1971, drawing attention to the importance of an environmental umbrella organisation, the Committee for Environmental Conservation (CoEnCo). 'The member societies of CoEnCo, of which the Council for the Protection of Rural England is one, have hundreds of thousands of members; but we are still not rich enough to make our weight felt against the great developers and exploiters in this increasingly professional world. Will somebody soon, please, aim the money where there are people who know how to use it now?' Privately, Lord Kennet had told Allsop that his activities should be brought under the wing of CPRE, even though its local branch had shown reluctance to oppose local oil exploration, because, in the words of one member 'that is what the government wants'. The *New Scientist* had earlier commented that the CPRE was 'above all the voice of the landed gentry' which had shown 'a curious reluctance to put up more than a token fight against the oilmen's invasion of the Hardy country'.[4]

Parliamentary Lobbying

Escalating the campaign to national level inevitably involved lobbying MPs in Parliament, and so it was Allsop's great good fortune to have Simon Wingfield Digby MP on his side. Wingfield Digby had received a number of letters of complaint from his constituents about the seismographic tests, and had put down a question to the Prime Minister asking if he was satisfied with the co-ordination between the Department of Trade and Industry (DTI) and Department of the Environment (DoE) over the issuing of exploratory prospecting licences. He had also contacted the office of the DTI Minister, Sir John Eden, seeking clarification regarding the extent of the legal rights of prospecting companies.

Two days later, he raised the question of drilling in West Dorset in a House of Commons debate on the government's Mineral Exploration Bill. This proposed to make available subsidies of £50 million over ten years to companies prospecting for minerals of all kinds - up to a limit of 35 per cent of their costs in each case. He told the Minister and MPs that Seismograph Services Ltd had entered private land without permission, and that its underground explosions had damaged property and threatened to pollute underground aquifers. But he posed a more fundamental question: 'At the end of the day, we have to ask whether, if oil were found in Dorset, it is a suitable area - it is an Area of Outstanding Natural Beauty - upon which to inflict these scars on the environment, especially at present when everyone is so much more aware of the importance of the environment.'[5] He argued that government subsidies to already-rich oil and gas companies were unnecessary, and called for the Bill to be amended to require planning permission for exploration as well as subsequent exploitation, and for the DTI to be required to consult the DoE over both stages.

Two months later, in January 1972, Wingfield Digby tabled a number of amendments to the Bill at Third Reading, the principal one seeking to remove oil and gas exploration entirely from the scope of the proposed legislation. He also asked the Minister to exclude prospecting in National Parks and Areas of Outstanding Beauty. The reply was a polite, but circumlocutory, 'No'.

> It is not my intention, and it is not the intention behind the scheme to lead to any sort of widespread desecration of the beauty spots, certainly not the National Parks or the nature reserves. But we need to know the location of the country's mineral resources. Once we have the knowledge we can weigh up, through the proper planning procedures, the balance of national interest and set the value of the mineral resources capable of exploitation against the undoubted value of the landscape which might in that process be desecrated. This is a judgement which is properly left to the process of planning and not one which comes within the purview of the Bill.[6]

Wingfield Digby replied with the confidence of one who no longer strives for ministerial preferment. He pointed out to Sir John Eden that the geological area of interest for oil and gas - the so-called Bridport Sands - centred around the village of Kimmeridge, which happened to fall within the Minister's own constituency of Bournemouth West. 'But none of these experiments has been going on there, although it is possible to prospect in a big city for petroleum and natural gas, as was done in West Berlin. So perhaps the Minister will direct his attention to his own constituents, and leave mine alone for a time...'[7]

In the end, the government got its way on the Bill, although it conceded that the question of whether planning permission was required for exploration which might cause environmental damage was 'a small grey area'. As an equally small gesture, it introduced its own amendment to the Bill requiring those mining companies in receipt of state subsidies formally to establish whether they required planning permission for exploratory drilling, and if so, to secure it before operations began. There was still a very long way to go.

1. Ministry of Town and Country Planning, *National Parks in England and Wales: Report by John Dower*, Cmnd 6628, HMSO, May 1945
2. 'Have you got oilmen at the bottom of your garden?', *Sunday Times*, 28 November 1971
3. 'A Priority for Parks', *Sunday Times*, 5 December 1971; 'Control over the Prospectors', *Guardian*, 6 December 1971, p.12
4. Legg, Rodney, 'Back to the Hills', *Dorset The County Magazine*, No. 25, 1972
5. *Hansard*, House of Commons, debate on the Mineral Exploration Bill, 10 November 1971, cols. 1047-1049
6. *Hansard*, House of Commons, Third Reading debate on the Mineral Exploration Bill, 18 January 1972, cols. 416-417
7. *Hansard*, ibid., col. 408

6

DEFENDING WEST DORSET (2)

We are people who
are concerned

CONCERNED ABOUT WHAT?

About oil fields
and the tide of mineral
development here

IS IT SERIOUS?

We have the facts -
and it is serious - it's why we exist

JOIN US
we are pledged to defend the
West Dorset Countryside

**Defenders of
West Dorset**

President Kenneth Allsop

Secretary Christopher Geering
26 North St. Beaminster

Defenders of

THE CERNE GIANT

West Dorset

I want to become a Defender of West Dorset
I enclose £1 (less if you cannot afford it)

NAME

ADDRESS

Telephone

The Cerne Abbas Giant's formidable weaponry lends a hand in recruiting supporters to the newly-formed Defenders of West Dorset in 1972. (Courtesy Tristan Allsop)

CHRISTMAS 1971 AT THE Mill provided Allsop with some respite, at least from the oil campaign. Following his appearance at the Bridport public meeting in November, Lawton Clark had gone strangely quiet. By mid-December, a UK Director of Berkley Petroleums (UK), Peter Morley Jacob, had heard 'absolutely nothing' and was unable to tell Allsop whether Mr Clark's silence meant that he had decided to 'pull up his stumps' or not.

To readers of his *Daily Mail* 'In the Country' column, Allsop was enjoying an idyllic, traditional family Christmas, hunkered down against the weather in his West Dorset fastness. The three children had converged on the Mill from various quarters of the country, and were allocated the task of collecting the Yuletide holly from nearby hedgerows.

> So off through the frost-crackling mud my children and their friends went to bring back the bounty, and I made for the coppice to see about that trunk section I had ear-marked as being a likely looking Yule log when I had been picking up lighter stuff. Sloshing through pulpy leaves I came to it. Just what was needed. That would have roasting flames roaring up the chimney. But I was lacking one minor essential: a horse team and chains...
>
> I slunk back to the house and applied myself to the urgent labour of reading a review book at the fireside. It was considerate of me, I decided, to let the children get the holly. As they sorted it out in the crowded kitchen, plaiting a garland for the brass knocker and hanging it over the fire's cross-beam, they would be enacting fun and mystery as perennial as 'the rising of the sun and the running of the deer'...
>
> I heard the youthful voices returning across the field and looked out of the window. Across the lattice of bare branches in the afternoon's deepening iron light I saw our commonest evergreen shining scarlet, a lamp held up bright through the darkness of the winter solstice.[1]

But privately, this shaft of optimism was not enough to lighten Allsop's mood. Spearheading the campaign against Berkley Petroleums in the run-up to Christmas had exhausted him, and the current hiatus now seemed to be rapidly filling with the demands of Powerstock Common. And then there was the day job. 'How can I get three country columns, two book columns and a *Nova* article written before I go on Monday? How can I undertake this filming job on this abominable limb?' he wrote in his new 1972 diary, the weekend before departing to South America for two weeks' filming.

An incident - heavy with metaphor - a few days before on Waterloo station had brought home to him that he no longer had the physical strength and stamina on his own to bear the weight of all his responsibilities. As he was leaving the ticket office, his recently-replaced artificial right leg slid on the slimy, wet platform. 'I went into splits, suitcases etc flying. Then the leg came off the stump. Terrible anguish. Amid curious eyes, had to try ramming the stump into the socket and obtain minimal suction to keep it there. Thank God I had an umbrella which kept me upright. Three young boys and a woman offered help, but I couldn't get a porter - two passed and refused a hand... Trouble was I also hurt my knee of left leg, so it was painful whatever I did.'

Back in Dorset feeling 'shocked and sick', he expected more practical and emotional support from Betty than she felt she was able to give. A few years earlier he had written privately about the 'curious calculus' that 'at the times when one needs just that little extra understanding - perhaps indulgence – [Betty] almost instinctively and exactly in ration withdraws that help.'

It was all too much. 'Life is a sewer. Everything depresses me - the ugly cancerous rusty tin farm buildings on the drive back, the brutishness of men who only use the soil as a sponge to be squeezed and don't care what squalor they live in... I can see no road to happiness - all are closed now. If I didn't feel so physically done-for - a complete crock - I would be better able to face up with vigour and less nauseating self-pity.'

It was not surprising, then, that when on 20 January Allsop returned from filming abroad, he took to his bed with 'flu. But the next day a call from Michael Hudson's wife, Ann, confirmed the return of the drillers. It forced him to get up and drive north along the Bridport-Beaminster road to Bingham's Farm. As he rounded the bend, a steel tower at least 120 feet high erected in a field adjacent to the road suddenly broke into view. Parked next to it was a Land Rover with the Seismographic Service Ltd (SSL) logo painted discreetly on the doors. Allsop pulled in and as he walked over to the driver, Michael Hudson arrived. Together, the two of them succeeded in extracting from the driver that four drills were being used - three tractor-mounted, and a 'Mayhew 1000', so-called because it was capable of drilling down a thousand feet in search of underground oil and gas reservoirs.

A mile back towards Bridport, a gathering of local councillors was being addressed by two SSL representatives, but attempts by a local reporter to join in were rebuffed: instead, he was told that a 'special show' for press and TV would be laid on the following week. Allsop's attempts a few days later to prise from SSL a map showing precisely where the test drilling and explosions were to take place were met with a blank refusal. 'Our sole duty is to collect data, and it would not be professional ethics to tell you what we are finding,' declared the head of the drilling team, Mr Woodliffe. 'We have informed the County Council of what we are doing and have therefore complied with our legal requirements.' But it seemed clear from the snippets of information that Allsop had managed to collect that the search was concentrated in an area bounded by Powerstock, Mangerton, Mapperton, Askerswell, Loders and Bingham's Farm on the Beaminster road - with the nearest drilling point just half a mile from the Mill. 'Bed at 12.30 and no sleep until 4.30 am,' wrote Allsop in his diary. 'Feel beset and overstrung by the oil situation: visions of sabotage by tyre slashings and cable cuttings…'

Later, a small notice tucked away in the back pages of the *Bridport News* of 3 March 1972 announced that Berkley Petroleums had submitted a formal planning application to drill an exploratory borehole at Welcome Hill, about three miles north-east of Bridport, and that any representations by members of the public should be sent in writing by 23 March to the Clerk of Dorset Council, Mr K. A. Abel. This marked a new and crucial stage in the campaign. Allsop was convinced that large-scale development of the heart of the Thomas Hardy country would be unstoppable if, as he expected, the drillers were to discover oil or gas.

'Our Vigorous Militancy'

A few weeks before, on 1 February, over fifty sympathisers had crowded into Dr Hudson's living room in Beaminster for the official launch of the 'Defenders of West Dorset' (DWD). A small committee was appointed with Allsop as President, Hudson as Chairman and Chris Geering as Secretary, with the immediate task of opposing the planning application for the exploratory drilling. Their chosen logo was the Cerne Abbas Giant, the huge, 180-foot tall figure of unknown antiquity, which, complete with club and rampant manhood, adorned the downland chalk above the Dorset village of that name. The knotty club in its right hand was understood as a symbol of Dorset's resistance to Roman, Saxon and now North American invaders. Local tradition also held that the Giant was a cure for barrenness, 'especially if the couple desiring issue actually consummate the marriage on the spot'.

Allsop explained to one supporter that the Giant had been chosen because it symbolised 'the ancientness of our countryside and our vigorous militancy', but, predictably, a number of the female members of the committee were not entirely happy with the choice.

Privately, after all the burdens and anxieties of the previous weeks, Allsop felt 'immensely relieved to unload the weight of work and responsibility on to other shoulders'. He was pleased that the DWD committee 'seems to straddle well all classes, types and politics. Let's hope it is a winner.'

But existing local environmental groups were far less enthusiastic, and resented what they considered to be Allsop's bid to muscle in on their territory. Relations were most fraught with the Council for the Protection of Rural England (CPRE), not just at county level, but nationally as well. Its national President, Lord Kennet (Wayland Young) had telephoned Allsop on 3 December 1971 and pleaded with him to work through CPRE rather than start another organisation 'of which there are too many already'. Allsop had first met Kennet two years earlier at a dinner party in Hertfordshire given by his then neighbour and local MP Shirley Williams and her then husband, the philosopher Bernard Williams. 'Don't like him,' Allsop wrote of Kennet. 'A vain and deeply self-satisfied man'.

Nevertheless, in a conciliatory bid to establish a co-operative relationship with CPRE, Michael Hudson - a member for eight years - had the matter raised at the next meeting of the CPRE's Dorset branch committee. However, the Chair, a Major R. H. K. Wickham, made clear he was not opposed to oil exploration locally, since he considered it was important in the depths of the Cold War that the government should establish the extent of the UK's strategic reserves. 'Since the Suez crisis there has been a stranglehold on prices, and the more minerals that are found from our own resources the better,' he wrote later to Hudson. Moreover, he had had no complaints about the activities of Seismographic Service Ltd. 'Hereabouts, we have had the utmost co-operation between the exploration companies, the local authorities and the owners and occupiers of the land anywhere near the routes of the "echo lines"… Personally, I should be very sorry to hear of another *ad hoc* society starting in this county. CPRE is long established and has the confidence of the County Council, who are, through their planning side, active members of CPRE.' He declined Hudson's invitation to attend the DWD's inaugural meeting on 1 February because 'I have a District Scout meeting that evening and will be chairman.'[2]

It was clear that Major Wickham was in favour in principle of exploiting any oil and gas found in Dorset, and therefore, logically, he supported the exploratory drilling in order to find it in the first place. Allsop was appalled by what he considered to be his complacency and collusion, privately describing him as a 'total simpleton'. For his part, Lord Kennet also accepted that the decision to allow exploratory drilling could not be logically divorced from considering the effects of large-scale exploitation if oil or gas were found - but there should be a presumption in favour of exploration, with the burden of proof that eventual exploitation would result in unacceptable environmental damage falling on the opponents, rather than the oil company. 'It seems to me difficult to hold that prospecting for minerals to find out whether they are there is in itself impermissible, unless one can conclusively show in advance that the exploitation of the minerals which might be found would be impermissible in a given area,' he wrote to Allsop. 'Can you do that in the question of Dorset oil?'[3]

Allsop's answer to that was straightforwardly: 'Yes'. He considered that by definition, in any National Park or an Area of Outstanding National Beauty, which had been established by the government explicitly to offer protection to the landscape against the scars of industrial development, there must be a presumption against permitting exploitation. Even in the case of overriding national interest, the onus of proof why this principle should be overturned should fall to the developer, not those seeking to uphold the law.

The stand-off eventually came to head at the annual meeting of the West Dorset CPRE Group on 22 April 1972, when Hudson launched a well-publicised attack on CPRE's 'conciliatory attitude' towards Berkley's planning application. A number of CPRE members in the audience applauded when he declared that an Area of Outstanding Natural Beauty should never be subject to this sort of development. The response of Major Wickham was to accuse DWD of being 'parochially minded' rather than looking after the interests of the whole country. 'What are they protecting Rural England against?' asked Allsop in his diary. 'The tragedy is that the public presumes that the countryside is in the safe custody of these fools and knaves. Feel sick and despondent.'

Not in my Backyard?

Relations were just as bad with the Dorset Natural History and Archaeological Society (DNHAS), of which Allsop was a member. The Curator and Secretary of the Society, Roger Peers, was based in the Dorset County Museum in Dorchester, and as such worked closely alongside the County Council.

Following the public meeting in Bridport Town Hall in November 1971, Allsop had written to Peers seeking the Society's support against the oil prospectors. His reply on 24 January was no more supportive than CPRE's: 'I am instructed to point out that while the Society is most anxious to prevent the unreasonable exploitation of the natural assets of the County it must take care not to acquire a reputation for opposing every proposal since if it does its opposition will cease to be of any value... If there is oil to be found in commercial quantities under Dorset then in the present state of the country's economy it seems to the Council (of the DNHAS) essential that it should be found and extracted so long as it can be done without unreasonable damage.'[4]

Already at loggerheads with almost every other environmental agency and NGO operating in Dorset, Allsop replied at length and with more than a hint of exasperation. 'I suspect that it is bootless to continue this discussion with you and your Council, since you present yourselves as so comfortably immoveable in your inaction. I object strongly to the ill-informed inertia with which you are treating this situation. The tragedy is that the public at large assumes that the existence of such organisations guarantees that these grave responsibilities are being properly discharged…'[5]

'My own reaction to your letter and all this talk about the complacency of established bodies, comfortable immobility etc, is of incredulity,' came the predictable reply a week later. 'Can you really be so out of touch with the local and sometimes the national papers, as well as the reports of all the existing bodies, not to realise that we and a great many people and bodies in Dorset have been slogging our guts out on actual, rather than imaginary, conservation matters all over Dorset for a very long time.' Mr Peers hoped that the objectives of DWD were not restricted just to 'Oil', but also to 'immediate and pressing problems' that he then proceeded to list at length. The implication was that Allsop was an ill-informed parvenu whose campaign in West Dorset was based solely on his own self-interest.

Peers might well have used the expression 'NIMBY' - the Not In My Backyard syndrome - but in 1972 it had yet to enter the vocabulary of environmental protest.[6] Others shared his view, including many local trade unionists who considered that Allsop was jeopardising local jobs. The Secretary of the Bridport and District Trades Council, Mr E. W. Evans, wrote to the *Bridport News* on 18 February arguing that 'the preservationists seem to give the impression… that people seeking work should go elsewhere. The natives are inclined to feel, with some justification, that similar advice might be offered to those who just want a nice country retreat.'

And some felt that Allsop was open to the charge of focusing not just on his own backyard, but even more narrowly on his own doorstep. In the first weeks of 1972 the columns of the *Bridport News* were dominated - in addition to oil drilling and the felling of the Powerstock oaks - by local controversies over the route of the proposed Bridport bypass, and the proposed closure of the Maiden Newton-Bridport railway line. Even the new Secretary of the Defenders, Chris Geering, wanted DWD to widen its horizons. He had first made contact with Allsop seeking his support against the demolition in Bridport of a ten-bedroom Georgian mansion, Wykes Court, to make way for a car park and allow lorries to make deliveries at the rear of shops in the high street. Allsop, however, had recruited him to the oil campaign instead. But Geering persisted, and on 29 February wrote a letter beginning 'Dear President', asking for Allsop's support on 'some of the minor battles I am currently involved in', and requesting permission to use the Defenders' headed notepaper in his campaigning.

By return of post, Allsop replied that he was wholly supportive on these other issues - but the time was not right.

> My hunch is that it would be wise not to press forward too fast with other matters (a) because we must get our priorities right and oil is the biggest threat and will need concentrated energy and (b) because we do not want to risk dispersion of our committee in possible disagreement about other things. Of course, this does not disbar you from any personal action you wish to take, but I feel it would be politic, for the time being at least, to keep our eyes fixed firmly on target number 1 - Berkley Petroleums. That is my feeling, but by all means raise the matter with the committee, although you should let them know my opinion on this. So, until this is cleared I think you probably should not use our note-head for the other matters. [7]

However, a few weeks later, on 7 April, a large picture of Chris Geering appeared on the front page of the *Bridport News* under the headline 'Oil Protesters Support Bid to Save Wykes Court'. In fact, the story underneath was about Geering's *request* to the DWD committee for such support 'because I feel that the same principle is involved here as it is in the oil affair. Chunk by chunk, the landscape that a lot of us have taken granted for so long is disappearing. It all matters now.'[8] It was a barely-veiled challenge to Allsop's authority as President, and was to contribute to Geering's resignation as Secretary of the DWD within the year.

The principal argument deployed by Allsop against the 'nimbyism' charge was that, regardless of the fact that it was taking place on his doorstep, the oil-drilling was first and foremost a *national* concern. To begin with, it threatened the destruction of 'Hardy country', so beloved of thousands of people living hundreds of miles away. At the same time it was just one instance of the mounting pressures from mining and industry that confronted all Areas of Outstanding Natural Beauty and National Parks - supposedly protected landscapes - across the whole of Britain.

The implication was that the campaign had to 'go national'. Accordingly, on 15 March 1972 Allsop wrote to *The Times* seeking support from its well-connected readers, reminding them that they had now little more than a week to submit letters of opposition to the Clerk of Dorset County Council. He also put in a plea for money to enable the newly-founded Defenders to fight an expected planning inquiry. 'The chosen site is (the irony of it!) on Welcome Hill, on the foothills of Eggardon, perhaps the most lovely and solitary heartland of this limestone region of coombs and deep lanes.' He made clear that their objective nationally was 'to bring about changes to Whitehall procedures and Westminster legislation to put an end to this random grabbing of resources (over and under the surface) which we should be cherishing.'[9]

At the same time, the local campaign was stepped up. A thousand car stickers proclaiming 'Oil means Spoil!' were printed for distribution among local supporters and Easter holiday visitors; 15,000 leaflets and membership forms introducing the Defenders of West Dorset were designed and printed, 10,000 of which Rodney Legg volunteered to distribute through the next edition of *Dorset The County Magazine*; and a standard letter setting out the DWD's objections to Berkley's planning application was posted to each member of the planning committees of both Beaminster and Dorset Councils.

Within a few days of the appearance of his letter in *The Times*, Allsop and the DWD received hundreds of letters of support from all regions of Britain and beyond, many enclosing copies of the objections they had sent separately to Dorset County Council. Some were posted from as far away as the USA and the Far East. Sixteen members of the Thomas Hardy Society of Japan pledged their support with fighting words and a donation of £25. Their President, Professor Mamoru Osawa, compared the campaign against the oilmen with 'the present ecological crisis of Japan'. Included among the correspondents from Britain were many of Allsop's distinguished colleagues, friends and admirers from across the media, arts and the academic world (see box below).

TV and Newspaper Journalists	**Academics/Foundations**
George Armstrong The *Guardian*	Corelli Barnet, University of Cambridge
Brian Inglis ITV	Lord David Cecil, University of Oxford
Ludovic Kennedy BBC	Frank Fraser Darling
Peter Snow BBC	Prof. Donald Davie, University of Stanford
Nicholas Tomalin *The Sunday Times*	Jacquetta Hawkes, Archaeologist
	Julian Huxley
Writers and Artists	Prof. John Lukes, University of Oxford
John Bayley	Alan Pifer, President of the Carnegie Trust
John Betjeman	John Sparrow, All Souls, Oxford
Kenneth Clark	
John Fowles	**The Church**
Roland Gant	Archbishop of Canterbury, Michael Ramsay
Evelyn Hardy	Fr. Brocard Sewell, Order of Carmelites
Richard Mabey	
Iris Murdoch	**Parliament**
Reynolds Stone	Robin Cooke MP
Sylvia Townsend Warner	Sir Robert Lusty MP
Laurence Whistler	Michael Shersby MP
Robin Wordsworth	Lord Hinchingbrook
	Lord Southborough
Film and Theatre	Lady Sylvia Sayer
Andrew Lloyd-Webber	
Christopher Lee	

Typical was the letter written later to the Environment Secretary, Peter Walker, by TV presenter Peter Snow, demonstrating why what was happening in a remote corner of Dorset was of concern to the whole of the country. He explained that he was writing 'not as someone who lives in the area but as a visitor who has with my family and friends enjoyed this part of the countryside for many years, and who hopes to continue to do so for many more. Such areas as Powerstock are not only necessary as areas of unspoilt beauty to those who live there but for many people like myself who live in crowded cities and need such an environment for our refreshment and health.'[10]

Meanwhile, over 500 letters of protest flooded into the County Council's post room, two-thirds from outside the county. This soon convinced Mr Abel that the discussion of Berkley Petroleums' planning application could not be restricted to local councillors alone. So on 11 April he wrote to all those who had made representations inviting them to a public meeting in Beaminster Town Hall, where local councillors could hear at first hand the views of both the developers, and their opponents.

'I would like to make it clear,' he wrote, 'that no decision will be reached on the application at this meeting as neither the Local Planning Authority nor the local authorities concerned have yet formed any view on the application. The object of this meeting is to hear a full explanation by the applicants of the exact nature and location of their proposals and to enable questions to be put to them.'

Allsop and the Defenders had just ten days to prepare.

1. Allsop, K, 'December', *In the Country*, Hamish Hamilton, 1972, pp.209-10
2. Letter from Major Wickham to Michael Hudson, 29 January 1972
3. Letter from Lord Kennet to Allsop, 10 December 1971
4. Letter from Roger Peers, Secretary of the Dorset Natural History and Archaeological Society, to Allsop, 24 January 1972
5. Letter from Allsop to Roger Peers, 23 February 1972
6. Letter from Roger Peers to Allsop, 29 February 1972
7. Letter from Allsop to Chris Geering, 1 March 1972
8. *Bridport News*, 7 April 1972
9. 'Oil in Hardy Country', Letters, *The Times*, 15 March 1972
10. Letter from Peter Snow to Secretary of State for the Environment, Peter Walker, 2 May 1972

7

A FRIEND OF THE EARTH

Early Friends of the Earth campaign posters displayed by Anfel Potter (centre) and colleagues in their cramped HQ in Soho's Poland Street in 1971. (Courtesy Friends of the Earth)

AT THE HEIGHT OF the oil controversy, a supporter from Kent wrote to Allsop drawing attention to the piecemeal nature of local environmental campaigns. In response to his question whether there was any 'sensible body' keeping an eye on the big picture, Allsop agreed that there was no such umbrella organisation. 'The CPRE is hopeless. My personal view is that the best body are the Friends of the Earth, who are young, energetic and idealistic.'[1]

In mid-1972 FoE in the UK was barely two years old. The initiative to set it up came from an American writer, environmentalist and mountaineer David Brower, who had established the first Friends of the Earth in San Francisco in 1969 as a 'non-profit organisation created to undertake aggressive political and legislative activity aimed at restoring an environment misused by man, and at preserving the Earth's remaining wilderness'. Brower's ambassador in the UK was a Scottish chartered accountant called Barclay Inglis, who from September 1970 worked part-time nurturing the fledgling organisation in London. In October, he opened a tiny one-room office in King Street alongside the bustling vegetable and flower market in London's Covent Garden, then a run-down area threatened with the kind of re-development that in the 1960s and early 1970s destroyed dozens of town and city centres across Britain.

The contrast between FoE's King Street office and the Travellers' Club half a mile away in stately Pall Mall could not have been starker. It was there, in November 1970 in this quintessentially English gentleman's club, that Inglis and two young colleagues - Graham Searle and Jonathan Holliman - launched FoE (UK) with a champagne send-off. Inglis as Chairman appointed Graham Searle, a 24-year-old postgraduate geologist at King's College, London, as FoE's first Executive Director. Searle had been Vice-President of the National Union of Students when future Labour Home and Foreign Secretary Jack Straw was its President, and had also chaired the NUS Committee on the Environment. In May 1971, FoE was officially incorporated as a non-charitable company limited by guarantee - deliberately not a charity, to allow maximum freedom in the conduct of its essentially political campaigns.

FoE had came into being in response to the failure of existing environmental organisations to give an effective response to the mounting threats to Britain's resources, landscape and wildlife. A cosy reliance on the old boy network and private negotiations with government officials behind closed doors was the *modus operandi* of bodies like the CPRE and local Naturalists' Trusts. In complete contrast, FoE's style was more open, media-oriented and often witty and engaging, borrowing much from the student protest movements in the US and Britain during the 1960s.

FoE first grabbed the headlines in May 1971 by dumping over 1,500 non-returnable bottles on the steps of Schweppes' head office in London, later publishing a set of posters that instantly grabbed media attention, declaring 'DON'T LET THEM SCHHH… ON BRITAIN'.

In the autumn of that year, FoE moved into a rent-free two-room office in Soho's Poland Street, subsequently launching a campaign against mineral exploration and mining in Britain's National Parks and AONBs. A particular focus was the activity in Snowdonia and elsewhere of the multinational mining corporation, Rio Tinto Zinc (RTZ). At this time FoE still had a tiny full-time staff of only eight, all well-qualified and most, like Searle, in their twenties. They offered technical competence, advice and alternative policy solutions that were well-researched and credible, helping the burgeoning number of highly decentralised, autonomous local action groups that had sprung up across the country.

Allsop first made contact with FoE - albeit indirectly - as early as October 1970 when it was still housed in King Street, above the radical publishers Ballantine Books. The latter provided FoE with its first commission - to produce *The Environmental Handbook: Action Guide for the UK*, tailoring the original American version to conditions in the UK. It was to be edited by John Barr, a freelance writer formerly on the staff of *New Society* and author of *The Assaults on Our Senses* - a book which Allsop reviewed, sympathetically, in July in the *New Statesman*. It was to Allsop that Barr turned to write an introduction to the *Handbook* (see pp.27-8), and his contacts at this time appear to have been with Barr rather than directly with FoE's small staff.

Allsop seems not to have spoken directly to Graham Searle until 17 December 1971, after hearing from the Countryside Commission that Searle was preparing a map of all the mineral workings across Britain. In early 1972, FoE published *Rock Bottom: Nearing the Limits of Metal Mining in Britain* - its evidence to the Zuckerman Commission (see below) - which Allsop described as 'obligatory reading'. On 11 February 1972, after a long telephone conversation with its joint author, Amory Lovins, Allsop wrote in his diary that 'FoE are the best hope for achieving results' and that the DWD should collaborate closely with them. Soon after, he wrote to Searle confirming that this was indeed the majority view of the DWD committee.[2]

Michael Hudson reported to the DWD committee on 9 March that he and Allsop had become members of FoE, and had jointly purchased a £25 share in RTZ in order to be able to vote at its AGM. The committee agreed that the growing *entente cordiale* between the two organisations should be strengthened by inviting Searle and his colleague Simon Millar to the next committee meeting, which Allsop offered to host at his home in the Mill.

Allsop became a frequent visitor to Poland Street during the spring of 1972, and it seemed not entirely out of the question that the Defenders of West Dorset might become *de facto* a local FoE action group. Over the coming months, FoE's influence could be discerned in the development of DWD's campaign against Berkley Petroleums (UK), and even in the content and approach of Allsop's television series *Down To Earth* (see Chapter 8).

Allsop and Friends of the Earth needed each other. FoE gave more attention than any other British environmental group to using the media to get its message across and project its own image. A later survey of Britain's environmental NGOs reported that FoE had established 'a consistently good working relationship with journalists and broadcasters... by understanding how the media work, the type of information wanted and when it is wanted. The media have been attracted by FoE's coherent arguments, good press relations and high quality publicity events. Information not readily available from other resources has been the basis for leading articles, even if FoE itself is not mentioned.'[3]

What Allsop needed was back-up in the form of well-researched briefings and campaigning advice. He also liked working with intelligent young people, as witnessed by his Rectorship at Edinburgh University. Later in 1972, when he had been released from his long-term contract with the BBC, he was happy openly to endorse the organisation in the introduction to *Project Earth*, Searle's campaigning guide for young people, and effectively FoE's manifesto. 'Those who ask what they can do, receive the reply, join FoE. The intention of this book is to enrol more for the rescue squad, to tell those still in their teens that all is not lost, and all is not hopeless - provided that all make their individual contributions.'[4]

In the bright, sunlit afternoon of Thursday 6 April, Graham Searle, Simon Millar and their respective partners were introduced for the first time to the ancient tumbled landscape of West Dorset. They had to concede that Allsop had a strong case when he described it as 'the loveliest part of all England'. Later, they dined at the Mill with the Allsops, the Hudsons, Chris Geering and his wife, and DWD solicitor David Lyon-Smith, before being joined by the rest of the committee. The main business of the meeting was to decide tactics for the forthcoming public meeting in Beaminster on 21 April, convened by Dorset County Council to examine Berkley's planning application. This was to be preceded during the morning by a visit to the proposed drilling site on Welcome Hill, where Lawton Clark and his Berkley colleagues would explain to local councillors the impact of their proposals, on the ground.

Allsop explained to the committee that he had secured - for free - the services of a Bristol barrister, Paul Chadd QC, a former Recorder of Bournemouth and a Thomas Hardy admirer. He had been active in a number of planning campaigns in Bristol, and had offered to represent the DWD during the public meeting. 'Sounds a splendid man, quick and humorous,' was Allsop's judgement. He would be supported by a firm of Bournemouth solicitors responsible for background legal research and correspondence with the County Council. Chadd had warned Allsop that the Council could make any rules they wished for the conduct of what was an informal public meeting. Later, Chadd was told that despite being a barrister, he would not be permitted to cross-examine Berkley's witnesses.

Around the log fire after dinner, Searle and Millar insisted that the Defenders should push to be represented at the morning site visit, so the objectors could put their case to the planners in the same way as the developers. Searle offered the services of either himself or Amory Lovins in challenging Berkley's presentation of the scientific or engineering issues.

Allsop had already telephoned Dorset County Council's Chief Planning Officer, Alan Swindall, to press the case for the Defenders to be represented at the meeting on Welcome Hill. He and Swindall had developed a reasonable working relationship over the future of Powerstock Common, but on this occasion Swindall insisted that this was a fact-finding event for councillors only. However, he promised that any information arising from statements by the Berkley Petroleums team would be made available to the wider public at the Beaminster meeting during the afternoon.

'Besides,' said Swindall, 'if we allow the Defenders to be present, we will have to invite the CPRE, the Ramblers and any other interested local groups.'

'And what's wrong with that?' Allsop had asked, curtly.

Eventually, reaching for a compromise, Swindall conceded that Searle might attend, but only as an observer and not as a participant. Allsop reluctantly accepted this, but the following day even this offer was withdrawn. The Conservative chairman of the Planning Committee, Mr R. G. Earle, took a harder line than his chief planning officer and was determined that troublesome local pressure groups should be put in their place.

A nine-page follow-up briefing paper from Searle and Millar landed on Allsop's doormat a few days later. 'What you want from the 21st is at least a Public Inquiry to precede the granting or refusal of permission to drill,' Searle wrote. 'The lawyer should therefore repeatedly stress the *national* importance of the decision - the words "Public Inquiry" should crop up time and time again.'

In addition, he drew attention to an important precedent. The so-called 'Westerdale Case' arose at a public inquiry into an application in 1968 by Home Oil of Canada Ltd for exploratory drilling in the North York Moors National Park. The Planning Inspector, Mr S. Rollinson, ruled that 'whilst there must be a formal decision relating to the application to explore only, the real problem will arise if gas is found. In the light of the licences to explore, which might be deemed to imply that extraction should be permitted; the very high cost of exploration; and the national interests involved, *I think it is logical to consider now, and as fully as possible, the impact which (eventual) exploitation might have on the area.*'[5]

Searle ended his note with some friendly advice that Allsop, later in the year, would have done well to recall: 'I hope this is of some use. Check everything we've written!' (See Chapter 10).

The Defenders may have been banned from participating in the Welcome Hill site visit, but there was nothing to stop them turning up in force to demonstrate from the public footpaths. Dozens of them converged on the site, many dressed in sage green T-shirts emblazoned with the threatening image of the Cerne Giant. Allsop arrived accompanied by the DWD's barrister, Paul Chadd, and Amory Lovins. Mingling among the crowd were representatives of the local and national press and television, including Nick Tomalin from *The Sunday Times* and Jack Pizzey from the BBC's *Nationwide*. The presence of the resplendently-bearded Admiral Sir Victor Crutchley (VC, *Croix de Guerre*), the 79-year-old owner of Mappercombe Manor and the Welcome Hill drilling site, provided an unmissable picture opportunity. Crutchley was not overtly hostile to the protesters, but as a former loyal member of the armed forces he took the view that if the government had granted Berkley Petroleums a licence to explore, then he should not stand in their way.

Councillor Earle, his back to the protesters, presided over an hour's session of essentially technical questions and answers between Lawton Clark's team and the members of the planning committee, after which the entire assemblage decamped in their coaches and cars to Beaminster Town Hall. Outside the hall, the milling throng of journalists made Fleet Street (Beaminster) look like its London EC1 namesake.

From the chair, Earle opened the proceedings by emphasising that this was not a public enquiry, but a public meeting to gather factual information. As he said this, he looked pointedly at Allsop. 'To those who would wish us to refuse this application, may I mention that the planning authority will need to give sound planning reasons if it is decided to refuse? Emotions are not enough. How much would they weigh in the balance?'

This remark demonstrated how difficult it was going to be to reconcile the fundamental differences of view between the various parties in the room. For there were basically three contending approaches that could be taken in considering Berkley's planning application:

1. To treat it simply as an application for a minor exploratory drilling operation, taking no account of subsequent developments if oil or gas were discovered;

2. To acknowledge the links between exploration and possible subsequent exploration, and to consider the environmental impacts of both;

3. To deny entirely the competence - both legal and technical - of the local planning authority to take decisions on what were clearly matters of national importance, that should be taken at a national level by a government minister.

The questions, answers and statements from the floor reflected all these different positions. Earle tended towards the first, but his Chief Planning Officer, Swindall, leaned in favour of the second. In a briefing paper he was to write a few weeks later for the members of the County Council's planning committee, he made clear his view that this was no run-of-the-mill planning application: 'The present application is, to the best of my knowledge, the first in this part of the country to be proposed in an Area of Outstanding Natural Beauty. The decision upon it may, therefore, create a precedent of some importance.' He stressed that the Council's decision on Berkley's plan for exploratory drilling would have to take account of the impact of the subsequent exploitation of any oil or gas deposits that were discovered - even though a separate planning application for this would be required. 'The drilling operation will involve an investment of some £100,000. If therefore the authority feels that there are no terms on which they would agree to the commercial production of either gas or oil if discovered, it is my opinion that they should refuse the present application.'

For Swindall, a refusal on these grounds was by no means out of the question:

The problem therefore lies in judging whether the present application will have *or lead to* a significant effect on the environment. In making this judgement the present quality of the area is of great importance. The site is within the Dorset Area of Outstanding Natural Beauty. Within this, however, West Dorset is of special significance. Not only is it an area of exceptional landscape beauty but its freedom from most forms of urban growth and commercial exploitation give it a peace and charm found in few parts of this country today. The local authorities administering this lovely area have a great responsibility and should jealously guard this heritage.

No specific *statutory* criteria are laid down regarding development within Areas of Outstanding Natural Beauty. There is, however, a general implication in the National Parks and Access to the Countryside Act 1949 that the planning authority will use its powers 'for the purpose of preserving and enhancing the natural beauty of the areas'.[6]

The business of the meeting got underway with Lawton Clark largely reiterating the points he had made to councillors during the morning. He said that the drilling equipment could be transported and erected in one day, but the narrow roads around the site would be completely blocked for this period. The exploratory drilling of the 6,000-foot hole would continue for up to six weeks, 24 hours a day, and the noise level would be comparable to 'two to three tractors working in a field'. In a bid to calm local opposition, he said that the chances of finding anything were no more than forty to one, and then it was likely that gas rather than oil would be found, enabling transportation by underground pipeline rather than road tanker. And he promised: 'If this is a dry well, Dorset will see us no more.'

Allsop asked a few technical questions, while Amory Lovins pointed out that if oil was discovered and extracted, it would supply precisely 72 minutes' worth of Britain's annual demand.

Paul Chadd QC, on behalf of the DWD, stuck closely to the brief set out in FoE's memo calling for the third approach to the application. He referred to the House of Commons statement by the Minister of Town and Country Planning Lord Silkin in March 1949, which set out the conditions that he considered should be met before any industrial development could be permitted in a National Park or AONB.

> The first condition is that it must be demonstrated quite clearly that the exploitation of those minerals is absolutely necessary in the public interest. It must be clear beyond all doubt that there is no possible alternative source of supply, and if those two conditions are satisfied then the permission must be subject to the condition that restoration takes place at the earliest possible opportunity.

Chadd argued that the information provided by Berkley concerned only the technical aspects of the proposed exploratory drilling, so that local councillors were not equipped to judge the wider issues of 'national interest', nor the extent to which currently unknown oil and/or gas reserves in West Dorset would contribute to this. 'This is a matter of such importance it would be wrong for the application even to be considered on the sort of technical information put forward to this room, an assembly totally unable to judge sufficiently to give approval or disapproval.' He concluded that it should be left to the Minister to make his own investigations, and then to judge the application from a national standpoint.

It is not hard to imagine the effect that this intervention had on the Chair of the Dorset County Council Planning Committee, who had just been written off as incompetent. After a pause, he asked: 'I take it that this is all the Defenders wish to say?'

Chadd: 'It is, sir. At a meeting like this it is impossible for them to do what I would do had I had the opportunity to ask questions.'

Earle: 'Nothing to the Planning Authority? You wish this decision to be refused but you do not wish to suggest any reasons why the Planning Committee should refuse? We are asking you to give reasons.'

Chadd: 'If, from what I have said, sir, you as a reasonable person cannot see reasons… I venture to think that the audience can see reasons why the Planning Committee should not allow the application in what I have said. This is an area of such outstanding beauty that the development ought not to be permitted.'

Rapturous applause went up from a large section of the audience. Chadd acknowledged this with a smart heel kick, the slightest of bows and a wry smile. From the floor, a Colonel Green pointed out to Earle that the County Council's own planning policy was reason enough - for it was they who in 1959 had pressed for the designation of West Dorset as an AONB, and that they had subsequently fought fiercely, and at great expense, against the erection by the Central Electricity Generating Board of electricity pylons across the landscape.

Even so, Chadd's contribution seemed both ill-prepared and badly judged. In a letter to Allsop a few days later, Amory Lovins tried to be charitable. He made the point that had the press picked up the point that Chadd had been allowed to attend only if he asked no questions, the Council would have been made 'a national laughing stock'. He had already sent the Bournemouth solicitors a long letter on ways in which they might strengthen their approach to the County Council.

Hudson and Allsop also asked Chadd for a draft of a supplementary letter from the Defenders to the Council listing the *planning* reasons why Berkley's application should be refused. The draft that followed made two major points of procedure:

- In view of the protection given by AONB status, the onus should be on the applicants to show that the application is absolutely necessary in the public interest, rather than the opponents to show that it was not;
- In any event, a proper environmental assessment required the consideration of independent technical advice, rather than just the partial information provided by the developers.

In addition, the letter provided the planning reasons for refusal that Earle had asked for:

- There had been no consideration of impacts on local flora and fauna;
- The application had not been referred to the Countryside Commission, as was required by the 1949 Act;
- The disruption of access roads had not been assessed;
- Nor had the impact of continuous noise from the drilling.

The Defenders' letter concluded by arguing that the County Council should either hand the issue over for decision to the Secretary of State for the Environment, on the grounds that they had inadequate technical information; or they should refuse the application, leading to an appeal by the developers which would trigger a public inquiry. Privately, Allsop was not optimistic about the ultimate outcome. 'We have all been feeling a bit depressed since the pretty naked display of 'pro-oilishness' by the decision-makers,' he wrote a few days later.

Unwelcome on Welcome Hill

The sudden slow and regular tolling of a solitary funeral bell resounded through the Sunday stillness, startling a cacophony of hoarse cawing from the ancient rookery in twelfth-century St Mary Magdalene's churchyard elms. Along the village street outside The Loders Arms, a melancholy morning mist wrapped itself around the sombre crowd of about a hundred mourners - the men dressed in black frock coats, bow ties and top hats, the women in heavy lace veils. The social mix was as varied as the Dorset landscape through which they had journeyed that morning: farm workers, a retired naval commander, schoolchildren, a young novelist, grandmothers, the local MP.

The six pall bearers lifted the black coffin to their shoulders, ready to lead the cortege up Smishops Lane, a holloway worn down over the generations thirty feet into the sandstone hill and tunnelled over in a green twilight of overarching trees. A simple wreath of hedgerow flowers - red campions, buttercups, dog rose and ragged robin - brought colourful relief to the otherwise muted palette of the slowly-winding procession.

It could have been scene from a Hardy novel, except for the inscriptions painted in white on the sides of the coffin: 'Welcome Hill, RIP' and 'Here lies an Area of Outstanding Natural Beauty, died of sickness which the Dorset County Council and others did not see fit to prevent.' Placards lifted above the cortege declared: 'A kill for the planners' and 'Dorset dies an oily death.' And at the rear of the cortege came a column of journalists - from the *Daily Telegraph*, *The Times*, the local *Bridport News* - and broadcasters from the BBC and Westward television, keen to capture the countrymen of Wessex challenging the North American oilmen.

Allsop felt uncomfortable in his black suit and wing collar, but at least relieved that on this occasion he could take a back seat. For the mock funeral had been organised not by the Defenders of West Dorset, nor by Friends of the Earth, but by Victor Montagu, the owner of Mapperton House, outside Beaminster. As Viscount Hinchingbrooke (a title he had disclaimed) he had been Private Secretary to former Prime Minister Stanley Baldwin, and until 1962 the Conservative MP for South Dorset. In view of his forthright opposition to the government's indiscriminate encouragement of oil exploration, the title of his 1970 book, *The Conservative Dilemma*, was especially apt.

Three weeks before the mock funeral, on 2 June, Dorset County Council's Planning Committee had given Berkley Petroleums - as Allsop had expected - the go-ahead for exploratory drilling on Welcome Hill. On the same day, he had received a personal letter from the Secretary of State for the Environment, Peter Walker, refusing his request that he should 'call in' the planning application for his own decision rather than the County Council's.

The argument was familiar: 'Applications to prospect and applications to exploit are different issues and each must be looked at separately, paying regard to the environmental and other effects of the operations at each stage. A permission to sink an exploratory borehole would not in any way imply that any subsequent application to exploit any deposit found would be granted.'

Already the 150-foot drilling rig had been erected on the skyline of Welcome Hill. The barbed wire and 'Keep Out' notice warned intruders to keep away, while at the entrance to the site, the 'Nettlecombe No. 1' sign was ominous.

Clerk to the County Council Mr K. A. Abel had stressed that the planning consent was subject to 'stringent conditions':

- The operation was to be limited to ninety days;
- The site would then be completely restored;
- If oil was found, the Council would be 'unlikely' to approve any well-head installation 'significantly' greater than the six-foot 'Christmas tree' structure promised by Lawton Clark;
- Any oil or gas would be removed from the site only by pipeline;
- The siting of any treatment or storage plant in the AONB would be 'unlikely' to be approved.[7]

Allsop was not convinced. In a statement issued on behalf of the DWD on 8 June, he described the Council's decision as a 'shoddy betrayal of responsibility and trust', which resulted from 'a combination of greed and naivety'.

I only hope that the names of our elected servants who collaborated in this transaction will go on some permanent roll of dishonour so that they will be remembered not only by us, but by future generations - the men who acquiesced in the rape of Thomas Hardy country.

And later, from the top of Welcome Hill surrounded by his fellow mourners, millions of television viewers saw him declare to the nation: 'What is happening here is a warning of what the next ten years could bring throughout Britain…'

Over the next few weeks, the feebleness of the County Council's 'stringent conditions' and of Lawton Clark's assurances at the public meeting became clear. Mr Clark had promised that the exploratory drilling would be over in six weeks— less than half the period of ninety days he was actually given by the Planning Committee. But even this more generous deadline, 31 August 1972, came and went, and still the foothills of Eggardon reverberated to the continuous growl of the drill - now rather louder than the noise of the 'two or three tractors' that had been promised. Heavier machinery had been brought on site in a bid to reach a final 8,000-foot-deep stratum of rock, which had begun to look promising.

The County's planners decided to extend their deadline by thirty days not once, but twice - first on 1 September and then again on 1 October. The Defenders' Secretary, Chris Geering, had expressed his irritation in a tetchy letter to Allsop as early as 17 July. 'What about action?' he wrote. 'Are we actually going to DO something? I feel rather frustrated about sitting here and sending out membership forms etc, but still the drill is grinding round…'[8]

Allsop's mood remained privately defeatist, but by now he was beginning to set his sights on wider horizons as he prepared to move to *The Sunday Times*. While acknowledging to Geering that that 'DWD has got awfully moribund', he tried to be upbeat, encouraging him to 'get everybody moving a bit'. 'I really think we *must* get well and truly ready to deliver a blast if the company are still trying to hang on at the end of this extension period.'

In the event, the blast came not from the Defenders. The final bombshell in the Battle of Nettlecombe was exploded by Berkley Petroleums themselves. On 24 October a spokesman revealed they were pulling out. 'We have decided that, on the basis of information so far gained, the cost of moving in a larger rig to drill to a greater depth would not be warranted,' he told the *Bridport News*. Tests on core samples taken from a depth of 7,000 feet had shown 'little worthwhile prospect'. The drilling rig had already been dismantled, and the work of removing all signs of Berkley's occupation of Welcome Hill had begun.

The champagne flowed at the DWD Committee meeting two days later at Michael Hudson's house in Beaminster. He warned against dropping their guard, but they were sufficiently optimistic to discuss other local causes they might begin to champion.

The following week, Allsop received a personal letter of congratulation from the redoubtable Lady Sylvia Sayer, the Chair and patron of the Dartmoor Preservation Association. No stranger to frontline environmental campaigning herself, she had often deliberately interrupted army live firing exercises on Dartmoor's military ranges. 'I am so *delighted* and relieved that Berkley Petroleums have pulled out,' she wrote, 'and I am absolutely certain that one reason for their departure is that you and your brave friends made it so hot for them.'[9]

'We're a bit jubilant here - but with reservations,' Allsop replied. 'The Department of Trade licence lasts six years, and their job lot of Dorset covers a lot of wild upland country. So we shall continue to be watchful for any renewed attempts to have another shot elsewhere in the AONB.' He refused to claim all the credit for Berkley's departure, 'but I like to think that in their deliberations about whether to carry on they did weigh the opposition they'd encountered as a factor in coming to a decision...'[10]

From Dorset to Snowdonia

The unspoken *quid pro quo* for FoE's contribution to the DWD's oil campaign was that Allsop should publicly throw his weight behind their own campaign against copper mining in Snowdonia in North Wales. Two weeks after the Beaminster public meeting, Amory Lovins wrote to Allsop asking if he would be one of a number of 'distinguished Patrons' of FoE's Snowdonia Defence Fund, launched to finance their submission to the public inquiry into RTZ's application to mine copper at Capel Hermon, in the heart of the National Park. Lovins was well aware of the potential conflict between Allsop's role as a leading television journalist and as an environmental activist, and so he sought to play down the political significance of acting as a Patron. 'Their duties are non-existent - the Patrons just lend moral support,' he wrote, adding that they were also approaching such other members of the Great and the Good as Sir Frank Fraser Darling, Sir Lynn Ungoed Thomas, the Bishop of Kingston, Lord Esher, Sir Geraint Evans, Sir John Foster and perhaps Sir Charles Evans.[11]

'The only possible embarrassment I can foresee is if you should want to do something about our Snowdonia campaign on your new show. How much of an obstacle might that prove?' Lovins asked. With the first episode of *Down to Earth* scheduled for transmission on 17 May, Allsop was understandably circumspect, and chose not to commit himself.

Lovins had fallen in love with the mountains of North Wales soon after leaving the United States in 1967 as a twenty-year-old student, for Magdalen College, Oxford. He was a brilliant polymath, a competent mountaineer and an accomplished writer and poet:

> I know just the place to show you what this low November sun can do. We'll take a stroll on to the Glyder ridge. It should be out of the cloud by the time we get that high. See there, while you lace your boots, look across at the little crag near the lip of Cwm Llugwy: if the wind catches the fine spindrift just right and whirls it into that warm patch of sunlight by the boulders - if we're lucky - there'll be a rainbow. They often roost just by those rocks. But only for a moment. Did you see it? Already the flash of colour has blinked and vanished. Today it will be even harder than usual to guess where the sunbolts will strike next.[12]

This passage is taken from Lovins' book *Eryri, the Mountains of Longing*, commissioned by David Brower, the American founder of Friends of the Earth, to draw public attention to the looming threat to the 'mountain wildness' of Eryri, the Welsh name for Snowdonia. On one of his climbing expeditions in early 1969, Lovins discovered that Rio Tinto Finance and Exploration Inc was undertaking exploratory drilling for copper near Capel Hermon in the Coed-y-Brenin forest, in secret and without planning permission. Over almost two years, the company drilled as many as 48 deep holes in the National Park before being instructed to stop, submit a planning application and eventually face a public inquiry.

At that time the multinational mining industry, particularly in the United States, had a reputation for 'an inflated sense of entitlement, a belief that it was above the rules, and a view of itself as the West's salvation'. This 'rape and run' attitude engendered in the industry both an obsessive secrecy, and a desire to manipulate both the regulatory framework and public debate on its activities.[13]

In Wales, Rio Tinto Zinc (RTZ) had manoeuvred itself into a position of considerable influence over the economic development of the Principality, in particular through the Welsh Industrial Development Board. This was a public agency whose Chair, Duncan Dewdney, was also Chair of RTZ Development Enterprises, as well as Chair and managing director of RTZ's Imperial Smelting Corporation in Avonmouth. In July 1971 RTZ also announced that it was establishing, together with half a dozen other mining companies, an 'Independent Commission on Mining and the Environment' under the chairmanship of Lord Zuckerman, a former Chief Scientific Adviser to the UK government. This was designed to demonstrate to the world the company's environmental responsibility, as well as to influence future government policy, and so it chose to play down the fact that two of its members had close connections with RTZ.

Over the next fourteen months, until Zuckerman had published his report, the Commission provided a convenient mechanism for deflecting embarrassing questions about mining in National Parks.[14]

In April 1971, an article by the *Daily Telegraph*'s mining correspondent, Edwin Arnold, had - unusually - put RTZ on the defensive. Arnold was no Friend of the Earth, for in the past he had frequently dismissed the arguments against opencast mining, but he reversed his position after doing a few key calculations. He worked out that a large operation yielding 100,000 tons of copper ore would involve shifting no less than 60.3 million tons of waste each year. This would mean that over an estimated fourteen-year life cycle for an opencast mine, almost 850 million tons of rubble would be generated - enough to bury the entire City of London to a depth 150 metres - higher than St Paul's Cathedral. 'Given the huge social costs of Snowdonia copper,' Arnold concluded, 'I feel as a nation we can afford to forgo that much domestic mine output, and buy in from the world market.'[15]

More hostile publicity for RTZ was to follow. FoE's *Rock Bottom*, published in January 1972, set out the arguments on which the bulk of RTZ's critics were to focus over the next year. This was followed in May 1972 by Richard West's book *River of Tears: The Rise of the Rio Tinto Zinc Mining Corporation,* published under the imprint of Earth Island publishers, with strong links to FoE. Lovins' book *Eryri, the Mountains of Longing* appeared around the same time. Together, they provided much of the intelligence for a BBC *Horizon* programme *Do You Dig National Parks?* broadcast on 22 May 1972, which Searle subsequently described as 'the single most effective blow to the chances of RTZ getting permission to mine in Snowdonia'.

RTZ had refused to co-operate in the making of the programme, but belatedly agreed to participate in a post-programme discussion. Chaired by Ludovic Kennedy, this was a live debate between Searle and Lovins on the one hand, and the Deputy Chair of RTZ, Mr Roy Wright, on the other. RTZ had demanded sight of the programme well in advance of transmission to prepare a rebuttal, but as was normal BBC practice, was allowed to see only the final edited version (as were Searle and Lovins) on the morning of the broadcast. RTZ's subsequent demand to be given 'a few minutes' at the beginning of the post-programme discussion to make a statement was also turned down.

In the unscripted exchanges watched by millions of viewers, it was Wright who came off worst. Uncomfortably on the back foot, RTZ decided to bring in the heavy guns and launch a summer counter-attack. On 27 June, at RTZ's request, the BBC's Director-General Charles Curran and its Head of TV Features, Aubrey Singer, met RTZ's Chief Executive Val Duncan and his Chairman, Lord Byers. Sir Val outlined five points of complaint about the conduct of the programme:

- The idea for the programme had been 'sold' to the BBC by Amory Lovins;
- There had been no consultation on the film with RTZ, and 'consequently it had been both inaccurate and slanted';
- RTZ was not allowed to see the film until immediately prior to the recording of the discussion, 'so it had no idea of the allegations being made against it';
- The request by RTZ's Deputy Chairman for five minutes at the beginning of the discussion 'to correct the wrong facts and impressions of the film' had been turned down;
- The programme had been 'considerably edited' so that some remarks were taken out of context, and the order of discussion had been changed.

The BBC responded by pointing out that during the making of programme, Lord Byers had refused to answer specific questions pending the publication of the Zuckerman Report, while his offer to provide information 'off the record' was unacceptable for a public broadcasting organisation. Curran also pointed out that programmes were never made available considerably in advance of transmission in order to avoid interested parties exerting unacceptable pressures for editorial changes.

A few months later, on 7 November, Duncan followed up the meeting with an enraged letter to Curran complaining that copies of the *Horizon* programme were being made available by BBC Enterprises to audiences around the country:

It is difficult to express in restrained language my feelings on discovering that the programme in its original objectionable form - unaltered, unedited and unexplained - is being used as a film in areas of exceptional vulnerability. We have heard that the film has been shown to the Snowdonia National Park Society and to Clifton College. It seems clear that these cannot be the only recipients of this benefit and that the BBC has elected for a policy of putting it about indiscriminately…

If it is the fact that there are elements in your organisation able to do these things and to continue to do them regardless of the views of the responsible controllers, then we should like to know, so that we can regulate our conduct and our self-defence accordingly. I hope I shall not appear peremptory if I ask for the most urgent of replies.[16]

Friends of the Earth were inevitably the prime target. In July, three weeks after the meeting with the BBC, RTZ's solicitor, Lord Goodman, wrote to the managing director of Allen and Unwin Ltd requesting that Lovins' book *Eryri* should not be published in the UK in its present form because of alleged 'inaccuracies', which were 'plainly defamatory'. These were set out in a ten-page appendix to the letter. 'We are sure... that with the knowledge you now have of the true position,' wrote Goodman, 'you will not publish the book in this country in the same form as it has been published in New York.'

Then, on 27 July, Goodman dispatched a further letter to the publishers Earth Island Ltd complaining about the 'highly defamatory' *River of Tears*, this time with a 37-page list of 'corrections'. 'The point will be reached,' wrote Goodman, 'when no matter how rich and important a corporation, it cannot for that reason alone submit to all forms of injustice, even from the smallest and most unimportant organisations.'

Allsop had been obliged to decline an invitation to chair the post-programme discussion of *Do You Dig National Parks?* because of his concurrent commitment to the *Down to Earth* series, so he was not a direct party to these exchanges. However, a red mist rose before his eyes as Searle and Lovins related the details of RTZ's onslaught. He consoled himself with the thought that revenge would not be far off, for on 9 June he had received confirmation of a new job on the campaigning *Sunday Times*.

1. Letter to Allsop from Ronald Burch, 28 June 1972
2. Letter from Allsop to Graham Searle, 23 February 1972
3. Lowe P and Goyder J., *Environmental Groups in Politics*, Allen & Unwin, 1983
4. Introduction by Kenneth Allsop in Searle G., *Project Earth*, Wolfe Publishing Ltd., January 1973
5. The Westerdale Case, APP/2488/A/42146/PC3A
6. Swindall, A. T., *Proposed Exploratory Borehole at Welcome Hill: Report by the County Planning Officer* May 1972
7. Letter by K. A. Abel, Clerk to Dorset County Council, in *The Times*, 5 June 1972
8. Letter from Chris Geering to Allsop, 17 July 1972
9. Letter from Lady Sayer to Allsop, 2 November 1972
10. Letter from Allsop to Lady Sayer, 4 November 1972
11. Letter from Amory Lovins to Allsop, 8 May 1972
12. Quoted in Lovins, Amory (ed. Cameron M. Burns) *The Essential Amory Lovins: Selected Writings,* Earthscan, 2011, p.6
13. Diamond, Jared, *Collapse: How Societies Choose to Fail or Survive,*

Penguin Books, 2005, pp.461-463
14. Searle, Graham, 'Copper in Snowdonia National Park', in Smith, Peter K., *The Politics of Physical Resources,* Penguin, 1975, p.100ff
15. Arnold, Edwin, 'Keep the Mines away from our Beauty Spots', *Daily Telegraph*, 17 April 1971
16. Letter from Sir Val Duncan to Charles Curran, 7 November 1972

8

DOWN TO EARTH

Allsop was a regular presenter for seven years on the BBC's late-night news programme *24 Hours*. He left the programme in 1972 to front Britain's first, but short-lived, environmentalist television series, *Down to Earth*. (Courtesy BBC)

A BBC PRESS NOTICE released at the end of March 1972 announced the launch of what was to be the first dedicated environmentalist series to appear on British television. To be broadcast from mid-May on BBC1, the series promised 'to bring environmental issues down to earth and into the home' and 'to show that environmental issues affect all of us, all of the time'. It would present 'positive and constructive ideas and arguments not only for halting the deterioration of our environment, but for improving it - and to get across to people that they have the power to do this, if they exercise it'. The new series would be presented by Kenneth Allsop, who would be leaving *24 Hours* in mid-April. 'I am delighted that the BBC has decided to give regular air time to this all-pervading and crucial subject,' Allsop was quoted as saying. 'The environment seems to me to be simply the most important subject a journalist can concern himself with today.'

Allsop had tried to raise the profile of the environment on *24 Hours*, notably in relation to the mounting threats posed by the extraction of china clay to the wildlife of the Arne peninsula, close to home in Dorset. He had had little success. Although during the 1950s and 1960s the BBC had gained a reputation that was second to none for filming natural history - with outstanding presenters like Peter Scott, Armand and Michaela Dennis, Hans and Lotti Hass and David Attenborough - it had steered clear of addressing wider issues of conservation and the politics of the environment.

This attitude within the BBC had begun to shift by the early 1970s, as threats to the planet posed by modern industrial society began to enter public consciousness. *Doomwatch*, the sci-fi series written by Kit Pedler and Gerry Davis, ran for three years on BBC1 between 1970 and 1972, reaching an audience of 13.6 million. And preparations for the world's first global conference on the environment in 1972, the United Nations Conference on the Human Environment in Stockholm, persuaded many in the BBC that it was time to pay more attention.

It was the BBC's Natural History Unit in Bristol that in September 1971 first developed the idea for a new environmentalist series. However, it was soon acknowledged that the NHU's culture, expertise and resources were not appropriate to handle the wide ranging - and essentially political - issues of pollution and resource depletion. This was a matter for News and Current Affairs.

On one of the dark grey, dead days between Christmas and New Year 1971, Allsop received a telephone call at the Mill from John Percival, a young filmmaker and BBC producer with environmental and anthropological interests, asking if he would be interested in fronting a new environmentalist series, provisionally entitled *Us*. Allsop naturally expressed great interest. After all, he was being offered an unprecedented platform from which, every week, he could seek to sell the environmental agenda to millions of television viewers.

However, at that stage he could not see how he could fit it around his existing commitment to *24 Hours*, especially since *Us* was to be produced 200 miles away in Manchester. But on the other hand, the future of *24 Hours* was becoming increasingly uncertain, and his enthusiasm for the new series was further increased by a memo from Percival a few weeks later, promising that the programme would 'attack and attack hard', yet be 'stimulating, exciting, and above all, full of the joy of living'. It was a far more important and enticing prospect than a proposed weekly wildlife quiz show, *Animal Stars*, that the Natural History Unit had offered him at the end of February.

Allsop announced his willingness to leave *24 Hours* and commit to the new series at a meeting on 10 March with Brian Wenham (Head of the Current Affairs Group), Paul Fox (Controller, BBC1) and John Percival. Subsequently, over lunch at Le Coq Hardi in Kensington High Street, Wenham agreed that the subject matter of the series was such that it fell within the terms of Allsop's existing contract guaranteeing him a minimum number of days annually on news and current affairs programmes. The way now seemed clear for a new, greener, chapter in his broadcasting career.

But what was soon to be renamed *Down to Earth* was still not a done deal: Fox was not convinced that there was a sufficient audience for environmentalism, citing the failure of a similar magazine series broadcast by NBC in the United States. Percival was 'put through the hoop' about this at a lunch with Fox, Aubrey Singer and Chris Brasher, but succeeded in convincing them that the proposal was viable. Yet another good lunch followed, at which Allsop, Percival and his assistant Angela Marks exchanged ideas for the new series, outdoing each other in how far they were prepared to push their environmental radicalism.

Just before the first day of spring, on Sunday 19 March 1972, Allsop gazed out at the daffodils in the garden through the window of his study at the Mill. On the portable Adler in front of him, he set out on five closely-typed pages of foolscap his philosophical thoughts and specific suggestions for the programme. These reflected closely the ideas and arguments he had presented two years before in a booklet for Penguin Education's *Connexions* series, then edited by a 29-year-old Richard Mabey.[1] *Fit to Live In? The Future of Britain's Countryside* sought to explain to students what was happening to Britain's environment, how the natural world had a value that could no longer be squandered and what should be done to save and improve it.

The memo was the product of a man with a mission. 'There ought to be a big printed notice up in the office cautioning against the words CONSERVATION, ECOLOGY, ENVIRONMENT, EXPONENTIAL GROWTH, ECOSPHERE, and suchlike,' he began. 'If we are to succeed in doing what we both believe to be crucial – i.e. insinuating these very issues into the consciousness of Everyviewer, then… it must not be done in terms which immediately make him feel inferior… In other words, we must be "popular" - we hope.' At the same time, 'the two imperatives and implicits which should be running through the programmes, unvocalised but ever-present, are the twin menaces: Population Growth and Economic Growth. I imagine that we would never actually tackle either head-on, because each is of apocalyptic size and needs 50-minute special documentary scope, but each as an issue is bound to arise again and again through immediate matters in the news. My feeling is that the oftener we can stamp question marks all over these two concepts, querying the wisdom of both, the healthier.'

As regards the tone of the series, Allsop warned:

> We must not expose ourselves to accusations of being (a) ecodoom-merchants or (b) elfin nature-lovers. I happen, privately, to be both - that is, the nearest I know to happiness is being in the countryside and also I am persuaded that the overall situation of life-on-earth is in danger to a point at which it is difficult to exaggerate or be melodramatic. All the same… I think our credibility as a programme will depend on our calmness and avoidance of hyperbole… We must be hard-nosed and authoritative.

There then followed a wide-ranging list of the dragons to be slain. 'How do we deal with such issues as the ICI reservoir at Cow Green and its drowning of that Ice Age colony of plants; how do we assess the worth of not permitting English China Clays to flay the Arne Peninsula because it is the last stronghold of the Dartford warbler? Because few of us would ever have seen those odd little botanical freaks… do we by the same token say that it doesn't matter if Concorde's boom shatters the window of Chartres Cathedral? Think of the jobs for aircraft technicians, the food for their children, and who would go and look at the windows of Chartres Cathedral anyway? Perhaps much of our programme will be posing such dilemmas…'

Farmers were another key target. 'Sanctified Mystical Bringers of Bread or licensed hooligans? We really ought to look at how farmers get away with murder on the justification that they're filling our bellies: their contempt for even the most rudimentary aesthetic rules, and the eyesores and squalid constructions they put up in valleys and on hilltop horizons because corrugated asbestos and old bedsteads are cheaper, and because local planning authorities can't touch them; their hunnish uprooting of hedges and hacking them off with those tractor-mounted mandibles; their record on DDT etc; their Belsens of pigs and calves and chickens to supply the Cheap Food which we're always told we get...'

And 'towns should be as much our terrain as the countryside... does the ever-expanding dormitory which surrounds every town have to be the usual subtopian smear? We should not regard ugliness, even when it's made of cement and girders, as an irrevocable permanency: it can, given the decision, be removed.'

Also in the firing line were environmental pressure groups and government agencies. 'Who are the people who are supposed to be ensuring that we hew to decent criteria in our treatment of our surroundings?' he asked. 'One can rattle them off: CPRE, National Trust, Nature Conservancy, Civic Society, Ramblers Association etc, but what sort of corporate fighting force does this miscellany of regiments add up to? What is the identikit local preservationist? Almost certainly a retired Service Officer, with a natural (ie induced) orientation towards acceptance of decrees and a natural respect for bureaucracy - which may be why they are ridden roughshod over so often by local authorities. This would be a good subject for a vivid graphic treatment.' And as for the Department of the Environment: 'We could question whether it's right for it to be such a ragbag, or whether this is good because it has fingers in most pies, and whether it makes cooing noises about the Greening of Britain without actually much affecting it.'

By the end of page four, Allsop's invective was beginning to flag, and the tone mellowed a little. 'While we shall be dealing a great deal in pragmatic situations, I think we should never forget what the programme is really about: life and beauty... I think, therefore, that we should be candid about praising the sight of meadows and woods, the pleasure of living creatures in the wild, the need for pleasant seemly towns, the response to landscape and to textures which also feel good in a tactile as well as a visual way.' Forgetting his injunction at the beginning of the memo, he concluded: 'I mean, why don't we have, as well as the hard facts, some poetry in it?'

Allsop dispatched the memo to Percival two days later. At the same time, he set the seal on the new direction he was taking by withdrawing from his commitment to the *Animal Stars* quiz series. With recording scheduled to begin on 5 April, it was fortunate that Tony Soper was available at short notice to present the seven programmes.

In a reply a few days later, Percival largely agreed with Allsop's approach, including 'a strong emphasis on the beauty of the earth'. But it seems unlikely that he forwarded the memo to his superiors.

On the Air

As they climbed the steps of the elderly De Havilland DH104 Dove executive aircraft waiting on the tarmac of London airport, nobody among the BBC production team seemed to appreciate the supreme irony of taking to the air to get to Manchester to present a pioneer environmentalist television series - and especially one called *Down to Earth*. Squeezed in alongside Allsop was an assemblage of eight other people: reporters, production assistants and a folk singer - plus three tortoises. This was the day, 17 May 1972, of the first live transmission of *Down to Earth*, and the team were due in Manchester at 3.00 pm in time for rehearsals and dinner, before the late night broadcast at 10.20 pm.

Allsop had set the scene in a BBC trailer broadcast the evening before. He promised a 'down-to-earth' approach to the environmental pressures and dangers that were 'mounting up against our everyday life' and to signpost what ordinary folk could do to tackle them. The approach would sometimes be light-hearted. For the first programme, Spike Milligan was drafted in to encourage grassroots action to clean up neighbourhood streams and ponds, while in later episodes spoof commercials would highlight the costs as well as the benefits of 'Bio-Glo' or 'The Real Thing'. The formula simultaneously borrowed from the satirical, early-1960s BBC series *That Was the Week That Was*, while anticipating by five years the environmentalist magazine *Vole*, to which several of the DTE team - John Craven, Gillian Reynolds, Miles Kington and *The Observer*'s Jeremy Bugler - would eventually be frequent contributors.

Added to the mix were the stunts that owed much to Friends of the Earth. As the first programme drew to a close, Allsop introduced the Plastic Banana Award. 'Every week we want to honour the creators of the grossest or ghastliest bit of environmental idiocy you've come across…Each week the person, firm or official department which licks all the others will be awarded ceremonially the *Down to Earth* Plastic Banana.' The large blow-up trophy was then paraded on screen by a fanfare of five attractive showgirls dressed in toy soldier uniforms, and viewers were invited to nominate the villain of their choice for the first presentation of the award the following week.

The magazine format, with individual items of five minutes or less, allowed DTE to range widely over the whole of the then-current environmentalist agenda. Prime targets were organisations and individuals responsible for local air, noise or water pollution, like the London Brick Company, the Wapping heliport or East Anglian agribusinesses. Urban planning conflicts were highlighted, including proposals for an urban expressway through Bath, or the redevelopment of Covent Garden in London. Not surprisingly, Allsop made sure that threats to wildlife and the countryside were given a fair airing, with the inclusion of items on government subsidies to farmers for ploughing up historic Wessex downland, and the illegal trapping and pickling for food of migrating songbirds in Cyprus. A contribution from Chris Brasher, then the BBC's Head of Features, also drew attention to the proposed construction by the Central Electricity Generating Board of a huge pumped storage scheme in a supposedly-protected area, at Dinorwig in the North Wales Snowdonia National Park.

But over the following few weeks it was the environmental complacency and connivance of British government departments, agencies and procedures that featured most prominently.

No punches were pulled in drawing attention to the failures and ineffectiveness of departments like the Home Office, the Department of the Environment or - with a name as Dickensian as its cosy and secretive relations with the industries it was meant to regulate - the Alkali Inspectorate. To Allsop, it sounded 'as if our Alkali Inspectorate wouldn't have criticised even the volcano which wiped out Pompeii', and so he gave out on air the name and address of the Chief Inspector. 'I expect he'll be delighted to hear from you,' he observed wryly.

In response to the launch of the Plastic Banana Award the team received a flood of nominations, but they felt that the first award should go to something 'really big'. 'Today,' Allsop explained during the second programme, 'Peter Walker, Secretary of State for the Environment, opened the £110 million Midland Links Motorway - the hub of which is the Gravelly Hill Interchange, already nicknamed "Spaghetti Junction". Despite Mr Walker's happiness that the scheme will bring "enormous social and economic benefits by diverting traffic from congested city streets, historic town centres and picturesque village greens" is it being welcomed quite so rhapsodically by the Gravelly Hill residents?' asked Allsop. 'Probably not by those who've been told that they'll get regular blood-test samplings because of the lead emissions from all those extra exhaust pipes - 100,000 a day whirling through that labyrinth...

'And who is it,' Allsop continued, 'who's thrusting the Britain of today forward to look like Los Angeles? Our own Department of the Environment. So, Peter Walker, it's all yours - our first Plastic Banana Award!' Cue five showgirls holding up the Plastic Banana, deflating on the last trumpet blast.

Response

'How did the programme go?' Allsop asked his diary, late at night after the first broadcast. 'Technically surprisingly smoothly (after two exhausting run-throughs) but I felt it was all too itty-bitty and *Nationwidey*, popularise though we wish to do…'

At the post-mortem the following day there was also much criticism from the programme team, including from Allsop himself, who expressed the hope that 'we shall rapidly learn from yesterday's mistakes and miscalculations'. The *Sunday Telegraph* considered that the programme, which had included an item on the health benefits of wholemeal bread, had 'tried to cram too much in, and grab too many quick effects. More roughage, Ken!'[2] The *Daily Mail* on the other hand complimented the programme on being 'a scrap book more than a text book - and not all gloom and despondency'.[3] However, by the third broadcast on 7 June Allsop was still privately voicing his disappointment. The programme was 'ill-prepared' and 'there should have been better thinking (from me included) into how we did Stockholm [the United Nations Conference on the Human Environment], which was a dull non-item.

And this was the major dilemma of the series. How could the programme simultaneously attract and engage ordinary men and women at their current level of awareness, while at the same time tackle in an intelligent way complex issues of science or high environmental politics? 'Does what's going on in Stockholm at the moment matter to those of us who live in Scarborough or Streatham?' he had asked the viewers when introducing the item. 'Twelve hundred politicians and pundits listening to each other give speeches may seem a bit remote from our own backyards.'

And so it did. Midway through the series, the BBC's Audience Research Department circulated an internal memo on viewers' responses. Around 2.5 per cent of the UK population had tuned in to the sample fourth programme on 21 June. Although this represented 1.4 million people, it compared poorly with competing programmes broadcast at the same time by BBC2 and ITV, with 8.8 per cent and 15.9 per cent respectively. On the other hand, approval ratings among those who *did* watch were increasing. As many as 84 per cent of the panel of viewers thought the series 'completely gripping', as opposed to the 15 per cent who reported that it 'didn't hold my attention'. The panel thought that Kenneth Allsop had 'added the necessary clear and professional punctuation to points made by the various outside speakers,' and its reporting of positive environmental campaigning made 'the fight for the future seem worthwhile'.

But the most serious threat to the series came not from the audience figures, but from political opposition from the BBC's senior management. The morning after Environment Secretary Peter Walker had been presented with his wilting plastic banana, producer John Percival was carpeted by BBC programme controller Paul Fox, and threatened with the sack for allegedly showing political bias.[4] The third episode, scheduled for 31 May, was subsequently pulled, ostensibly to allow coverage of the return to Britain of the Duke of Windsor's coffin, and of the Cup Final. Allsop had little doubt that 'the main reason was our Plastic Banana award to Peter Walker... Much antipathy directed at JP [Percival] and his "opinions".' He thought the series would be allowed to proceed under sufferance, but with the clear message: 'You are being watched!'

He was right. Two weeks later the BBC's internal TV Programme Review Board spotlighted *Down to Earth*, and concluded that 'the programme itself deserved the BBC's plastic banana... for appearing not to realise that it was taking sides in controversies.' The Director, Public Affairs, considered that 'insofar as it made the BBC appear to be campaigning on those issues which were evidently controversial, that was wrong.'

This reflected exactly the views of the Director-General, Charles Curran. Curran's predecessor, Sir Hugh Carleton Greene, had presided over a liberal regime which by the end of his tenure in 1969 had established the principle among broadcasters that reporting and comment should be as free on the BBC as they were in the press. Curran's was a considerably more conservative approach, reinforced after June 1970 by sensitivity to pressures from the new Conservative government, exemplified by Home Secretary Reginald Maudling's bid to stop the broadcasting in January 1972 of *A Question of Ulster*. Peter Walker himself had also intervened over *Up the Rent*, a documentary on Britain's poor record on housing and homelessness.

Curran later set out his views at length in some autobiographical reflections published in 1979:

> Any institution like the BBC which depends fundamentally on the general assent of the public for its continued existence... will inevitably reflect the society which it serves. It cannot be the instrument of total revolution. It will most often be the vehicle of conformity... In their efforts to achieve a fair presentation of the range of opinion it is, in my view, a cardinal error for broadcasters to plan the presentation of one view of a subject without a specific intention to return to it in order to present the other views which may be in circulation... The moral responsibility of the broadcaster is not simply to keep the ring open for all opinions, but to see that everybody has a chance to appear in it.[5]

This was not at all Allsop's view of his role as a journalist, nor of the purpose of a campaigning environmentalist programme like *Down to Earth*. In a valedictory article in *The Listener* marking his departure from *24 Hours*, he declared that he had 'never been persuaded by the concept of "balance" most vociferously demanded by those who think you have not been sufficiently unbalanced in their direction'.[6] Mary Holland in *The Observer* wrote that 'In an underhand way, it could be the most subversive programme to appear on television for a long time.'[7]

A confrontation seemed inevitable, and it was not long in coming. Once again the treatment of Environment Secretary Peter Walker was the focus of the row. In a five-minute live interview on the 21 June edition of *Down to Earth*, Allsop questioned the Minister - uncontroversially - about the drive to clean up Britain's rivers. Then, in the light of Walker's recent attendance at the Stockholm environment conference, he quizzed him about the relationship between economic growth and environmental degradation:

> Mr Walker, as a Conservative, and a member of a Conservative government, you must be inevitably pledged to and committed to the idea of a profit-motivated and consumer-geared society. Now, at Stockholm you made what struck me as being quite a remarkable statement when you said that you were 'aligning yourself with the new generation of young who are insisting on looking at the world's problems afresh and calling for action'. But you see, many of these people are totally opposed, implacably, against your outlook on a profit-motivated society. How do you reconcile this?

The question seemed to catch Walker off-guard. He gave a rambling reply focusing on the increasing separation of the ownership of companies from their day-to-day management, and listed such advantages of capitalism as innovation, diversity of products and wider opportunities. But then he conceded: 'I believe that the Conservative Party's got to face this issue, as other parties... *Laissez-faire* capitalism always did have and always will have massive disadvantages and must be curtailed.'

It may be that Walker felt he had been bowled a googly and subsequently complained to the BBC's senior management - although Percival noted that the DoE's Head of Information, Henry James, had expressed himself 'well pleased' with the interview. In any event, the BBC's Head of TV Features, Aubrey Singer, accused Percival of allowing 'leading and biased' questioning, and demanded to see the transcript. Percival enclosed with his reply a memo pointing out that there was never any suggestion during the interview that Allsop was endorsing a particular political view. The politics of the environment were not the politics of left and right, but those of growth and anti-growth. But in a separate letter to Allsop, Percival made clear that a proposed item on oil exploration in Dorset would be too sensitive to air, and warned that henceforth all items contained in the programme must be cleared with higher authority before they were transmitted. 'Doesn't it make you proud to work for such a fearless and impartial organisation?' he asked.[8]

Singer had also written directly to Allsop, complaining about his very public participation in the televised, mock funeral procession on Welcome Hill (see pp.88-9). 'Surely it is difficult to be anchor-man on *Down to Earth* and take part in such demonstrations,' wrote Singer. 'Having been seen in this way on a nationwide bulletin, anybody appearing on it and being interviewed by you in the studio will be bound to think he is talking to somebody with a totally committed position.' He concluded the letter with a warning that if there were to be any more such public manifestations 'then I think we'll have to seriously consider whether or not we alter your role in the programme.'[9]

Singer was also doubtless stung by the article in *The Listener* that had appeared a few days before, in which - without warning - Allsop had aired his views on the treatment of *24 Hours* by the BBC's management. He must have been aware that Allsop's observations applied equally to *Down to Earth*:

> *24 Hours* was never prized as highly as it deserved for the staunch course it hewed, in defiance of political pressures from without and wan support from within. Pretty well from the beginning *24 Hours* was sold short. It has always scraped by on a paltry budget compared with any similar operation. It never received from the planners the promised regular timeslot, which meant that it was never, from its fluctuating base, able to aim at a recognizable size and type of audience - a programme going out at 10.10 pm should be structured and paced differently from one going out at 10.50pm. *24 Hours* has always been the BBC's moveable snack bar. If there was an over-run, *24 Hours* was run over.

Never slow to take offence, Allsop was enraged by Singer's letter. Replying on 1 July, he 'objected most strongly to your improper suggestion that my integrity as a presenter of *Down to Earth* would be affected if the topic of mineral extraction was under discussion. If you are about "seriously to consider altering my role in the programme", I shall be obliged if you will promptly inform me of the result of those considerations as I must, of course - as there is nothing in my contract which forbids me taking part in non-political activities - in turn consider the action I shall have to take.'[10] Once again, Allsop believed that the Director-General was the main originator of the complaint, and so immediately despatched a letter to him in similar vein. The charge of lack of impartiality, he wrote - fearlessly (some would say recklessly) - 'is possibly the gravest charge which can be made against an interviewer... I shall naturally wish to be shown in precise detail when and how I am alleged to have committed this misdemeanour...'[11] It is not known whether he ever received an answer.

Grounded

In the event, *Down to Earth* was not formally taken off the air, but the BBC's senior management seemed to go out of their way to minimise its audience. What should have been the fifth programme on 14 June was pulled to make way for the European Football Championships, a decision Allsop attributed to Paul Fox. '[This] would seem to amount to deliberate sabotage, a determination to sink a programme he never really wanted,' he wrote in his diary.

More was to come. The following three programmes appeared fortnightly rather than weekly, after which there was a long, three-week break before the next one on 9 August. The final broadcast went out on 23 August - over three months from the start of what was supposed to have been an eight-week series. The time slot allocated to the programme on a Wednesday evening was also continually changed, with starts ranging between 10.10 pm and 10.45 pm. The broadcast scheduled for Wednesday 19 July actually went out on the Thursday. One viewer wrote in to complain that this was 'the first weekly television programme to go out once a fortnight', while another pleaded for an earlier time slot 'when a wider audience can see it'.

These were just two of the hundreds of letters Allsop received during the brief life of the series. Almost all were supportive, and he replied to them all. He remarked later that nothing he had done hitherto in journalism had elicited such a response from the public. Brief as it was, the series helped establish Allsop as a kind of unofficial ombudsman, to whom viewers could turn for help in staving off the pressures that were threatening their local environments from every direction.

He had returned to *24 Hours* for its last programme on 14 July. Before the broadcast, he attended a 'swarming' farewell party. 'Everybody pretty pissed,' he noted, including the presenters. He had brought with him a blown-up copy of an appreciative letter sent to him by former Director-General, Sir Hugh Carleton Greene. He pinned this in a prominent position on the wall, and from across the room tried to induce Paul Fox to look at it. But Fox would not play ball, and so Allsop 'exchanged some barbed, smiling insults'. Despite their political differences, Allsop still retained a grudging respect for him.

'So, for now, goodbye' was how Allsop wound up *Down to Earth*'s last edition on 23 August 1972, referring to the end of 'this present series'. Three days later he told the *Guardian* that he had been given hints - 'well, maybe' - of a spring comeback, but in reality he must have realised that the absence of 'the kind of cheering we all hoped for from the managerial hierarchy' meant that *Down to Earth* had, literally, been grounded.[12]

Martin Jackson in the *Daily Express* wrote an appreciative review that could have been penned by Allsop himself (and may well have been prompted by him). Jackson confirmed that the series had become an embarrassment to the BBC, which as a result had 'shifted and buried' its scheduling.[13] It was 'the first genuine attempt by television to popularise the environment issue, to take it out of the laps of the landed gentry and gin-and-tonic suburbs and make it the concern of us all,' he wrote. Inevitably it was indiscreet and irreverent, and stepped on Establishment corns. 'Unfortunately, these are timid days at the BBC... It is not just *Down to Earth* that they buried last night. It is a whole area of inquiring, investigatory television which we are now in danger of losing.'

Producer John Percival was not offered any further work by the BBC on his existing contract, and it was made clear to him that he was a marked man. 'The ostensible reasons for killing the show were that it was poorly made, tasteless and ill-informed,' he said later. 'There may have been some justice in all these accusations, but the real reasons had more to do with the political pressures, and the attacks engineered by big business.'[14] Percival left London to live on an organic smallholding outside Bruton in Somerset. In 1976 he managed to persuade the BBC to finance *Living in the Past*, another controversial series following the experiences over a year of a group of volunteers trying to live under Iron Age conditions.

For Allsop himself, it was the first time in twelve years that he was without a regular platform on television. 'I have no clear-cut outlet for environmental issues on television,' he wrote later to John Lucas, an Oxford politics don and friend from his Merton College days. 'Not, in the Controller's view, a subject guaranteed to get the audience which all-in wrestling does.'

1. Allsop, K., *Fit to Live In? The Future of Britain's Countryside*, Penguin Education, 1970
2. *Sunday Telegraph*, 21 May 1972
3. *Daily Mail*, 22 June 1972
4. Andresen, M., *Field of Vision: The Broadcast Life of Kenneth Allsop*, Trafford, 2004, p.495
5. Curran C., *A Seamless Robe. Broadcasting - Philosophy and Practice*, .Collins, 1979, pp.115 ff
6. 'Goodbye to 24 Hours', *The Listener*, 22 June 1972
7. 'Missing those dear familiar faces', *Observer*, 23 July 1972

8. Letter from John Percival to Kenneth Allsop, 28 June 1972
9. Letter from Aubrey Singer to Kenneth Allsop, 26 June 1972
10. Letter from Allsop to Aubrey Singer, 1 July 1972
11. Letter from Allsop to Charles Curran, 1 July 1972
12. 'Allsop Shifting', *Guardian*, 26 August 1972
13. 'The BBC buries its head in the earth', *Daily Express*, 24 August 1972
14. Andresen, op. cit., p.500

9

CROSSROADS

Conflicts of interest with his other roles meant that *Fit to Live In?* (1970) was Allsop's only explicitly environmentalist tract among his fourteen books. There would have been more had he chosen to become a full-time writer. (Author's collection)

ON THE AUGUST BANK holiday weekend of 1972, Kenneth Allsop could take time to relax and reflect that he had arrived at one of the biggest crossroads in his life. Three days before, on Wednesday 23 August, the last episode of *Down to Earth* had brought what had been a less than successful series to its finale. It also apparently marked the end of twelve years of regular appearances on the BBC. BBC1 Controller Paul Fox a few weeks later wrote to the Assistant Head of Programme Contracts asking whether Allsop's long-term contract as a freelance guaranteed him *work* as well as a certain level of income. 'At the moment, there are few if any prospects of work for him in Current Affairs or Arts,' he concluded.[1]

Bank holiday Saturday was also the occasion of his last 'In the Country' piece for the *Daily Mail*. After almost two years, churning out the regular 500-word columns had become something of a chore - although their subsequent collection into a book proved to be a considerable financial success. But any residual sadness he might have felt at leaving the *Mail* was eclipsed by his new position as a regular columnist on *The Sunday Times*, which had started two days earlier.

The paper's editor, Harold (Harry) Evans, had successfully established *The Sunday Times* as a campaigning newspaper, and had had his eye on Allsop since the spring, partly as a result of the national publicity he had generated over his Dorset oil campaign. Evans offered him not one, but two substantial columns that would alternate weekly. The first, of between 1,000-1,500 words, would cover the environment as part of the 'This Britain' series, while the second would focus on contemporary social and cultural issues on the 'Look!' pages in the Review section. These would be shorter pieces of between 600-800 words. Not only did Allsop manage to negotiate 'very reasonable terms', but he was also promised a far wider degree of editorial freedom than he felt he had on the *Mail*. 'Splendid news,' he wrote in his diary.

That Saturday's *Guardian* included an interview with Allsop in which he played down the significance of the changes. 'I'm shifting the balance of my life a bit,' he said. 'I've always straddled writing and television, but now the emphasis will move more towards writing.'

In fact, the career options facing him at this time were much wider than he made out. *Down to Earth* and the national publicity generated by the Dorset oil battle had secured him the reputation as Britain's foremost environmental campaigner. At the end of August, he was beginning to draft the foreword to Graham Searle's manifesto *Project Earth*, in which he openly encouraged its young readership to join Friends of the Earth.[2] By October, Allsop's relationship with FoE was such that he was considered a leading candidate to be its next chairman. His diary entry for 26 October 1972 notes: 'Telephone call from Graham Searle: Will I become chairman of FoE? Said I thought "No" because (a) the additional burden and (b) counter productive for waging campaigns."

It was probably true that the public's confidence in him as an environmental commentator would have been compromised by such an overt association with Friends of the Earth, particularly among older and more traditional conservationists. It was for that reason that during the campaign against Berkley Petroleums he and Michael Hudson had been careful not to publicise too widely their support for, and in some respects, dependence on, FoE. In any event, his confrontations with Aubrey Singer at the BBC over *Down to Earth* were a reminder (if he needed one) of the conflict of interest between his roles as activist on the one hand, and journalist on the other.[3]

But his refusal to take up a formal role within FoE sprang from more fundamental reasons. Allsop simply disliked organisations of any kind - even those whose values he shared. By nature, he was not a 'joiner', nor a team player. He cherished his independence too much.

Another avenue he might have pursued was as a full-time writer of books. His term at Merton College, Oxford, had given him a taste, which still lingered, for a semi-academic existence, with the time and space to think and write. He admitted in one newspaper interview that he fancied 'taking himself off to the country to write books, rather like an eighteenth century botanising parson... I don't feel there is enough time in life for reflection. In my life, one is always decanting before the bottle is wet.'[4]

Many years before, he concluded that he would never be a novelist like his boyhood hero Henry Williamson - despite his early success with *Adventure Lit Their Star*. He had written a number of non-fiction works like *The Bootleggers* and *Hard Travellin'*, which were very well received, and which reflected his fascination with the development of American society and culture. At the same time, he was of course also an accomplished ornithologist and observer of the natural world; but rather than following the lead of the Rev. Gilbert White in cataloguing the detailed comings and goings of the local wildlife, his preferred focus was the mutual relationships between man and the landscapes and wildlife around him. 'The Wildlife of London', an extended essay written in 1969 for *The Sunday Times Magazine*, highlighted the extent to which wild birds and mammals had accommodated themselves to the man-made buildings, bombsites, railways, parks and gardens of the capital.[5] This article was to have a profound effect on a young Richard Mabey, who was inspired to write *The Unofficial Countryside,* and devote much of his future work to exploring the wildlife of these urban 'edgelands'.[6]

Given his commitment and passions, it may seem surprising that by mid-1972 Allsop had produced rather few environmentalist publications focusing explicitly on the politics of the environment and how they could be influenced. There was the occasional article, review or introduction to the works of others, but his most substantial contribution was *Fit to Live In? The Future of Britain's Countryside* (see pp.99-100). His limited output was largely explained by his role as a leading BBC news anchorman. But with this behind him, in the spring of 1973 he was to begin discussions with publishers Sidgwick & Jackson on a proposed polemical, autobiographical book provisionally entitled *The Destruction of Britain*. But events were to get in the way.

The author John Fowles was sceptical about Allsop's expressed desire to be a full-time writer. Exactly two years before, on August bank holiday 1970, Fowles had driven the ten miles from his home in Lyme Regis to have lunch with him and Betty at the Mill. 'I didn't really believe his modest desire to be thought of as a writer,' he recalled. 'Writers don't live in such décors. And can't function behind such a persona that men like Allsop are condemned to wear - eternally genial, shrewd, wise, relaxed...'[7]

In reality, Allsop, too, knew that he needed to be actively engaged in the world, not withdrawn from it. As Fowles observed, his friend was 'a would-be knight, and I'm a would-be peasant'. A few weeks later, on 16 October, it was Allsop's turn to analyse Fowles: 'In many ways, I envy him his detachment, his refusal to be sucked into struggles and controversies - I think basically out of despair, a certainty that you can't win,' he wrote. 'I wish often that I could quit, but how can you sit back and let the bastards run things without interference?'

The BBC Natural History Unit?

Yet another career option had been presented to Allsop earlier in the summer of 1972: he could continue his long-term association with the BBC, but take an entirely new direction within it. David Attenborough, then Director of Programmes, Television and a member of the BBC's Board of Management, called him into his Lime Grove office on 26 July and encouraged him to apply for the job of Head of the BBC's Natural History Unit (NHU) in Bristol.

Since its foundation in 1957, the NHU had established itself as the Corporation's - and indeed the world's - centre of excellence for natural history broadcasting. Attenborough himself had been pressed to become its first Head, but he had preferred to stay in London with his family, and continue making his successful *Zoo Quest* series from there. The Bristol post was subsequently filled by Nicholas Crocker, then the West Region Television Outside Broadcast Producer. Although intending to stay only briefly, Crocker led the NHU for fifteen years, but by 1972 it was time for him to retire and hand over the reins to a successor with fresh vision.[8]

Allsop liked and trusted Attenborough. 'DA is a nice man: extraordinarily without bullshit for his power-position,' he wrote in his diary. 'The job is being internally boarded but he would make it all proper for me to be included in the six candidates… and, although he declared that he couldn't rig the board, he indicated that he would like me to have the job.'

Allsop had already established a close relationship with the NHU, contributing to a number of programmes in the *World About Us* (WAU) series, fitting them around his commitments to *24 Hours* and his other TV and radio programmes as best he could. From 1970, he wrote and delivered voiceovers for WAU programmes on Majorca, Suffolk, chimpanzees and the black rhinoceros, and he both wrote and narrated *The Wildlife of New York City* episode (which was to be three years in the making - see below). In a letter to Suzanne Gibbs, the NHU producer of *Save Our Suffolk*, he declared: 'I very much enjoyed doing it. I only wish one somehow had more time for this sort of subject - more important, really, than all the summit political stuff…'[9]

Staff at the NHU were not slow to pick up the hint. On 6 November Sheila Fullom, a researcher and assistant to the NHU's Executive Producer, Christopher Parsons, rang Allsop suggesting they discuss the possibility of his working for the NHU on a more regular basis. 'It could be an alternative to the life sentence of *24 Hours*,' he wrote, before meeting her for lunch a few weeks later.

But the meeting was not a success. She appeared subdued and anxious - quite possibly because she was a little awestruck in his presence. 'These Natural History people don't advertise well the tranquillity and healing quality of the countryside,' he wrote. 'I rather brutally concluded the discussion by saying that I really wasn't prepared to serve an apprenticeship or go on a trial… Bristol must tell me (a) how much work they want in the year and (b) how much money would be guaranteed for it.'

Nicholas Crocker subsequently estimated that they could offer him only about £2,500 worth of work a year. Allsop was an expensive commodity, and this figure compared poorly with the £8,500 he was guaranteed from Current Affairs and Arts under his existing BBC contract. The salary that David Attenborough offered him eighteen months later to head up the NHU was around £7,000.

The day after their meeting, Allsop telephoned Attenborough to say that he was very flattered to have been asked, but he had to decline the offer. The salary and his new commitment to *The Sunday Times* were sufficiently respectable reasons for turning down what, on the face of it, was a plum job. But there were other reasons, too. It would almost certainly have meant turning his back on a lifetime of print journalism, and for the first time becoming a full-time employee and administrator in the BBC - one of the 'grey men', about whom he was so dismissive.

Two years before, on 24 October 1970, he had recorded in his diary a 'Reflection on the present state of the BBC and the squalid gang who now have power there'. 'All my life I have worked for Organisations, mostly of leviathan size, but have both deliberately on occasion and perhaps deliberately on their part, never been committed to them, or sucked into their vortex. Why is the Organisation - which theoretically should at least by its nature have one advantage, that of rehearsed efficiency - be invariably run by second-rate people? Obvious answer: the bright, creative, independent minds can't be vapourised into becoming contributors to the pervading grey mist the Organisation executives both produce and flourish in.'

David Attenborough would have had an element of sympathy with this view, for within six months of his interview with Allsop, he himself was to resign as Director of Programmes, Television, to go back to filmmaking - and with the Natural History Unit - in Indonesia.[10]

Although Allsop had reported how much he enjoyed doing the *Save Our Suffolk* programme, it seems to have been the subject matter rather than the process that he found attractive. Making films was a very different enterprise from writing articles, or planning and conducting interviews. Messages had to be simplified, shortened and in most cases subordinated to the pictures on the screen. They involved working in a team and making compromises. A week after his first letter to Suzanne Gibbs, he wrote another, this time complaining at 'having a fairly horrible time trying to get the footages and corresponding correct number of words together, and I'm not a bit sure I've managed it...'

The problem was even worse with *The Wildlife of New York City*. Allsop was first approached to write the script and commentary in February 1970, but it was over three years before the programme was to be screened. His two trips to New York were difficult to arrange around his *24 Hours* commitments, and much of the footage had to be filmed in his absence.

Eventually, in the spring of 1973, closeted in a Bristol hotel, he was forced to do multiple re-writes into the early hours. 'Deeply frustrating - excluding and junking 80 per cent of the material - and ideas - fighting to get in,' he wrote to Sheila Fullom on 21 March. 'Feel as though I've done 15 rounds with Cassius Clay,' he wrote in his diary later that evening. 'The experience has resolved me *never again* to take on writing a film: I *hate* it and the agonizing effort isn't worth *any* sum of money.' An invitation five days later to script a new series ('"Civilization"-style') on 'The Garden Through History' came at exactly the wrong time. He refused immediately, 'my heart leaping with fright at the prospect of again being sucked into the fearful morass of script-writing'.

Allsop was experiencing at first hand the truth of Marshall McLuhan's famous 1960s epigram 'the medium is the message'. The requirement of television for speed, conciseness and visuality, particularly after the advent of colour, tended to dictate the content and presentation of the programme.[10]

From the beginning, Allsop had firm views on the approach *Wildlife of New York City* should take. In an early draft storyline written in August 1971, he wrote:

> What this film will be about is nature's resilience and adaptability. It will make the point that more creatures and other living things, in numbers and variety not commonly noticed, are remarkably tolerant of a man-made environment, even at its most messily butchered and de-natured...
>
> Most wild creatures don't either prosper or adapt. They give up and go away, falling back before man's machinery and his elimination of their habitat. This should in no sense be a complacent film, leaving the impression: 'It's not really so bad: even when we've done our worst nature manages to make the best of it.'
>
> So the film will certainly not make light of pollution, slums, overcrowding, out-of-scale building, industrial vandalism, anti-planning, over-planning, no planning, squalor, ugliness, cancer conditions, and the rest of the blights that man piles one on top of another to create the degree of imbalance he's shown to be possible. Indeed the film will, as a sub-theme, be pointing to the loss and waste, and by speaking in *absentia* of the wildlife driven out will be showing the negative alongside the positive... The mood of the film should not be breezy, well-I-never, chuckle-chuckle, as we see raccoons rummaging in dustbins, etcetera, but reflective: an essay more than a report.

Attached to the storyline was a draft forty-page shooting script, ending with a 'philosophical end thought':

> Although it might seem that the Infernal City, the 'parasite on concrete', did all it could to exterminate everything which lay in its path, it may finally have rendered itself uninhabitable for human beings. One thinks of those elaborately immense Mayan cities and temples lapped over by jungle in Mexico. Perhaps the ultimate city, New York, will kill man off first, perhaps the actual 'greening ' of America will start here, for the artefacts of man are but a temporary interruption of nature, a roadblock quite quickly overcome.

The final cut of the programme was not the 'chuckle-chuckle' report Allsop had cautioned against, but neither was it a 'reflective essay'. It focused on the birds and animals making the most of the degraded New York environment, but there was little footage devoted to the now locally-extinct species like the peregrine or the black bear. His 'philosophical end-thought' that maybe man could not adapt so readily to the megalopolis as other species, was dropped.

A row over his Bristol hotel expenses almost aborted the entire project. An NHU memo records that a furious Allsop had declared that this was 'positively the last film ever to be made by him, and that he will not come to Bristol any more'.[12] A placatory dinner with the NHU team and concessions over his expenses were just enough to ensure that the programme was completed, only days before its transmission on 20 May 1973.

But, subtly, he was to have the last word. While filming in New York at the beginning of May 1972, he was invited to appear on the *David Frost Show*. In 1961 Frost had been the front man of the highly successful BBC television satire show *That Was the Week That Was*, and later went on to host his own, lucrative late night chat show in the US, commuting weekly across the Atlantic, first class, by Concorde. The closing frames of *The Wildlife of New York* were to include an extract from this interview, interwoven with lengthy footage of a slimy, unattractive insect exploring a jungle of tangled electric wiring.

After introducing Allsop and explaining to the live audience why he was in town, Frost asked him if there were any especially endangered species of animal or bird New York.

Allsop, sucking his cheek, thought for a moment, and ignored the question.

> Not the cockroach! There's one particular species called colloquially the 'Brown Bandit' which has found its way to the United States, and discovered an incredibly suitable environment inside television sets. And what better? Here you have warmth, security, entertainment - a sort of womb with a view! And here it lives, nibbling away at the insulation. We're being nibbled away at this very moment…

Frost: 'And are there many people with one of these creatures in their television sets?'

Allsop: 'Everybody! (*Loud laughter from both sides of the camera - Frost excepted*).

But apart from his difficulties over the kind of programmes it was producing - indeed with the medium of television itself - Allsop had additional, personal reasons for saying 'no' to the Natural History Unit. As the fifth most handsome man in the world, he enjoyed (or sometimes not) the attentions of many women. One of the team producing *The Wildlife of New York* (let us call her 'Irene') soon developed a flirtatious relationship with him, and by December 1970 was writing long, conspiratorial letters to him almost daily, about the possibility of his working more closely with the NHU, or about arrangements for the first trip to New York in March 1971.

Although Allsop genuinely appreciated Irene's conscientious hard work, there is no evidence that her feelings for him were reciprocated. Indeed, in his diary Allsop noted his 'strong forebodings about being so intimately engaged with her on (the New York) project'. These anxieties subsequently proved to have some foundation, and while filming he described 'the strain of her flirtatious, knowing fatuousness' which was 'beginning to wear my nerves thin'. Furthermore, Irene began to deploy her undoubted organisational talents to plan the future direction of Allsop's broadcasting career. She suggested to her boss that Allsop might write and present a documentary on the development in Britain of more compassionate attitudes to wildlife. Seemingly unprompted, she then began to collect research material in preparation for the new programme - and indeed for other subjects she considered he might tackle. Later, in August, Irene began - again uninvited - to act as his unofficial publicity agent, seeking to arrange appearances for him on *My Kind of Music* and *Desert Island Discs*. She explained to the producer of the latter that Allsop was 'the professional woman's piece of crumpet... Mr Allsop works with this unit from time to time, and has a freshness and flair combined with enthusiasm and wit, that make him a most agreeable character...' To Carole Stone on *My Kind of Music* she wrote: 'He is a gentle, phlegmatic, humorous character behind the façade of intellectual sophistication that he presents on *24 Hours*. He is modest about his musical appreciation, but is in fact a recognised jazz expert...'

Then in September, Allsop received from Irene a note forewarning him of the proposal for a new environmentalist series (eventually to become *Down to Earth*) and indicating that she would love to work with him on such a series. This seems at last to have provoked an angry confrontation, for in early November she wrote a tearful response that it would 'take time to pick up the pieces and stick them together again... but will my faith in the human animal ever be restored? I doubt it. It is fatal to have a trusting nature...'

The suspension of what Allsop regarded as Irene's encroachments on his personal and professional space was only temporary, and eventually he felt obliged to write a letter of complaint to her superiors. But he did not immediately post it. He was 'fluctuating about whether it will sock her too hard - and yet this situation about which I have a persecution complex must be solved.'

It was. On Friday 25 August 1972 he drafted his first column for *The Sunday Times*. He 'combed it through with double the usual care' to make sure everything was right in this, his first, piece. Cloistered writer; full-time campaigner; BBC administrator; wildlife filmmaker - these were 'the roads not taken'. He was an activist, not a naturalist; an oppositionist, not a manager. Allsop was leaving the crossroads behind him, and he knew, with Robert Frost, 'how way leads on to way', and doubted if he should ever come back.[13]

1. Memorandum from Paul Fox to BBC's Assistant Head of Programme Contracts, 21 September 1972 (BBC Written Archives)
2. Searle, G., *Project Earth*, Wolfe Publishing Ltd, 1973
3. See Chapter 8, p.107
4. Interview with *Oxford Mail*, 16 May 1969
5. Allsop, K., 'The Wildlife of London', *Sunday Times Magazine*, 23 March 1969
6. Mabey, R., *The Unofficial Countryside*, 1973
7. Drazin, Charles (ed.), *John Fowles: The Journals*, Vol. 2 Vintage Books, 2007, pp.90-91
8. Parsons, Christopher, *True to Nature*, Patrick Stephens Ltd, 1982, pp.57-61
9. Letter from Allsop to Suzanne Gibbs, 4 November 1970 (BBC Written Archives)
10. Attenborough, David, *Life on Air,* BBC Books, revised edition 2011, p.240
11. McLuhan, Marshall, *Understanding Media: The Extensions of Man,* Mentor, 1964
12. Natural History Unit Memorandum, 19 April 1973
13. Frost, Robert, 'The Road Not Taken', in *The Poems of Robert Frost,* Random House, 1946, p.117

THE SUNDAY TIMES

Venice lurks under all that spaghetti

NEWFOUNDLAND dogs have webbed feet: true or false? True, apparently; at least I've read it in a serious guide to the island. Birmingham has more miles of canal than Venice: true or—hey, wait a minute! What kind of Sunday quiz show is this?

True, I believe. At least, it has been stated in print in an official report. For Venice is small and Birmingham is large. And Brum is spaghetti junction for canals as well as motorways. The whole system meets in Cambrian Basin, a few yards away from the Council House, right in the middle of the city. You might never guess, if you whizz round the ring road —I hope, incidentally, that they do eventually take up the imaginative suggestion to hold motor races round it—yet it is all there, just below ground, approached down steps and through holes in walls.

Slowly, Birmingham is realising that it is sitting on a leisure goldmine, urged from within by the city architects' department. 1969 saw the first canal-side walk —small beer, and backed by tall flats, but a beginning. A canal pub, the Longboat, was rebuilt, with sympathetic housing behind it. Gas Street Basin and the land around, owned by the British Waterways Board, had a scheme designed for it by John Madin and passed by the city; it is dormant now, perhaps because BWB is scared of its own future. A pity, because it includes a hotel, pub, flats and moorings—all this within 400 yards of the city centre. If the board really has to disappear as a senseless adjunct of necessary reorganisation of water undertakings, it would be a splendid swan-song.

Now, simultaneously, have come two more proposals from the city; a towpath walk and a suggestion for a marina under Spaghetti Junction. To take the

Cambrian Basin, Birmingham

latter first: three canals meet under Spaghetti—and, as I said earlier this year, the astonishing skyscape of flyovers makes it the biggest landscape opportunity in the country at the moment. The land is largely owned by the

Keeping an eye on RTZ

A PECULIAR letter was recently received by two unconnected organisations which had bought copies of a film from BBC Enterprises, which markets TV programme material here and overseas.

The film was Do You Dig National Parks? which Mike Barnes made for the Horizon series and which was transmitted on May 27, after David Attenborough had given it full support and the green light. The documentary examined the activities of the mining company Rio Tinto-Zinc in Snowdonia National Park, the quest being for copper. Having refused repeated invitations to co-operate in the production, RTZ had a last-minute

by Kenneth Allsop

like a hard-boiled egg and chucked the toxic silt into a river system; in Sumatra it has obtained exploration rights over an

Subject Called Ecology In A Place Called Capel Hermon, was put on in September 1971, the World in Action staff (who had hitherto understood that the programme was mandatory under the IBA rules) were staggered that Harlech's North Wales region chose that evening to opt out and run a Welsh language replacement—a singular bit of rejuggling. A Subject Called Ecology has never been shown in North Wales.

And how far-flung are the pies in which RTZ's long fingers are to be discovered! The unofficial "commission" on mining and the environment, set up by six mining companies including RTZ

In August 1972 Allsop joined *The Sunday Times*, contributing regularly to the campaigning 'This Britain' column. After just three months, he took on one of the world's biggest multinational mining companies, Rio Tinto Zinc – and faced the consequences. (Author's collection)

LIKE A WELL-TRAINED falcon suddenly unleashed, Allsop arrowed straight for his prey and showed no mercy. 'I hate the CEGB with an ineffable hatred,' he began his first 'This Britain' column, 'for its stupendous record of uglification'. The targets of the article, headed 'Glossing over a Bad Image', were the Central Electricity Generating Board; its programme of erecting electricity pylons across the Dorset Area of Outstanding Natural Beauty; and the attempts by its public relations men to diffuse the opposition by creating token nature trails and field study centres.

By joining what was then Britain's leading campaigning newspaper, *The Sunday Times*, he had - for the first time in his career as a journalist - been given a new freedom to say exactly what he felt. His debut column appeared at the same time as Editor Harry Evans was putting the finishing touches to the leader that was to launch the newspaper's brave and ground-breaking Thalidomide campaign. For week after week, Evans hammered home the message that the Distillers Company must pay full and speedy compensation to the hundreds of children in the UK deformed by the Thalidomide sleeping pills taken years before by their mothers during pregnancy. Allsop felt that at last he was among friends.

Frank Giles, Deputy Editor and Foreign Editor, later wrote of Evans' 'crusading zeal' for the causes he believed in:

> Open government, the showing up of secrecy and deceit in high places, the right and duty of the press to report fully and accurately upon matters of public interest, a preference for evidence over propaganda - above all, perhaps, the importance of what has been called the citizen as victim - victim of misused power or business ruthlessness or racial prejudice or inferior services.[1]

But Giles qualified his eulogy by pointing out that 'Evans had tended to take on staff with too much liberality, and then failed adequately to monitor the performance of some of them.'

Giles had been the other front-runner for the editorship when Evans was appointed, but the contrast between the two could not have been greater. Giles was an establishment figure with a military and diplomatic background. He had worked in the Directorate of Military Operations in the War Office from 1942-45, subsequently moving to the Foreign Office where he worked as private secretary to Britain's Foreign Secretary Ernest Bevin, and then in the British

Embassy in Moscow with Sir Archibald Clark Kerr. Giles recalled that because of his time at the Foreign Office he 'had been persistently described and regarded as some sort of superannuated Foreign Office hack, a smooth-tongued go-between who had somehow, and inappropriately, strayed into the steaming jungles of real journalism.'[2] Evans concurred: 'Some of the new young Turks at *The Sunday Times* regarded his debonair style with suspicion, comparing him to the actor Ian Carmichael,' he wrote in his autobiography. 'But he was a steadfast and calming influence on the paper.'[3] Allsop was one of the older 'young Turks' on the paper, and was later to find himself on the receiving end of this 'calming influence' - when calmed was the last thing he wanted to be.

For the first six months, most of Allsop's fortnightly 'This Britain' columns hit out at the environmental 'barbarians' he had already listed in his draft prospectus for *Down to Earth* (see pp.100-101). Apart from the CEGB, his targets included:

- The Ministry of Agriculture Fisheries and Food (MAFF), for handing out grants to farmers for grubbing up wildlife-rich hedgerows and draining ditches;
- The Department of the Environment and the Forestry Commission for their failure to take effective action against Dutch Elm disease in what was supposed to be 'Plant a Tree' year;
- The Shell oil company for continuing to market to farmers the deadly pesticides aldrin and dieldrin which threatened peregrines and other birds of prey with extinction;
- Farmers and gamekeepers for illegally trapping and killing birds and animals, and the manufacturers of the snares they used.

In addition, in November he used almost 2,000 words to pay tribute to his hero, the nineteenth-century rural visionary from Wiltshire, Richard Jefferies, who a century before had contributed to a debate in *The Times* on the causes of rural poverty and unrest. After drawing attention to the current urban desolation of Jefferies' native Swindon, and the forlorn neglect of his beloved Coate Water, Allsop concluded (probably rightly, given the frequent opaqueness of Jefferies' prose) that 'Swindon - and Britain - doesn't comprehend a word he wrote.'

Whenever he could, he used the column to draw the attention of his national readers to the local issues on which he had been campaigning in Dorset. When Dorset County Council in early October extended by three months Berkley Petroleums' planning permission for exploratory drilling below Eggardon, he attacked the Department of Trade for granting the licences; called county councillors 'spineless' for failing to live up to their responsibilities to safeguard protected landscapes; and more or less accused civil servants in the Department of the Environment of lying.

But he knew there were limits to how far he could plug his own local agenda in a national newspaper. His solution was to do an informal deal with his neighbour and colleague Brian Jackman. So it was Jackman who wrote an extended piece calling for the Purbeck Hills in Dorset to be made a National Park, and another attacking the Forestry Commission for their plans to cut down Powerstock Forest. In return, Allsop used one of his columns to spotlight the proposed demolition of the Electric Palace cinema in Harwich. This was to make way for a road widening scheme to accommodate juggernauts plying their trade with Britain's new Common Market partners across the North Sea.

After a few weeks at *The Sunday Times*, Allsop was pleased to receive a letter from Harry Evans complimenting him on his articles thus far, and it seemed as though his stream of pugnacious, campaigning articles could continue indefinitely. During the first week of January 1973, he returned to the subject of Berkley Petroleums Ltd. The company had abandoned the drilling on Welcome Hill in October. It had promised on several occasions before that if the exploratory well should prove to be dry (which it had), then 'that will be the last Dorset will see of us'. However, a spokesman announced on 4 January 1973 that it was returning to West Dorset and Somerset to make more seismographic tests. 'The answers given by the survey at Nettlecombe near Powerstock - although no oil or gas was discovered - are sufficiently encouraging to warrant us looking further north,' he explained. Under the headline 'The word of an oilman...', a short update by Allsop on 7 January invited readers to 'Watch this space...' But watch as they might through the dark weeks of early 1973, no follow-up article appeared. That was because Allsop's progress as a campaigning environmental journalist had for the moment been stopped in its tracks - by Rio Tinto Zinc.

Keeping an Eye on RTZ

It was to be only three months before Allsop was at last given the opportunity to throw down the gauntlet to RTZ. In early December 1972 a copy of Amory Lovins' *Eryri, the Mountains of Longing* had arrived in the offices of *The Sunday Times* following the delay in its publication caused by RTZ's threats of legal action against Friends of the Earth (see p.95). Allsop was given the go-ahead to write a review of the book, but the story was brought up to date when his former colleagues passed on information suggesting that the BBC had finally capitulated to RTZ's demands for the withdrawal from circulation of the *Horizon* programme *Do You Dig National Parks?* Chairman and chief executive of RTZ, Sir Val Duncan, had written to the BBC's Director-General on 15 November seeking 'to make quite sure that this film is put to bed as unworthy of the BBC.

May I please have your personal assurance that this will be done?'

Allsop was handed a copy of a letter to Friends of the Earth from a Mr Ron Crofts from BBC Enterprises asking 'for purely contractual reasons' for the return of its copy of the *Horizon* programme, which FoE had been showing to audiences around the country. A similar letter had been dispatched to another purchaser of the film, the Concord Educational Trust, which was asked to destroy the copies in its possession.

On 17 December 1972 *The Sunday Times* published Allsop's article under the headline 'Keeping an Eye on RTZ'. This focused on the impact of RTZ's mining activities around the world, and the 'difficulties which arise for nosey parkers' who questioned their business operations.

The article described the source of the company's annual £24 million profits from its operations across the world's five continents: mining for zinc in Australia, nickel in Rhodesia, copper in the Transvaal and the Soviet Union, diamonds in South Africa, uranium in Canada and bauxite in Brazil. 'To grub out copper in Bougainville, RTZ has spooned out a mountain like a hard-boiled egg and chucked the toxic silt into the river system,' he wrote. At home, the company had drilled 48 bore holes without planning permission in the Snowdonia National Park, threatening 'enormous devastation on a scale so far seen only by Bougainville villagers, whose reluctance to vacate their ancestral land above the mineral caches was overcome by police using tear gas and clubs.'

'Wherever comment and critical interference have occurred, RTZ has moved swiftly to defend its interests,' Allsop observed. He acknowledged that the request from BBC Enterprises for withdrawal of the *Horizon* programme had not originated from the BBC Controllers nor the Board of Governors, but internal investigations were proceeding to establish 'whose ear was bent' further down the organisation. The article then reviewed the attempts by RTZ over the previous months to suppress other critical broadcasts and publications, and to 'pack' organisations and commissions with RTZ place-men.

Finally, Allsop quoted the condescending threat from Lord Goodman to Earth Island Publishers. 'Our clients,' Goodman had written, 'are a large and rich corporation engaged in activities which are indispensable for a great many human purposes. It is because they are large and rich that they have been reluctant to take action against your organisation. The point, however, will be reached when no matter how rich and important a corporation, it cannot for that reason alone submit to all forms of injustice, even from the smallest and most unimportant organisations.'

'The point is also reached,' Allsop retorted, obliquely alluding to Lord Goodman's famous girth, 'when richness and largeness swell so monstrously that from that altitude of power it may seem that all other organisations are small and unimportant - including human beings - and that they can be either frightened into silence or squashed. It seems to be becoming increasingly urgent that the distinction between national need and corporate greed should be more firmly marked - and that this mining giant, so skilled in underground methods, should be held in a very bright light of public notice.'

A metaphorical standing ovation burst from Allsop's current and former colleagues. Jon Tinker from the *New Scientist* wrote sending 'congratulations on your magnificently scurrilous piece', and offering assistance 'as an old RTZ-baiter'. Allsop's producer on *Down to Earth*, John Percival, thought the article 'quite simply, one of the most powerful and one of the most courageous pieces of journalism I have read in a very long time'. Amory Lovins thanked him for his 'lovely article'. 'You've done some strong and brave journalism here; it will help the fight a lot. Courage! I think we can win.' He promised to provide some more information 'in case RTZ try to jump on you'.

It was not long in coming. On 20 December 1972, just three days after the article had appeared, Harry Evans received a long letter from RTZ's lawyers, Clifford Chance, complaining that there were 'so many inaccuracies and misleading statements' in Allsop's column that 'the article cannot conceivably be defended as fair comment'. The assertion that RTZ had refused to co-operate in the making of the *Horizon* programme was 'misleading'; there had been no 'jiggery-pokery' or communication with anyone in the BBC other than the Director-General seeking the withdrawal from circulation of the *Horizon* film; the references to RTZ's alleged attempts to pack government agencies and committees with their own representatives were 'seriously defamatory'; the account of RTZ's global activities was 'seriously distorted'; and it was 'entirely without foundation' that the corporation had abused its powers by pressurising the authors of critical publications.

Two days later, a further letter arrived from RTZ containing the draft of a grovelling apology that it demanded *The Sunday Times* should publish, and make in the High Court. In addition to the items to which it had already drawn attention (above), the statement stressed that since the unilateral declaration of independence (UDI) by the Smith regime in Rhodesia, 'RTZ has ceased to give instructions to Rio Tinto Rhodesia, has cut that company out of its accounts and derives no profit therefrom'. Its proposed draft statement concluded: '*The Sunday Times* is particularly anxious to emphasise that this apology and retraction is made after the most careful investigation of the facts, and from their conviction that there were no facts to support the various allegations.' The satirical magazine *Private Eye* noted the irony that while RTZ's writ complained of the allegation that it had tried to silence its critics, one of the effects of the writ would be exactly that: to silence any further criticism of RTZ.[4]

RTZ's writ and draft apology were intended to force a humiliating capitulation on the part of *The Sunday Times*, but there was no possibility that Harry Evans nor James Evans, the senior lawyer in the newspaper's parent company, the Thomson Organisation, would ever agree to it. Nevertheless, from Allsop's perspective as a respected journalist, the most damaging accusation was that there were 'no facts' to support his allegations.

Boxing Day 1972 was 'pretty hellish' for Allsop, 'trying to tackle the appalling task of composing my rebuttal of the RTZ writ'. In addition to his own shorthand notes of various interviews, Allsop's internal report drew heavily on a closely-typed five-page foolscap note from Amory Lovins of Friends of the Earth, countering the RTZ writ line-by-line with detailed background material, evidence and some minor corrections to the article. 'I am always here with information,' Lovins wrote. 'You have my full support - physical, moral and every other way. Guts and dedication deserve support.' It was 2.00 am before Allsop's paper was finished.

Two days later in London, Allsop presented his evidence to James Evans. He provided full details of RTZ's refusal to co-operate over the making of the *Horizon* programme, based on a lengthy interview with the producer, Mike Barnes. Barnes had revealed that when it was announced in the *Radio Times* that there would be a live studio discussion after the programme, the chair of RTZ, Lord Byers, had suggested having lunch with Barnes to 'discuss the situation'. Barnes refused, suggesting that any comments or proposals should be put in writing, which he said 'made them very angry'.

On the allegation that RTZ was seeking to extend its influence on public bodies, particularly in Wales, Allsop pointed out that his reference to the appointment of Duncan Dewdney, the Chair of RTZ Development Enterprises, as Chair of the Welsh Industrial Development Board, had come straight from a *Times* Diary piece on 22 August 1972.

As evidence that RTZ had sought 'to suppress and muzzle comment on their activities', Allsop cited the correspondence between Val Duncan and Charles Curran the previous November. Duncan had declared - with reference to BBC Enterprises making available to the public copies of the *Horizon* film - that the object of his letter was to 'make quite sure that this film is put to bed'. Curran had replied that Duncan's letter was couched in 'extreme terms', and that there was no major fault in the Snowdonia programme apart from a couple of small issues of presentation.

Allsop did, however, concede that his description of RTZ's worldwide operations contained a few minor errors. 'Compression probably leaves one open to accusation of inaccuracy here - yet I think RTZ's objections are hair-splitting.'

In the event, on 31 December, *The Sunday Times* printed 'an interim statement' pending its investigation of 'a number of matters raised by Rio Tinto Zinc'. The statement came nowhere near to being the humiliating apology that RTZ had demanded. Instead it focused only on Allsop's reference to Rhodesia, and accepted RTZ's assurance that its profits since UDI had not included any profits from that country. 'Kenneth Allsop did not intend to suggest that RTZ had been guilty of any infringement or other impropriety in relation to "sanctions" or similar legislation,' it stated, 'and we are sorry if any contrary impression was given.'

'Not very happy that it has been done,' wrote Allsop in his last diary entry for 1972, 'but I suppose James Evans's reasoning that this may take some of the wind out of their sails is logical.'

On 4 January 1973 a small group gathered in Thomson House in London's Gray's Inn Road to discuss future tactics. They included James Evans; *The Sunday Times*' counsel Andrew Bateson QC; BBC producer Mike Barnes; Amory Lovins and Simon Millar from FoE; the Gallaghers from Earth Island Ltd; and Allsop himself. Their conclusion was that while concrete evidence was available to support most of Allsop's allegations, more information was needed to justify the use of pejorative words like 'nobbling' and 'jiggery-pokery'. Andrew Bateson proposed that the newspaper's tactics should be to pick holes in the letter which had accompanied RTZ's writ. 'We have just enough ammunition for this - such a move would be to get them to be more specific, rather than their "chuck-the-book-at-them" attack.'

Pinioned

On the evening of 9 January 1973 Allsop sat alone in the silence of his drab and dusty fifth-floor flat in Colville Gardens. Despite the central heating, he had wrapped a blanket around his overcoat and thick pullover, and pressed a hot water bottle against his back. The table in front of him was littered with crumpled sheets of paper, most of them with just one incomplete sentence, impatiently sten-gunned down with a line of xxx's. A half-empty bottle of Teachers stood within easy reach, next to his silent typewriter.

He picked up his ball-point pen and turned to the blank, ninth page of his new diary.

> 9.30 pm. In very bad shape. Have had to abandon the *Sunday Times* article - not gone beyond the first fumbling sentence. Exhaustion; illness. I am afraid it may be a breakdown as severe as that of six years ago: the same dreadful tiredness and pervading pit-of-existence feeling, and the continuing dull lumber ache and chill. If this is the onset of another bad betrayal of the body it is the last I will take.

The thought of death is a refuge and yet is unbearable - so much which is dear, never to be seen again - unthinkable, and yet I constantly think of that likelihood. But there must be a maximum of pain and debility with which anyone can put up with reasonable dignity and self-respect. My limits are clearly demarcated in my mind. A thing - life - can be clung on to too desperately - until it becomes despicable.

We cannot know whether this recurrence of a previous kidney complaint had been brought on by the continuous stress since Christmas of defending himself against the RTZ writ, but his severe depression and writer's block almost certainly were. It was to last many weeks, fed by the gathering evidence that he was being marginalised, and deprived of his public platform, at least as an environmental campaigner.

Following the meeting with James Evans at the beginning of the month, decisions on the newspaper's strategy and tactics against RTZ passed to Harry Evans, Frank Giles, Peter Crookston (editor of the 'Look!' column) and *The Sunday Times* lawyers. At the end of February, Allsop wrote to Jon Tinker: 'The ST so far has been taking a satisfactorily tough line in replying to the multitude of complaints they made about the article, but of course it's now grinding through the slow-motion mincing machine of the law and it's impossible to predict what the outcome will be.' Left out of the loop, Allsop continued to write his 'This Britain' column, but he complained that ever since the RTZ article Deputy Editor Frank Giles 'seems to go over my stuff with an X-ray'. In any event, for most of March the column was taken over by a three-part series by Ian Jack on 'Great railway routes of Britain'. Then, over the following weeks, Allsop felt obliged to retreat to safe ground with articles on Nicholas Pevsner's *Buildings of Britain* series; the joy of naturalists' society reports; the potential contribution of waterless toilets to combating the effects of drought; and a children's safari in Kenya. His fortnightly 'Look!' columns were equally unchallenging, covering MAD magazine; 'Vera, the fair cop from Rotting Hill'; and personal memories of Evelyn Waugh. However, there was to be one remarkable exception...

Meanwhile, at the beginning of the New Year, Allsop had resumed a relationship with the BBC, albeit in a low-key way. He was certainly not embarking on another twelve-year stint. 'I don't think I could do that again - it was murderous,' he told the *Radio Times*. 'I saw my style then as an E-type Jaguar: this time I'm coming back as a stately Daimler.'[5] This was an exaggeration on both counts: he continued to drive an E-type, and the two programmes he was given to front were something less than flagship-grade. *Edition* was to be a weekly, late-night, half-hour programme on BBC2 covering developments in newspapers, publishing and public relations. *Week by Week* was to be a ten-minute filler before the nine o'clock news went out on BBC1, looking back at the events of that week in randomly chosen years between 1924 and 1964. Allsop called it the 'Nostalgia Programme'.

If he had hoped that his work at the BBC would provide him with some light relief from his trials at *The Sunday Times,* he was to be gravely disappointed. On 13 February 1973 he was summoned to a meeting with Malcolm Walker, the newly appointed assistant to Paul Fox, to discuss some previous episodes of *Week by Week.* Walker, whom Allsop privately described as a 'short back and sides brash careerist', thought the programme should adopt a light touch to keep the ratings buoyant, whereas Allsop wanted to approach the events of 1914 or 1947 with the seriousness he considered they deserved.

At their meeting, Walker talked about 'getting more air' into the programme. '"Not so low key",' Allsop reported, 'without ever actually saying "castrate it". I told him that he would have to get Jimmy Young - this was my style - and said (knowing full well he had an unsuccessful brief stay with *Play School*) that as I knew nothing of his background and experience on programming, I can't guess his criterion. He brought up the "complaints" about my reference to the Labour Government in the '47 programme - then later showed me a draft of a letter to be approved by Fox, crawling to a woman who had written complaining. I rang Fox's secretary and said I wanted to be consulted as it was apparently laying "blame" on me...'

A week later, Walker rang to deliver the contents of a 'vitriolic' memo from Fox complaining about the contents of the previous week's programme on 1964 and the election of Harold Wilson's Labour government.

Allsop concluded: 'One should not really be working for these cheap hucksters who are afraid of their own shadows... But I am weary of battling - all one's life one has been pitted against dishonest time-servers. I wish to God I could escape. I feel tainted and soiled by the lot of them.'

He had had enough. On 13 March he gave notice to Walker that he would do no more *Week by Week* programmes after his contracted thirteen, 'as the programme is not developing as I was led to believe that it would; not requiring any kind of thoughtful comment, and little more than links of film.' As a result, the series ended earlier than planned, on 11 April.

Disarray on the Home Front

Allsop's problems in London were only compounded by developments back home in Dorset. The champagne celebration that greeted the news the previous October that Berkley Petroleums was abandoning its hunt for oil and gas marked the start of a period of complacency among those Defenders of West Dorset who had at last scented victory. The fact that all had gone quiet on the western front conveniently suited Allsop's busy new commitment to *The Sunday Times,* and despite his encouragement to Chris Geering in September to convene an early DWD committee meeting, none was held throughout the autumn. Geering's increasing frustration at the lack of activity and direction eventually led to his resignation as Secretary, further reducing the organisation's effectiveness.

But the prospect of victory was suddenly snatched away with the announcement in January 1973 that despite its earlier promises, Berkley Petroleums was back - this time to survey a large tract of countryside in North Dorset and across the county boundary into Somerset. A new seismographic investigation would be conducted along two parallel lines running roughly due north, from Melplash to Martock and from Broadwindsor to Lopenhead. A third line was to run east-west near the county boundary. About two-thirds of the territory involved fell within Somerset, with the remaining one-third in Dorset.

Allsop's letters to the local and national press denouncing the trustworthiness of the oilmen emphasised that the Defenders of West Dorset were still in business and would continue the campaign against the invasion of one of Britain's AONBs. However, instead of reinforcing his commitment and leadership, the resumption of drilling served only to add to the mounting depression and sense of defeat triggered by his separate experiences at *The Sunday Times* and the BBC. Friday, 23 February 1973, he recorded, was 'a pretty unproductive day. Feel to have slowed down permanently: have no attack left in me; the most mundane little tasks require immense psychological and physical effort, and take preposterously long. Bed midnight, feeling hopeless.' Locally, he was inclined to pass the baton to others, particularly as Somerset rather than Dorset was to bear the brunt of this new phase of exploration. His letters to the press were worded carefully, promising only that the DWD's help would be 'available to all seeking *guidance* or *support* in *their* resistance' (author's italics).

On the previous day, 22 February, around fifty members had attended the DWD's first Annual General Meeting at The Bull in Bridport. Allsop took a back seat during the meeting, and the chair was taken - quite appropriately - by Dr Michael Hudson. He began the proceedings by reviewing the events of the past year. Membership had grown to six hundred, with a further hundred non-subscribing 'sympathisers'. Locally, the DWD had succeeded in demonstrating the unreliability of Berkley Petroleums' statements, as a result of which many landowners north of Beaminster had refused the company's requests for renewed exploratory tests in the area. At national level, the Defenders had acted as a catalyst, bringing mineral exploration to the nation's notice in the press, radio, TV and in Parliament. Their campaign was being used as a model case study by the Stevens Committee, appointed by the government to enquire into the future of Britain's National Parks and Areas of Outstanding Natural Beauty, which he hoped would result in more effective legislation.

But Dr Hudson was defensive in more than just a titular sense, claiming that the organisation had been 'by no means inactive, though it might not have featured in the press recently'. He sought to counter the accusation that the Defenders had failed because Berkley Petroleums had returned to the area, by redefining the concept of 'success'. 'Whether people in West Dorset agree with our views or not, we have aroused general interest in environmental problems on our own doorstep. Our real energy has not been in outright antagonism, but against an all-pervading apathy. And to help foster a sense of awareness of what we stand to lose in this country will be a worthwhile end in itself.'

He reported that the DWD was now affiliated to, and represented on, the executive committee of the Dorset branch of the CPRE, and had passed on its experience to the Somerset CPRE. (However, what he was not able to report then was that six months later, the Chairman of the Dorset branch, Major R. H. K. Wickham, confirmed once again to its annual meeting that the CPRE would not object, as a matter of principle, to oil exploration in the county. 'I can assure you that it is vital in the interests of the national economy that exploration of the underground resources of our county should go on,' he said, 'so that we know where the coal, the gas, the oil - whatever it is - is available as a reserve in case of emergency and for future generations.')[6]

But Hudson implicitly accepted that the Defenders needed a new *raison d'être* when he drew attention to potential new areas of engagement. These included:

- Action against the proposed closure of village schools, particularly Toller Porcorum primary school;
- The fight against the closure of the Maiden Newton to Bridport railway line;
- The removal of electricity pylons around Eggardon;
- The route of the proposed Bridport bypass;
- The establishment of an early warning system, through local wardens, to pass on information on key planning changes.

However, his concluding remarks revealed a certain lack of strategic direction when he called for views on how the movement should develop in the future. Allsop might well have felt that his own re-election *nem con* as President was not an unmixed blessing.

The sound of screaming police sirens and the blare of fire engines echoing around the whole of central London increased Allsop's anxiety and sense of foreboding. As the taxi crossed over Holborn Viaduct, the driver looked up at him in the mirror. 'Car bomb outside New Scotland Yard this morning. Didn't go off, but they've been stopping traffic and checking suspect cars ever since.'

Lunch on Thursday 8 March at the London Stock Exchange Tower in the City was the earliest convenient slot that Harry Evans could find in his crowded diary. He had a meeting there that morning, and it wasn't too far for Allsop to travel from *The Sunday Times'* office in Gray's Inn Road. The memo he had received from Allsop five days before seemed urgent and strangely hush-hush. 'To keep the investigation absolutely watertight against leaks I think - don't you - that any further discussion should be verbal, with no memoranda put through inter-office channels, and closely confined to the essential people.'

Allsop's feeling that he was being pinioned had grown steadily during the previous weeks, as both the BBC and *The Sunday Times* had sought to tighten their grip over what he could and could not say. His feelings of anger and paranoia were mixed with a growing anxiety, for Evans had given him a contract to use his skills as a campaigning environmental journalist, and if he could no longer do this, his future with the newspaper looked bleak. He needed a big and bold story to demonstrate to Evans that he was indispensable.

When he read a *Daily Mail* 'exclusive' on 3 March, he knew his opportunity had arrived.

Home Secretary Robert Carr was planning to meet with leading anti-pornography campaigners, including Mary Whitehouse, the President of the National Viewers and Listeners Association (VALA), and the secretary of the Festival of Light, Steven Stevens, to discuss their demands to reform the obscenity laws, draft new legislation to cover broadcasting and review the position of the British Board of Film Censors. To Allsop, this was just the latest example of the cosy relationship that had developed between the Tory government and VALA to extend both moral - and political - censorship in the UK.

His memo to Evans was headed: 'PRIVATE AND CONFIDENTIAL':

> I don't think it is paranoid to suggest that the VALA/Festival of Light axis is extending from being a hit-and-miss tyranny of the bigoted and silly. It has certainly achieved some McCarthyite success at affecting broadcasting policy - and possibly the cultural-informational scene generally. Anyone working within, for example, the BBC knows that Mrs Whitehouse and the attitudes she so vocally represents have had a real effect in altering what is said, and how things are done... Her campaign permeates through heads of departments to programme-

making levels. There are implicit edicts which are now taken into account - oftener in an anticipatory sense, ie: a sentence is struck from a script or an item watered down to ward off what will be regarded as inevitable trouble from that quarter. So the censorship which the Whitehouse militants have sought to impose does work to a disturbing degree.

Allsop went on to explain that VALA had set up a highly-organised, covert system of precipitating complaints from 'average viewers' (in fact, VALA 'guerrillas') to BBC Controllers and/or the presenter or producer concerned.

It could, I suggest, be public service journalism to gain some detailed documentation about how VALA conducts its campaigns and how it deliberately goes out to get one particular person or programme... It would seem to me to be worth financially staking the right undercover person for, say, three months to get close to the centre of the organisation. We would need a person acceptable as a zealous crusader who, by being able to devote more unpaid time to the cause than can most people, could, with luck, infiltrate to the secretaryship or assistant to Mrs Whitehouse herself, or at least on to the main committee.

The investigator would have to be carefully selected and the cover story meticulously prepared, and the whole plan carried out with great confidentiality and a minimum number of people in the know... I have a couple of thoughts of staff people who could pull this off, although of course it might entail some subterfuge: assumed name, and so on.

Despite Allsop's request for complete secrecy, Evans had shown the memo to his deputy, Frank Giles, who would have regarded it as yet more evidence that Allsop was a loose cannon - and possibly mentally unstable. Evans decided that he would use the Stock Exchange lunch not to discuss this cloak-and-dagger plan, but Allsop's future role on the paper.

Allsop and Evans admired and respected each other's skills and experience. They had both served in the RAF during the war, and started in journalism the hard way, as junior reporters on provincial papers straight from school. So the lunch was friendly and informal, but Evans had to pass on the news that the future of the 'This Britain' column was uncertain in view of the imminent departure of Features editor Peter Crookston for a job on *The Observer*. Until his successor had been appointed, the Mary Whitehouse project would have to be put on hold. Over coffee, Evans then raised the possibility that Allsop might take over *The Sunday Times* book reviews.

Allsop's answer was rendered completely inaudible by an enormous explosion that sent a shudder through the entire Stock Exchange Tower, rippling the surface of the coffee and rattling the spoons in their saucers. They both rushed to the window and saw, less than half a mile away, a huge plume of smoke billowing from the vicinity of the Old Bailey. It was the biggest bomb explosion in central London since the Blitz, the result of the Provisional IRA's first operation on the English mainland. Later, Allsop learned that one person had been killed and 180 injured as the car bomb hurled nearby vehicles into the air, wrecked a pub opposite and smashed hundreds of windows.

Back at his flat later that evening he might well have felt that his position at *The Sunday Times* was in a similar state of ruin. He knew that his days as a campaigning environmental journalist on the paper must be numbered - but there was much that he still wanted to say, even if, somehow, he had to put it in a farewell, valedictory statement.

Over the previous two years Allsop's preoccupations had expanded from local threats to the West Dorset landscape, to national environmental issues and policies, and now to global threats to the planet as a whole. In particular, he wanted to highlight the impact of the construction across Latin America of the proposed Trans-Amazonia super highway, not only on the rainforest and indigenous cultures, but also on opening up the area to multinational mining consortia wishing to exploit what he described as 'an El Dorado of oil, diamonds, iron ore, copper, uranium, gold, diamonds and manganese'. However, he could not do it in 'This Britain', both because the subject matter was international, and also because of its high political sensitivity. And in any event, in mid-March 1973 'This Britain' was temporarily suspended to make way for *The Sunday Times'* extended coverage of the Ulster crisis.

Yet a unique opportunity arose during the week beginning 12 March, when Peter Crookston edited 'Look!' in the Weekly Review Section for the last time before moving to his new job at *The Observer*. Allsop had developed a good relationship with Crookston over several years, and seems to have persuaded him to include the piece on the Trans-Amazonia highway in the 'Look!' pages - bizarrely amid the usual articles on fashion and culture. An added benefit of this ploy for Allsop was that Frank Giles was likely to pay rather less attention to scrutinising the contents of the Weekly Review than he would the main news and current affairs section.

Allsop's article 'Axes of Self-Destruction' was as hard-hitting as 'Keeping an Eye on RTZ' had been a few months earlier:

What will happen when the Amazon has been tamed? When the mahogany trees have been burned off the planned cattle range the size of Scotland, how long will pasture support the five million beef steers? Only briefly, some agronomists think, before the maimed ecology lapses into sterile earth. How many bumper harvests of corn will be creamed off the compost of ages before the minerals are exhausted in soil stripped of its leaf canopy? And how will such apparently uninvolved places as Britain and North America be affected when the great green lung which supports almost half the planet's oxygen has been deforested...?

Meanwhile, those Amazonian aborigines who hadn't already dwindled from VD or TB, or been purposefully disposed of by machine-guns and germ warfare under the aegis of what used to be called, with surely the keenest of black irony, the Indian Protection Service, must undergo the necessary shake-out...[7]

Then, for the first time in *The Sunday Times,* and as if there would never be another opportunity, he included a statement of his profound personal disappointment and pessimism about the future of the planet, even though this was barely relevant in a piece on the Amazon.

I suppose it's a sign of something - maturity or disenchantment - that one comes to admit that younger convictions were hollow. After the war, I was excited that on the bomb rubble would arise slender towers shining in parks, a new airy London - I didn't foresee prison blocks of bleak concrete. I was once certain that education could save the countryside - but overlooked that hordes of binocularised birdwatchers could smother a rare bird with enthusiastic attention...

A Sense of Betrayal

Three weeks later, on 10 April, 'the slow-motion mincing machine of the law' finally produced a resolution of RTZ's libel case against *The Sunday Times.* In the High Court in front of Mr Justice Bean, Mr Brian Neill, the QC for RTZ, read from a statement that had been agreed with the newspaper during more than three months of negotiations.[8] Compared with the grovelling apology that RTZ had demanded immediately after the publication of Allsop's article in December, the statement on first reading seemed to concede rather little. Times Newspapers accepted RTZ's assurance that its profits since UDI had not included any profits from Rhodesia, an accusation which Allsop anyway had not made. And *The*

Sunday Times had already apologised for any impression it may have conveyed that UK sanctions against the regime had been infringed by the company.

The statement said that after investigating other matters referred to in the article, the newspaper accepted that there were 'a number of passages which *could be taken* as impugning the integrity of RTZ in the conduct of its business and, in particular, implying that the company had at various times tried by improper means to suppress legitimate comment and criticism of its activities.' (author's italics) The statement therefore did not concede that *The Sunday Times* had in fact impugned RTZ's reputation, only that some readers might be inclined to that conclusion.

However, it was the last two sentences in the statement that incensed Allsop. '*The company* (i.e. Times Newspapers) *now acknowledged that the relevant facts did not justify any such imputation. It had apologised to RTZ, and agreed to pay the company's costs.*'

James Evans had warned Allsop the previous week that there seemed to be no alternative but to retract those parts of the article which were 'unprovable', but *The Sunday Times* had now gone further and accepted that there was no evidence for any of Allsop's allegations about RTZ suppressing the criticisms of its opponents. This was in spite of the detailed, six-page dossier based on interviews with many of the people involved that he had prepared on his 'hellish' Boxing Day 1972. It seemed to him that his reputation as a journalist was being publicly sacrificed by the newspaper as the price for reaching a low-cost settlement with RTZ.

Why the climbdown? One explanation is that during the spring of 1973 *The Sunday Times* was involved in a far bigger legal battle, involving both the House of Lords and the European Court of Human Rights, to lift a legal ban on revealing the negligence of the Distillers Company in failing to test adequately the effect of the Thalidomide drug on pregnant women. It could have been a case of clearing the decks for action. There is also the possibility that Frank Giles was from the start uncomfortable with the way that Allsop and Friends of the Earth were undermining the global reputation of one of Britain's foremost and most strategically-important companies. Giles and Sir Val Duncan, the Chair and Chief Executive of RTZ, knew each other well, both having attended Brasenose College, Oxford, in the late 1930s.

Whatever the newspaper's reasons, Allsop felt betrayed, and also depressed that even a campaigning newspaper like *The Sunday Times* could not be relied upon to stand up to the 'barbarians'. Then a letter from Harry Evans confirmed that Robert Lacey - a journalist with less sympathetic views than Peter Crookston - was to take over as Features Editor.[9] 'Life doesn't get less worrying,' he wrote in his diary. 'Oh for the liberation of money - not for itself, merely to be immune and independent and free to write calmly and pleasurably'.

A week's trip to Nairobi with Betty to cover a children's safari provided a brief Easter respite. As he flew out of London on Maundy Thursday, 19 April, he left the gales and wild rain behind him, as well as the news, buried deep in its annual report, that RTZ was finally to abandon copper mining in Snowdonia.

*

1. Giles, Frank, *Sundry Times*, John Murray, 1986, p.156
2. Giles, Frank, ibid., p.200
3. Evans, Harold, *Good Times Bad Times*, Weidenfeld and Nicolson, 1983, p.15 (In the early 1970s on BBC TV, Ian Carmichael played the monocled 1920s aristocrat, Lord Peter Wimsey.)
4. *Private Eye,* 'Saint of the Year', 29 December 1972
5. *Radio Times,* 30 December 1972, p.4
6. *Bridport News,* 2 November 1973
7. 'Axes of Self-Destruction', *The Sunday Times*, Weekly Review Section, 18 March 1973, p.33
8. *The Times*, 11 April 1973, p.5
9. Letter from Harold Evans to Allsop, 9 April 1973

11

RED LETTER DAY, BLACK LETTER DAY

The Peregrine – Allsop's favourite bird. ' Such perfection and flair and nobility brought down by our foulness – destroyed by persistent toxics so that their stoops are misjudged and they break their necks on the ground…' (© Kevin Law/Wikimedia Commons)

BY THE EARLY 1970s the remote mountains and moors of mid-Wales were rapidly becoming a green Mecca for Britain's environmentalists and birdwatchers. In a seven-acre disused slate quarry on the edge of Machynlleth, the Centre for Alternative Technology had begun to attract growing numbers of visitors to its displays of renewable energy, organic gardening, low energy housing and composting toilets, while every weekend ornithologists from around the country converged on Tregaron thirty miles to the south, drawn by the prospect of glimpsing the rare red kite. Today, thanks to the successful reintroduction programme by the RSPB and Natural England, motorists travelling west from London along the M40 have become almost blasé at the sight of these splendid birds of prey with an arm's length wing span, wheeling in groups low over the motorway and the adjacent Chiltern Hills. But in 1972 there were just 26 pairs in Britain, all of them confined to the oak-covered hills and valleys of mid-Wales. There they shared the skies with a pathetically small number of other birds of prey, including the fastest bird in the world - the peregrine - reduced locally by continuing human persecution and insensitivity to only six breeding pairs.

The scarcity of these raptors attracted not only benign, middle-class birdwatchers to the area, but also a few young working-class men from mainly English industrial towns, intent on stealing, and often selling, both eggs and young chicks to a global market of collectors and falconers. The 1954 Protection of Birds Act had been strengthened in 1967, so that any wild bird, its nest and eggs were protected by law, with special penalties for particularly rare species like birds of prey. But enforcing the Act over hundreds of square miles of mountain and moorland was a hit and miss affair, and the fines imposed by local magistrates on those who could be caught were not much of a deterrent.

On the afternoon of Friday 18 May 1973, Allsop received a phone call at the Mill from Richard Porter at the RSPB's headquarters. Four men had been caught with fifteen ravens' eggs, together with climbing equipment and egg boxes, and two others were found at a peregrine's eyrie, clearly casing the joint. Questioning by police had led to a search of a house in Coventry, the home of a man believed to be the head of an egg collecting ring supplying rare British eggs all over the world. The four were due to appear before Landovery magistrates two weeks later.

Seizing an unexpected opportunity to mix business with pleasure, Allsop threw a few clothes into a suitcase, and with Betty set off at speed in the E-type Jaguar, crossing the Severn Bridge in the early evening, heading northwards towards the hotel they had booked at Devil's Bridge, near Aberystwyth. At

Rhayader, they turned on to 'a stupendously beautiful, wild mountain road'. Just short of the Cardiganshire-Radnorshire border, Betty suddenly called a halt. She had seen a brown bird on the hillside, tugging at a white 'blotch' - probably a dead sheep. Allsop stopped the car and at first glance assumed it was a buzzard, but then as it raised its head, he realised it was, in fact - a golden eagle. 'We got out of the car, and although only two hundred yards away, it did no more than hop heavily a few feet, and didn't take to the wing until Betty waved her arms. Then it spread its immense tip-turned wings and planed like a heavy bomber along the scree. Much more dappled and pale rufous that I would have expected...' Alone on the mountain road in the gathering twilight, they watched it for a full ten minutes: it was definitely an eagle.

'Hawks and owls have always been high on my emotional register,' he had written two years before to BBC Natural History Unit producer Richard Brock. 'Something to do with keeping them as a boy (kestrels and tawnies), and, like JA Baker, I've always been a "hawk hunter" - in pursuit, I suppose of the outlaw wildness which they exemplify.'

Despite the rare magnificence of seeing a golden eagle, for Allsop it was the peregrine that was 'our most beautiful bird, as irreplaceably important to our heritage as Snowdonia or Salisbury Cathedral... Even the most ardent birdwatcher has probably not often had a peregrine enter his life,' he wrote. 'In my case, it has, across the years, been just an occasional vibration of streamlined wings, a pulse of excitement and delight, the sense of a fiery spirit blazing fast across the edge of one's consciousness.'

At the end of January 1973, he had used his *Sunday Times* column to draw attention to how the continued use by farmers of the organochlorine pesticides dieldrin, aldrin and heptachlor posed a threat to the peregrine's survival. These had been responsible since 1956 for a steady decline in peregrine numbers At the end of the 1960s a 'gentleman's agreement' between the government and the industry to phase out the use of the chemicals had been undermined by pressure on farmers from the manufacturers' salesmen to stockpile them before the onset of a complete ban. 'So much stockpiling was done that aldrin is still slopping liberally about in some parts,' Allsop wrote. 'A few days ago there was a nasty little disaster in East Lothian when 20 wild geese were found dead - similar to a worse incident in the same district last winter when hundreds of birds, including greylags, pheasants and kestrels died from dieldrin overkill.'[1]

In preparing his article, Allsop had interviewed Derek Ratcliffe from the Nature Conservancy, a world expert on peregrines.[2] He had expressed concern that there had been a slackening in the self-imposed discipline on the use of dieldrin. 'I think things are going rather as the agro-chemical camp wants them to,' he said. 'They've made the right noises. Public concern has faded. There's a general assumption that everything's alright now. It isn't. It's a very delicate see-saw situation, and it could easily tip disastrously in the wrong direction again.' Indeed, an ominous new pattern had emerged in which traditional peregrine eyries on sea bird colonies like the Bass Rock, the Isle of May and St Kilda remained deserted. 'Here they would feed on kittiwakes, petrel and auks,' Allsop reported. 'And it is in such species that alarming residual levels are occurring - and not just of PCBs, DDE and dieldrin, but also of lead, zinc, copper and antimony.'

And then, of course, there were the nest robbers…

On Saturday, 19 May the Allsops set off to drive the 35 miles east to Newtown to meet the RSPB's Welsh Officer, Roger Lovegrove. As the E-type nosed its way up the winding road from Devil's Bridge, a red kite suddenly emerged, sailing in the blustery wind above the oak slopes dappled in the afternoon sunlight, whistling like a shepherd summoning his dog. Further on, the scrub oak gave way to dense Forestry Commission plantations as the road began to follow the infant River Wye, streaming down from the slopes of Plymlimon to the north. At Llanidloes, the landscape opened out as they entered the broader valley of the Severn, flowing fast towards Newtown. They turned down a narrow lane on the western outskirts of the town to a recently renovated watermill straddling the Mochdre Brook. Allsop pulled into the drive surfaced with slate chippings, noticing the flit of pied flycatchers and grey wagtails along the bank, and the bubbling call of curlews from the adjacent hayfields.

Sitting alongside the mill stream, Lovegrove explained in his still-discernible Devon accent that he had been a secondary school teacher for ten years, before giving it up to work for the RSPB. Now, with a tiny staff and a band of part-time volunteers, he was responsible for covering the whole of Wales, as well as its offshore islands, driving in excess of 20,000 miles every year visiting his parish.

'The peregrine is still having a rough time in Wales,' Lovegrove explained. 'This year there have been only six or seven successfully breeding pairs - a desperately slow recovery rate. Where you have such low numbers, stealing eggs from birds which are unlikely to lay again that season will soon push them past the tipping point… Egg collecting has always gone on, but after its Victorian heyday it seemed to be tapering off as the traditional collectors got too old. But now there's a new breed of young men in their twenties. The irony is that, as television and organisations like the RSPB have increased public interest and concern for birds, for some this has created an obsession for collecting - sometimes for its own sake, but sometimes to make a lot of money.'

Lovegrove described the steps the RSPB had taken to install wardens to protect particularly sensitive sites. For some, there was 24-hour surveillance, but for others a lack of resources meant there could be only periodic visits, 'and that leaves 23 hours a day when the nests are unprotected.'

He went on:

> A few weeks ago, I came across a silver-grey Ford Capri parked close to a peregrine's eyrie. It was empty, but when I returned two hours later, there was a forty-year old man in an oilcloth jacket sitting in the driving seat, and I noticed that behind him was stacked camping equipment and sleeping bags. I knocked on the window, introduced myself, and as politely as I could asked what he had been doing. He was very reluctant to volunteer anything about himself. 'I've just been for a walk up in the hills. And what business is it of yours?' he replied sharply.
>
> I wasn't going to be put off, so I asked him if he had friends with him, which he denied. I was just about to give up and leave, when a girl RSPB volunteer appeared, drew me to one side, and said she had spotted two men on top of the cliff looking at us through binoculars. She and I then left the Capri and walked to a cottage up the road to phone the police. While we were away, one of the two men walked down the hill to the car, while the other walked separately down a dried-up stream bed. Then the local bobby arrived in his white van and took their names and addresses. They were all from Luton. One - in his twenties with long hair - could only be described as a yob. The other was about the same age, and I've never seen anyone looking so evil in all my life. They were obviously working as a team - a few weeks later they were seen together in another county, this time in kites' and buzzards' territory.
>
> But on this occasion, they had no ropes or climbing gear or eggs on them, and we couldn't prove that they knew there was a nest nearby. That's always the case - for every one we catch, there are nine who get away with it.

Allsop had been taking detailed shorthand notes, and he continued scribbling for some seconds after Lovegrove stopped speaking. Then he looked up and said, 'But you had more luck with Ian Huggard, I understand?'

Huggard had been convicted a year before after bragging in the pub that he had just taken three clutches of red kites' eggs. He was just 22, and worked in Hereford as a lorry driver's mate. Lovegrove recalled: 'When the police searched his digs, they found a collection of 96 eggs - kites, hen harriers, ravens, golden plover, choughs - all of them with index cards showing when and where they had been taken. Just think of the impact of that - there are only 90 pairs of choughs left in the whole of Wales!... The trouble with the Protection of Birds Act is that you can only prosecute when you can prove that the eggs have been taken in the last six months - not for those stolen earlier. The law needs to be changed so that it's an offence to be "in possession of eggs which were illegally taken" no matter when, or by whom.'

The Sunday Times' cuttings library had more details on the Huggard trial. In May 1972, in the first case of its kind in Wales, Huggard had been convicted by Tregaron magistrates for taking three red kites' eggs from Forestry Commission land near Cwmystwyth. The offence related to only one egg from each clutch, rather than all of them. He was fined a total of £75 - £25 for each egg, the maximum under the Act. He was also ordered to pay £150 in costs. Allowing for inflation, that was £900 and £1,800 respectively at 2013 prices.

The four men accused of taking the ravens' eggs - the immediate reason for Allsop's trip to mid-Wales - eventually appeared before Llandovery magistrates in Camarthenshire on 1 June 1973. Two of them were sheet metal workers from Coventry, both 25; the other two were landscape gardeners aged 29 and 33 from Middlesex. One of the sheet metal workers, David Neville, was well-known to the RSPB as a dealer who had sold eggs on the American market. His notebook showed that his recent visit to mid-Wales was a planned expedition to raid the nests of ravens, kites and buzzards. It also included details of dozens of egg collectors across Britain.

Between them, the four men were fined a total of £76, with £40 costs - in today's money just £209 each, with £110 costs.

After breakfast on Sunday morning, Allsop crossed the quiet road from The Hafod Arms and walked the few yards to the bridge spanning the 300-foot ravine down which the River Mynach thundered to its rendezvous with the larger River Rheidol. He leaned over the parapet, and pulled a cigarette from the Philip Morris carton in his right jacket pocket. Through the scrub oaks clinging to the rocks he could just make out the grey wagtails looping and playing in the rainbow spray far below. William Wordsworth and George Borrow had once climbed down the precipitous stone steps to the bottom of this waterfall, but then - he reflected ruefully - they each had the advantage of having two legs.

It was Sunday, but there was no chance of getting a copy of *The Sunday Times* here. His thoughts turned to how he would put together his piece on the nest robbers. How long would it be before there were no peregrines' nests to rob, he wondered? As if poisoning them with pesticides, shooting them and destroying their habitats with blanket conifers were not enough, robbing their nests was effectively delivering the *coup de grâce*. As for the law, the Protection of Birds Act was full of loopholes, the resources for policing it were lamentably small and the fines imposed by local magistrates were just derisory…

Allsop could feel he was descending rapidly into gloomy despair, but this was suddenly arrested by Betty calling across the road. 'Ken, it's almost half past ten and we need to pick up Colin now.' The RSPB's Colin Helliwell lived in the next valley and had promised to show them the only peregrine's eyrie left in Cardiganshire.

Sitting almost doubled up on the E-type's narrow rear seat, Helliwell gave directions back to the mountain road to Rhayader. With the bright morning sun in his eyes, Allsop drove slowly upwards through the old lead mining village of Cymystwyth. At the top of the hill the landscape below them opened up. Spread before them was a wide, flat bottomed valley with massive extrusions of dark grey volcanic rock, looming 700 feet above the road. The face of the rock had been scraped off sheer, and was pocked with galleries, shafts, terraces and overhangs, with slaty scree sliding down from the old mine workings like volcanic shoots. Two waterfalls crashed down vertically in white ragged ribbons to the broad River Ystwyth bubbling and meandering through the boulders and the scree. Alongside, sheep grazed on a flat green table of pasture and wandered among the scattered ruins and shells of stone buildings and tin sheds, silent now for forty years.

Allsop parked the Jaguar, and the three of them scrambled over a heap of scree and clinker to an informal watching bay scooped out of the spoil. Almost as soon as they were settled, two red kites sailed slowly over the mountain ridge, closely followed by two buzzards. Then, out of the camouflaged invisibility of a rocky overhang 300 feet above, a pair of peregrines emerged at the same time. The female (the falcon) ringed upwards, and she and the tiercel (the male) played in headlong stoops and flicks of the wing, and quickly saw off the larger, but much slower, buzzards. With all of the raptors in the air at the same time, it was easy for Allsop to note the differences in their size, colouring, and the 'jizz' of their movements.

The peregrines returned to their eyrie about fifty feet down the rock face, and through his binoculars Allsop could make out the white splashes on the tufted grass, and the head of a single chick - the eyass - looking over the rim of the nest. Helliwell explained that it was just under three weeks old, and the first chick to have successfully hatched in Cardiganshire for six years. The previous year's clutch had been taken by one of the Coventry sheet metal workers - the police had found the eggs with a data card giving precise details of the time and location of the robbery.

Allsop heard clearly the *chakchakchak* of the peregrines as they left the eyrie and spiralled up across the valley, and he could easily make out the tiercel's moustacial stripes as it flew closer to them. Then a kestrel appeared, and the tiercel made three magnificent stoops at it, swooping down at speeds approaching 200 mph. This brought out the falcon, and the pair circled in wide glides for some time, climbing until they were just small cruciform black specks against the cumulous clouds above the valley.

Allsop had watched the gala performance for almost two hours. It was his red letter day.

All Guns Blazing

The euphoria didn't last long. After arriving back in Dorset in the late afternoon of Monday 21 May, Allsop soon realised that this was not going to be a good week.

After giving Amanda a hug, saying hello to the dogs and taking the suitcases upstairs, he picked up *The Sunday Times,* still unread on the table in the hallway. He looked briefly at the front page, then turned to his 'This Britain' column on page fifteen, headlined 'Tyneham Dream Fades'. He smiled as he read through the first few paragraphs, pleased that he had regained his old pugnacious form. But his jaw stiffened towards the end when he realised that several key paragraphs had been cut. He had been censored.

Tyneham was a small coastal Dorset village in the western Purbeck Hills. Its limestone cottages, Elizabethan manor and 700-year-old St Mary's Church had for centuries sheltered behind the 500-foot Gad Cliff, facing the sea at Brandy Bay a mile to the south. But in 1973 Tyneham was - and still remains - a ghost village. The streets were silent; the manor house had been razed to the ground; and house martins flew through the empty black sockets of the windowless cottages.

Thirty years before, at the height of the Second World War, as the military prepared for the D-Day landings, Tyneham's 225 residents had been given just one month's notice to leave, 'in the national interest'. The army needed more space for tank training and gunnery practice. Before they left, a week before Christmas, one resident left a hand-written note on the door of St Mary's Church. It read: 'Please treat the church and houses with care; we have given up our homes where many of us lived for generations to help win the war to keep men free. We shall return one day and thank you for treating the village kindly.' The Churchill cabinet gave the residents a promise that as soon as the war was over they could return, but in 1948 a compulsory purchase order was issued for the land. Tyneham was to stay under the permanent ownership of the Ministry of Defence.

The village was just one small part of a much larger area of Purbeck that had been annexed by the Royal Armoured Corps for tank training, gunnery and missile practice before and during the war. The ranges covered an area the size of Warwickshire - almost 8,500 acres of limestone hills, cliffs and heathland, together with an additional 'outer sea danger area' stretching thirteen miles out into the English Channel. Despite being part of the West Dorset Area of Outstanding National Beauty, designated by the Nature Conservancy as a Site of Special Scientific Interest, and declared a Heritage Coast by the Countryside Commission, this spectacular landscape was almost entirely out of bounds to the general public.

During the previous year's August bank holiday - in 1972 - Allsop had interrupted the contemplation of his future to join a protest meeting in the car park at Tyneham, on one of the few days of the year when the army opened up the road to the village. This was the first mass rally ever to be held there, and also the first to bring together a variety of local conservation groups - the Defenders of West Dorset, the Campaign for the Relief of Wildlife (CROW) and the so-called '1943 Committee' - in a joint bid to get the Army to hand over all the Purbeck ranges to the National Trust. The demonstration had been organised by an umbrella group: the Tyneham Action Group, whose 1,500 members were drawn from the local CPRE, Ramblers, Open Spaces and Purbeck Societies. For a time Rodney Legg had chaired the Group, until he was deposed for his radicalism by some of the Dorset old guard.

In blazing sunshine, holidaymakers in bikinis picnicked by their cars and mingled with the conservationists, half-listening to the two hours of speeches or casually leafing through the scores of leaflets handed out by the activists. Despite the carnival atmosphere, many of the protesters pressed for direct action to liberate former public buildings like the church and the post office, but were dissuaded by the substantial size of the police presence.

Allsop was the principal speaker at the rally. He was determined to take on the Ministry of Defence in his *Sunday Times* column, but at that time there was no obvious 'hook' on which to hang the story. His notes were filed away until April 1973, when he heard that the Defence Lands Committee chaired by Lord Nugent of Guildford was about to make recommendations to the government on selling, or at least improving public access to, MoD land across the country. But Allsop's hopes were not high, for eight of the Committee's fifteen members were nominated by interested government departments, and four were serving or retired service officers. Only two had a track record in environmental protection:

J. S. Cripps, former Chairman of the Countryside Commission, and Jack Hargreaves, the veteran presenter of the BBC's countryside series *Out of Town*.

Allsop's pessimism seemed to be confirmed when, in response to a question from the left-wing Labour MP Arthur Latham, the Department of the Environment indicated that if the MoD were to release any of its land on Purbeck, it would be sold back to the previous owners or their descendants, in accordance with convention - the government's so-called 'Crichel Down' rules. It would be given neither to the National Trust, nor to the Nature Conservancy.

Following the RTZ case, Allsop had been obliged for months to steer clear of political controversy in his column, and his (interrupted) lunch with Harry Evans in March seemed to suggest that his days were numbered on the paper, or at best that he might soon be taken off writing on the environment. He had nothing to lose. So he came out with all guns blazing.

Allsop had two prime targets. The first was the Army's PR department, which had sought to argue that its closure of thousands of acres of the Purbeck landscape had protected what was 'a most magnificent natural wilderness' from damage by modern farming practices and disturbance by visitors. The second were the government's nature and conservation agencies, which - as in the case of Powerstock Common - had done little to give substance to the protective designations they had bestowed upon the area.

'None of these paper garlands has been a serious obstacle to the guided missiles of Chieftain tanks which whanged into crags where peregrines once nested, were lobbed out into a 14-mile ocean sector banned to lobster boats, obliterated 95 miles of ancient footpaths and rights of way, and severed the prehistoric Ridgeway, as well as the newly-created south-west peninsula coast path'. Then he laid into the possibility that the Department of the Environment might sell the land back to the former owners. Allsop revealed that these former owners were all ex- or serving senior military officers, who could not be relied upon to put the needs of the environment first:

- The western section of the ranges would be offered to Colonel Joe Weld, the Lord Lieutenant of Dorset, who occupied Lulworth Castle and its extensive park, and operated the Lulworth Cove 'beauty spot';
- Heath Range in the north had been owned by the family of Colonel Ashley Bond of Creech Grange, a quarter of a mile outside the eastern boundary of the danger area. Allsop pointed out that in 1968 Colonel Bond's ball clay mining company had been bought out by English China Clays, and the reversion of ownership to him would increase the temptation to mine the sensitive heathland to an even greater degree;

- The area around Tyneham House, including 800 acres of wooded valley, had been owned by the cousin of Colonel Ashley Bond, Major General Mark Bond. Although General Bond was still a serving Rifle Brigade officer, he was in favour of the land being handed over to the National Trust to protect it both from insensitive tourist development, and - if it was to be developed for housing - from being 'swamped by stockbrokers'. But he was insistent that rather than being managed in the interests of wildlife and the landscape, it should be farmed conventionally, raising the prospect of its transformation into what Allsop described as a 'grain prairie'.

Allsop argued that the so-called Crichel Down rules had now been superseded, and that 'established procedure' was for other interested government departments or agencies to be offered first refusal. In this case, the ranges could be offered to the Nature Conservancy, which could then develop a future sensitive management strategy with the National Trust, the Dorset Naturalists Trust and Dorset County Council. 'What is lamentably lacking is centralist idealism - and that should not be a naïve word to use in these times of beleaguered countryside,' he concluded.

The article as it appeared in the newspaper was hard hitting enough, and it might therefore be concluded that the paragraphs struck out with a blue pencil must have been truly incendiary. There is however, a more prosaic (and more amusing) explanation: a case of cock-up rather than conspiracy. Unknown to him, Allsop's article had been printed opposite a very expensive, full-page advertisement by the MoD encouraging young graduates to become Army officers. It sought to counter the traditional image of the Army as class-ridden, with the rank and file drawn from 'the sons of the soil', and the officers, the gentry. The advertisement concluded: 'There's no disguising the fact that to become one of the nine full Generals in the British Army you have to be very, very good indeed. Neither nepotism, wealth or social standing will get you there...' This, opposite Allsop's article revealing that three senior Army officers - two of them related - together owned a very large chunk of West Dorset!

On Tuesday 22 May, Allsop called Rodney Legg (who had helped research the article) to explain that he was not responsible for the cuts and to dictate a letter of complaint that Legg was to send to *The Sunday Times*. 'He went on for about an hour and a quarter, spelling out just what he felt about this issue and that,' Legg recalled. 'He was probably ticking off a list as he went, and interspersed superfluous apologies for things that had not been done, or might be taken wrongly.'[3] Allsop then rang Tony Crook, editor of *The Sunday Times*' 'This Britain' column. He established that the cuts were apparently made by

Harry Evans following complaints from his deputy, Frank Giles. Giles was from a military background and was a Governor of Wellington School, which - with its close Army connections - traditionally sent many of its pupils to Sandhurst to be trained as Army officers. He would not have been best pleased. So in a bid to get to the bottom of the 'misunderstanding', Allsop fixed an appointment to see Giles on the afternoon of Thursday, 24 May.

As he jotted down a reminder in his diary, he noticed the entry for the preceding day, Wednesday, when he was due to see the Controller of BBC2, Robin Scott. Two weeks before over lunch, Will Wyatt, the producer of *Edition*, had broken the news to him that Scott wanted a new presenter for the series when it returned in the autumn. This was ostensibly because Allsop was expensive, and his other commitments were preventing him from devoting sufficient time to the series.[4] But Allsop discerned a more sinister motive. A small number of viewers had complained that he had referred in one programme to Greece as 'a military dictatorship', and he believed he was now being charged with 'gratuitous editorialising' - even though his description of the colonels' junta was factually quite correct. Already, there was no love lost between Allsop and Scott. 'One fumes and despairs at being in any way forced to have any dealings with such dangerous fools,' he wrote later. But his wish was now being granted. He had pulled out of *Week by Week*, and now he was being sacked from presenting *Edition*. This really was the end of his connection with the BBC.

That evening, he tried to put the forthcoming confrontations with Giles and Scott to the back of his mind. The following day was Amanda's 25th birthday, but because he needed to be at the BBC, he would be unable to join her and Betty at a celebratory visit to the Chelsea Flower Show. Instead, Betty had prepared a special pre-birthday dinner and drinks for the three of them at the Mill. The weather outside was dull and sultry, but the evening went well, presents were opened and Amanda reciprocated by handing her father a cheque for £100 in repayment of a loan for the repair of her car that she had crashed in Norwich. 'That is a very sweet gesture,' he wrote, adding - curiously - that the money was coming 'out of her inheritance'.

'A Deadline which has Priority'

Outside London's Waterloo Station, the minicab driver looked at his watch for the third time since he'd arrived, and then rifled through his fare book to make sure he hadn't made a mistake. No, Wednesday, 23 May 1973, 3.50 pm. He got out of the car and walked to the public call box across the road. In his office in the BBC's Television Centre, Will Wyatt picked up the phone. 'Sorry to bother you, sir, but has Mr Allsop arrived?'

He had been due at the station over an hour ago, and both Wyatt and the driver agreed that this was completely out of character. 'Can you just hang on for the next train, and I'll make a few calls?' Wyatt asked. He first rang the AA to find out if there had been any major hold-ups or accidents on the A30, just in case Allsop had decided to drive. Everything was normal. Then he made several attempts to ring the Mill, but the phone was always engaged.

Around five o'clock, the *Edition* production team were getting distinctly edgy, especially Wyatt, who knew that Allsop was due to meet Robin Scott in just over half an hour. The phone call from the taxi driver confirming that Allsop had not arrived on the following train was his signal finally to contact the police. After taking down the details, PC David Emmett from the Bridport station agreed to make some investigations. All Wyatt could do was wait.

PC Emmett arrived at the Mill at about a quarter to eight during an unseasonably cloudy, wet evening. The shutters on the downstairs windows were closed, and the curtains drawn in the bedroom above the front door. He tried the front and back doors, but both were locked. It was then that he noticed the dark green E-type parked in the garage.

He found out from a neighbour that the Allsops' home help in Powerstock had a spare key. Two hours later, she unlocked the back door for him and a colleague. Inside, through the gloom they noticed that the front door had been bolted from the inside, and that the telephone was off the hook. They went upstairs towards the main bedroom.

He was in bed in his pyjamas, propped up in a half-sitting, half-lying position against the pillows. His eyes were closed, he was pale and there was no pulse. A clipboard and paper leaned against his raised left leg, a ballpoint pen resting loosely in his right hand. On the bed was an open copy of a book placed face down. It was *The Collected Dorothy Parker,* with two passages underlined: 'There is nothing good in life, Mrs Parker said, that will not be taken away', and 'she could find no other means of dealing with the pain of being'. A small plastic container with just three small capsules left inside was on the bedside cabinet. In a partially-opened drawer below was a bottle labelled 'Sleep', containing 92 capsules, and two more bottles of pills on the bottom shelf.

A pathologist was later to confirm that two varieties of barbiturates had been found in Allsop's body, in quantities which together represented four times the lethal dose. He estimated that when he was found, Allsop had been dead for about eight hours.

Allsop's friend and GP, Michael Hudson, was summoned from his home in Beaminster and arrived at the Mill half an hour later. Shocked and clearly upset, he struggled to remain professional as he examined the body.

Around 11.00 pm a taxi pulled into the lane leading down to the Mill.

Betty and Amanda were startled to see the lights burning from every room in the house…

The inquest was formally opened on Friday, 25 May, and then adjourned until the following Wednesday, 30 May - the day after Allsop's funeral. The presiding Deputy Coroner for West Dorset, Mr Arthur Lyall, invited statements from PC Emmett and Dr Hudson. He then described the paper on the clipboard, which he said contained only 'some observations of birds taken from the room', and also some words which were 'indecipherable'.

Much was made during the proceedings of the remorseless pain Allsop had endured from the stump of his amputated right leg, and his tendency sometimes to exceed the prescribed dose of painkillers if the episode was particularly painful. Dr Hudson said: 'He went to great lengths to conceal his suffering, but I was aware of the effect it produced in him. Over the years he had been treated with a variety of drugs and appliances to overcome his disability, but none had ever been successful. In the last two or three years, Mr Allsop had found that the most effective combination of drugs to control the severest attacks was a mixture of aspirin and barbiturates, but he took these only on a very occasional basis and only when he was in the very worst attacks. On these occasions he would tend to take rather larger than normal doses.' Dr Hudson reported that he had had a phone conversation with Allsop on the evening before he died, in which he had 'casually' remarked that his leg had been very painful for a couple of days.

The Deputy Coroner concluded that there was nothing to indicate how the overdose had come to be taken, and declared an open verdict on the grounds it could have been an accident. The headline in the *Western Gazette* told the story: 'Open verdict on broadcaster who suffered intense pain.'[5]

When he reached his verdict, the Deputy Coroner was unaware of the brown foolscap envelope addressed to Betty that Allsop had left alongside a pile of papers on the chest of drawers in the bedroom. The policemen had apparently not noticed it in their preoccupation with the scene around the bed. When Betty came to open it, the first sentence was enough to tell her what it contained: 'My dear, I am sorry to cause you this last distress…'

Although friends and relatives soon got to know how Allsop had died, it was almost twenty years before it formally became public knowledge, when his daughter Amanda published the suicide note in *Letters from My Father*.[6]

The letter was calm, well-crafted and almost matter-of-fact. Like a draft of one of his *Sunday Times* articles, the 1,300 words were typed and corrected with a felt-tipped pen as though ready for publication. Characteristically punctilious, he had recorded the time in the top right-hand corner at which he had started to write - 8.45 am, soon after Betty and Amanda had left on the coach for London. He therefore had most of the morning to compose the note, although the clear way in which his thoughts were marshalled suggests weeks, or even months, of prior rehearsal. As much as providing an explanation for his action, the intention of the letter was to absolve Betty from any responsibility for what was his own 'internal decision', and to acknowledge the good times that he and Betty had shared.

He begins by explaining that after she and Amanda had left the house, he had sat on the bed for some time 'trying to force myself (literally) to pull myself together and grind into action again, but sat filled with grey frustration at the disappointment of the new limb.' But contrary to the impression given at the inquest, he was not in acute physical pain. Rather, the kidney trouble that had once more flared up in January had returned 'with a dull ache',[7] and there was a lump on his stump, probably caused by the replacement limb he had been sent ten days before. At first this had been far more comfortable than the existing one, and he had even wondered if, after thirty years, he had finally found his 'Cinderella' of legs. But then it began to lose suction and the day before (Tuesday) he had called Roehampton hospital to arrange yet again for another repair.

> And quite suddenly all these lines intersected at what I saw was a terminal point... I feel utterly worn out by the pain and the strain, by the struggle to maintain the outward appearance of capability and normal physical output...

His exhaustion was compounded by despair at man's destruction of the natural world, a feeling made worse, ironically, by the 'red letter day' that he and Betty had enjoyed in Wales only three days before:

> I'm so glad that we had that morning watching the peregrines together: that was one of the happiest times of my life, a fulfilment. Yet I suppose now I can see that there was something of this finality in that: the only peregrines left in Cardiganshire, and their single baby on that high eyrie ledge looking across that wide, bare, beautiful valley and its crashing white ribbons of water down the scree, looking into an emptiness for itself. The tiercel and falcon, when they ringed up into the bright sky and fell in those tumbling dives down the crags, free spirits, were so right, and everything which we represented - our race which poisons them and shoots them and steals their eggs and young - so wrong. We are the predators and killers, not those peregrines, for they and the few of their kind which survive, but

not for much longer, live exalted lives, true to their nature, and we degrade and damage their world which is so beautiful and complex and balanced.

And as if in personal atonement for the folly of the human race, he wishes his body could be laid out on the hillside, 'some last useful thing, by providing a meal for the foxes and buzzards up on the Knoll - such a slight recompense is their due.'

He is glad about a number of things: their children; the love and support Betty has provided; his success at holding off the power saws from Powerstock Forest; 'and to have been able to write a few things which - I don't know - perhaps might help, temporarily at least, to keep the barbarians at bay from the decent and worthwhile things which are so vulnerable.' He allows himself a brief moment of black humour while regretting his 'rottenly unprofessional behaviour' in letting down Will Wyatt by failing to show up for that night's programme. 'But for once, you might say, there's a deadline which has priority.'

There is a third line at the 'intersection' - his failure to fulfil his potential as a writer. He should have devoted 'less effort and time on instant consumption stuff, more on what might have mattered a bit more for a bit longer'. He believes he could have brought 'a small spotlight of illumination on to our period if I could have had time to produce that autobiographical reflection upon the suburban boy growing up on the edge of the countryside'. He wishes he could have had 'a sustained go at the wreckers and spoilers in the Sidgwick book[8] - and on the origins of fascism which despite all those hours at Merton went unfinished'.

In this regard, the Dorothy Parker book does contain an important pointer to Allsop's state of mind, possibly more revealing than the underlined sentences read out by the Coroner. A few pages earlier, on p.vii of Brendan Gill's Introduction, there is a disquisition on the effect on writers, like Dorothy Parker, of falling into obscurity.

> There are writers who die to the world long before they are dead, and if this is sometimes by choice, more often it is a fate imposed on them by others and not easily dealt with. A writer enjoys a vogue, and the vogue having passed, either he consents to endure the obscurity into which he has been thrust or he struggles against it in vain, with a bitterness that tends to increase as his powers diminish. No matter how well or badly he behaves, the result is the same. If the work is of a certain quality, it survives the passing of the vogue, but the maker of the work no longer effectually exists. Even though

he goes on writing, he dwells in the limbo of the half forgotten, and his obituary notices are read with a flippant, unthinking incredulity: who would have guessed that the tattered old teller of tales had had it in him to hang on so fiercely? What on earth had he been waiting for? Hoping for? Dreading?

A protracted life in death is all the more striking in the case of writers who make a reputation in youth and then live on into age…[9]

The very first paragraph of Allsop's letter reflects this theme. He writes: '30 years has been a long time to keep this broken mechanism at full steam - long enough, I am decided. How dismal to putter down to a stop, to disintegrate - especially when you have had such a head start as I.'

One can imagine Allsop reading Brendan Gill's words and recalling the John Llewellyn Rhys Prize for literature that he had won for *Adventure Lit Their Star* at the early age of twenty-nine. He might well have reflected on the winners who followed him and who went on to achieve literary acclaim - Elizabeth Jane Howard, V. S. Naipaul, Margaret Drabble, Melvyn Bragg - success that for one reason or another had eluded him. And at the same time he may have pondered the progressive silencing of his voice on the BBC and at *The Sunday Times*, after years of celebrity, and when there was so much more that needed to be done to stave off ecological disaster. As Allsop teetered on the edge, it was almost as though Gill was telling him: 'Go ahead, jump!'

His letter ends simply. 'I shall have some blue vinney and some onion and a glass of wine. Then I shall get off this bloody leg and lie down.' The last words he wrote on the clipboard as he drifted into unconsciousness were not at all indecipherable, contrary to the Coroner's report. They reaffirmed his lifelong joy at the natural world: 'It's beautiful to hear the birds - mistletoe thrush, wren, and I can see the flycatcher hunting in the deep leaves. How sublime it is…' Then his writing trails off, and the pen slips from the paper.

A few weeks later, as Betty was beginning to recover from her initial numbness and shock, she and Amanda drove over to Lyme Regis for tea with John Fowles and his wife Elizabeth. Betty told them that she had no doubt about the principal reason for her husband's suicide. 'She blamed it all on "the oil" and all the letters he got from people who needed help over similar problems; Ken's feeling of hopelessness and defeat,' Fowles recorded in his journal. 'It seemed clear that it was a case of over-involvement, a kind of fixing of the battlefield against his own chances - as if, because he had "failed" as a novelist and hated his involvement with the BBC, he decided to make total victory his goal in an area where it cannot be got.'[10]

Whatever its prime motivation, was Allsop's suicide a spur-of-the-moment decision, or had it been long planned? Two years before, in March 1971, when he experienced a major relapse of his kidney complaint, he had drafted a handwritten note to himself in the middle of a sleepless night:

> The horrible loneliness of yet again in the silence and emptiness, staring into these dead hours, tired, tired, tired and unable to sleep, because of the endless debate in my mind about the pointlessness (or point?) of prolonging years which increasingly by now seem to me to have been misused or unused, nothing of any real value or originality accomplished to be left behind, and nothing of that kind to come. The pain is back and I wonder if there can be any purpose served in obediently seeing this boring and repellent illness given the slow-motion treatment it's supposed to have…

Years later, in 1980, Jacky Gillot, a BBC television and radio presenter and the wife of John Percival, Allsop's producer on *Down to Earth*, also took her own life, and Betty rang John Fowles to break the news. She began to talk about the parallels with her husband's death. 'She spoke of the cunning of suicides: how Ken had seemed to be through his crisis, how he had embraced her that last morning when she had had to get up early to go to London, how happy their previous evening had been, a birthday dinner somewhere for Mandy, and so on. How she had later realised his recent peace and apparent settling for his fate in life had been because he was decided on death, and was only waiting for the right opportunity…'[11]

When he woke up to that grey, wet Dorset morning Allsop knew that later in the day he would have to face the humiliation of effectively being sacked from the BBC by Robin Scott, and, on the following afternoon, probably by Frank Giles from *The Sunday Times* as well. He was too exhausted to handle yet more confrontations. And it was one of the few occasions when he was left on his own in the house. Although it was certainly unfortunate that it should be Amanda's birthday, this was the moment. In his diary for Wednesday 23 May 1973, he wrote in large, underscored, capital letters: END.

1. 'Fabulous Falcon in Danger Again', *The Sunday Times,* 28 January 1973, p.14
2. Ratcliffe, Derek, *The Peregrine Falcon*, T&AD Poyser, 1980

3. Andresen, M., *Field of Vision: The Broadcast Life of Kenneth Allsop*, Trafford, 2004, p.523
4. Andresen, op. cit., p.518
5. *Western Gazette*, 1 June 1973
6. Allsop, Amanda, *Letters from My Father,* Alan Sutton, 1992, pp.171-74
7. See pp.128-9
8. See pp.114
9. *The Collected Dorothy Parker*, Introduction by Brendan Gill, Duckworth, 1973, p.xx
10. Fowles, John, *The Journals* Charles Drazin (ed.), vol. 2, Vintage Books, 2007, p.126
11. Fowles, John, op. cit., p.246

12

AFTERWARDS

Allsop's simple limestone headstone in the corner of Powerstock churchyard. Betty's ashes were buried with him eight years later. (Courtesy Tristan Allsop)

THE VILLAGE OF POWERSTOCK had never seen anything like it throughout the many centuries of its somnolent obscurity. On the afternoon of Tuesday 29 May 1973, dozens of villagers stood outside their front garden gates in the grey drizzle to witness the arrival of the black Daimler hearse as it negotiated its way slowly past the Humbers, Jaguars and Range Rovers parked awkwardly between the less stately - but more colourful - Ford Escorts, Austin Minis and Hillman Imps belonging to the villagers. At the primary school, the lunch break had been extended to allow children and teachers to peer over the fence, in truth not so much to pay their last respects as to spot the local and national celebrities as they walked up the hill towards the twelfth-century church of St Mary the Virgin. At the lychgate, the recently-appointed Bishop of Salisbury, the Right Reverend George Reindorp, stood awaiting the arrival of the cortege, his white surplice beginning to flap in the gathering westerly breeze. Behind him, the grey mist was at last clearing the slopes of Eggardon Hill a mile away.

Inside, the church was full to capacity. In the front row sat Betty, her pale and dazed face only partly obscured by the black hat and gauze veil she wore. Alongside her were Tristan, Amanda, Fabian and a few close family relatives, while in the pews behind colleagues from Fleet Street, the BBC and the arts whispered quietly to one another. Paul Fox, Aubrey Singer, John Percival and Will Wyatt sat separately, squeezed in beside villagers, local journalists and representatives from the Defenders of West Dorset, the CPRE and the local Naturalists' Trust.

As the coffin was carried up the aisle towards the beautiful Norman chancel arch, many in the congregation must have recalled the last funeral Allsop had attended, less than a year before on Welcome Hill. On that occasion they were mourning the threatened death of Dorset's natural beauty at the hands of the oil men. Some doubtless pondered that while that threat had not yet gone, its principal opponent now assuredly had.

The organist played the last few notes and the subdued hum of conversation faded to silence. Bishop Reindorp began by welcoming the congregation and explaining that he had particularly wished to take the service himself, even though it was only a few months previously that he had first become acquainted with Allsop, when he was interviewed by him for an edition of the BBC's *Conversations* series. He spoke of Allsop's brilliance as a journalist and broadcaster, and his deep, fearless but controversial commitment to the natural world and the Dorset landscape which he loved.

Tributes came from the 78-year-old Henry Williamson, standing tall but frail at the lectern. He related the story of how he had first met Allsop as an unknown, fifteen-year-old boy impassioned by nature writing, who had cycled all the way from London to Devon to meet him. He concluded his tribute by reading some poems by D. H. Lawrence. Then it was the turn of the distinguished classical guitarist, and Allsop's Dorset neighbour, Julian Bream, to continue the tributes musically.

Amanda had been the last of Allsop's children to see him alive, and she appeared to be the most emotionally affected by the funeral. Nevertheless, she summoned the courage to read a poem by Thomas Hardy that was uncannily appropriate. In the poem, 'Afterwards', Hardy wonders if, and in what circumstances, people might remember him after his own death, and perhaps recall his reputation as a nature lover. The second stanza describes the flight of a nightjar on a hill that could well have been Eggardon:

If it be in the dusk when, like an eyelid's soundless blink,
The dewfall hawk comes crossing to alight
Upon the wind-warped upland thorn, a gazer may think,
'To him this must have been a familiar sight'.

The poem then brings to mind Allsop's role as a wildlife campaigner:

If I pass during some nocturnal blackness, mothy and warm,
When the hedgehog travels furtively over the lawn,
One may say, 'He strove that such innocent creatures should come to
    no harm,
But he could do little for them; and now he is gone'.

Amanda then read the final stanza, as the funeral bell slowly tolled out from St Mary's tower across the village below:

And will any say when my bell of quittance is heard in the gloom,
And a crossing breeze cuts a pause in its outrollings,
Till they rise again, as they were a new bell's boom,
'He hears it not now, but used to notice such things'?

Afterwards, the Bishop of Salisbury led the silent congregation out into the rain across the wet grass towards the open grave in the north-east corner of churchyard. Allsop's final resting place was just over a mile in each direction from the two places he loved most in the world: his home at the Mill to the west, and the airy promontory of Eggardon to the south-east, where with his friend Brian Jackman he had looked down on the kestrels, hobbies and harriers gliding on the thermals below. Brian was there among the many friends and strangers as the coffin was gently lowered into the grave. Later, he noted that they 'stood with heads bowed in homage to the gifted, kind and tortured spirit who had burst into our lives like a comet and lit up the sky before he fell to earth'[1]

On television the day after Allsop's death, *Nationwide* presenter Michael Barratt used the closing minutes of the programme to pay tribute to his former colleague. He told millions of viewers that 'as a human being and as a professional commentator, he was a man anyone would boast about knowing and working with… We all miss him and his example terribly.'

For many, in the days that followed, it was difficult to believe he had gone. On 10 June, twelve days after he had been buried, Allsop's last column on 'The threatened eggs of Wales' appeared in *The Sunday Times*, completed by Brian Jackman using the meticulous notes scribbled during the recent Welsh birdwatching weekend.[2] A radio appeal that Allsop had recorded on behalf of the 18,000 members of BLESMA - the British Limbless Ex-Service Men's Association - was also broadcast posthumously on Radio 4 on *The Week's Good Cause*. This was introduced on Allsop's behalf by the actor Kenneth More, who had played the injured flying ace Group Captain Douglas Bader in the film *Reach for the Sky*.

Hundreds of letters to Betty from Allsop's friends and colleagues expressing condolence and grief arrived at the Mill, and hundreds more poured into the BBC from ordinary viewers who felt they had lost a friend. One example, from Mrs Phyllis Greenaway of Selsey, summed up the feelings of millions of others:

'I have never before wept for someone I have not met, though it is true that your husband could not have seemed like a stranger. He was our favourite man, with all that he strove for and all he achieved in a comparatively short space of time - which will last forever, and confound the enemies of goodness.'

In Memoriam

Not long after the funeral, a modest white limestone headstone was placed above the turf-covered grave. It bore the simple, carved inscription: 'Kenneth Allsop 1920-1973 FIDE ET AMORE' ('By faith and love'). A young medlar tree, which Allsop had ordered for his garden only the day before he died, was planted behind the headstone, promising small white flowers in the spring, and shade from its spreading dark green leaves in the summer. This was appropriately bucolic for its surroundings, but to his close friends and colleagues it seemed hardly a sufficient memorial to a pioneer environmentalist who had left such a legacy of inspiration to others. Something more significant and publicly visible was called for.

So during the summer of 1973, an informal committee of family and friends was formed to look at the options. In addition to Betty and Amanda, it included Brian Jackman, Rodney Legg, John and Elizabeth Fowles, Richard Mabey, BBC producer John Percival and Dr Michael Hudson. The first and most obvious choice they considered was the purchase of the windswept hill top on Eggardon, an option which appealed particularly to Betty, Amanda and Brian Jackman, who on so many occasions had accompanied Allsop on his birdwatching expeditions to the summit. But support in the committee was by no means unanimous. Eggardon was not under immediate threat, and anyway the National Trust had expressed some interest. Moreover, John Fowles in particular felt that securing and preserving it 'lacked the kind of challenge he was always so ready to meet himself'.[3] In addition it was expensive: for half of the hilltop site, the owner was asking £42,000 - the price of prime agricultural land rather than wind-blasted rough grazing.

It was clear that whatever site was eventually chosen, a large sum of money would be needed, together with a public appeal to secure it. It was at this point that Graham Searle, the Executive Director of Friends of the Earth with whom Allsop had collaborated closely over their respective campaigns on oil and mining, stepped forward to offer administrative support. Searle was shortly to leave FoE temporarily for New Zealand, and was succeeded as Director by Richard Sandbrook, who soon after joined the informal memorial committee and became its secretary. This was the first open acknowledgement of how close Allsop's relationship with FoE had become during the last eighteen months of his life.

Out of the blue, in mid-September 1973, Betty received a letter from the agent of Baroness Wharton, a large landowner whose holdings included the island of Steep Holm, fifty miles north-east of the Mill, in the middle of the Bristol Channel. The island was - and still is - a large hump of Mendip limestone covering fifty acres and rising abruptly 250 feet from the sea. It was a wild, uninhabited place of high cliffs, dense undergrowth and panoramic views towards the Brecon Beacons to the north, the rolling hills and moorland of Exmoor to the south, and the Somerset coast to the east. It had been used by the military since Victorian times as a defensive redoubt, and batteries of nineteenth-century brass cannon still stood on the cliffs, subsequently scarred with the buildings and abandoned hardware from two world wars. But it was its wildlife that made Steep Holm so important. It was home to the largest herring gull breeding roost in England, and its prominent position provided a vital link in bird migration routes to and from Britain. Its unusual - almost Mediterranean - flora included the beautiful Wild Peony, a species found nowhere else in Britain. For all these reasons, it had been officially declared a Site of Special Scientific Interest by the Nature Conservancy.

'The Baroness wishes to sell the island,' the agent wrote, 'she thinks, to someone, or some group... who would perpetuate its present use as a bird sanctuary and as an unspoilt site for botanical research... It occurred to me that, though not in Dorset, it might well be an appropriate memorial to your husband in view of its ornithological interest.'

It was certainly a more prominent and impressive block of limestone than the small headstone in the corner of Powerstock churchyard.

Betty's report on this development was met with mixed feelings in the committee. Although Lady Wharton was prepared to sell the island for £25,000, Brian Jackman especially wanted to hold out for Eggardon. As far as he knew, Allsop had never even seen Steep Holm, let alone visited it, and it was certainly outside the English countryside that he had loved and campaigned for. Moreover, landing on the island against the racing tides of the Bristol Channel was difficult, and in practice this would limit access to a small elite band of dedicated naturalists. John Percival was also sceptical, arguing that the island's flora was similar to 'the average British bomb-site, with elder, privet and brambles'. In addition, he considered that the extreme number of gulls would always make the island unattractive to other rock-nesting birds.

John Fowles, however, was enthusiastically in favour. 'For all its inscrutables, such a project seems to me in a way much closer to what Ken stood for than the buying of some piece of already reasonably "safe" ground (such as Eggardon Hill) because of personal association. To me that would seem a little like a green gravestone.'[4] Later, in a draft memo to Betty, he set out his vision for the island:

- Establish a Field Study Centre in the Victorian barracks for serious students and naturalists, with, eventually, guided nature trails for school parties and limited numbers of other day-visitors;
- Install a permanent warden to manage the Centre and keep ornithological records;
- Enhance the island's attractiveness as a bird reserve and migration staging-post by improving the water supply, nesting sites and food sources;
- Clear away as much as possible of the military litter left behind after the last war.

'To sum up,' he wrote, 'we want to save and rehabilitate Steep Holm for the benefit of nature and naturalists everywhere; and we feel certain that Kenneth himself would want it to be saved by a communal effort.'

But that was the key question: what *would* Allsop have wanted? He had told Brian Jackman that the only memorial he needed was a pile of his bleached bones picked clean by the hawks and foxes on some windswept Dorset hillside. If there had to be a public appeal, he would probably have wanted the money to go to Friends of the Earth for one of its more urgent conservation campaigns. And that was certainly the view of several FoE staff members who argued that if a site were to be purchased, it should be one which was more immediately threatened, and biodiversity-rich, than Steep Holm.

On Monday 12 November 1973, Amanda, Rodney Legg, Brian Jackman, Richard Mabey and John Percival gathered at FoE's Poland Street headquarters in London's Soho to make the final decision. Betty was unable to attend, but by now she had been persuaded by Fowles' enthusiasm - and she at least had *seen* Steep Holm, on a holiday visit to Penarth on the Welsh side of the Bristol Channel. With FoE's new Director Richard Sandbrook acting as an independent secretary, the discussion ebbed and flowed like a Severn tide, but eventually, Jackman's was the only remaining dissenting voice. So Steep Holm it was.

At this time, Sandbrook was attempting to steer FoE through its own financial crisis, and he and the Chairman, Charles Levison, were understandably concerned at the short- and long-term financial implications of their involvement in the purchase of the island. Would Friends of the Earth (or its research arm Earth Resources Research that was then being set up) last long enough to own and manage Steep Holm in perpetuity? Their solution was to hand over fundraising and the eventual ownership of the island to a separate charity and company limited by guarantee: The Kenneth Allsop Memorial Trust. In the spring of 1974, Betty, Amanda and Fabian Allsop, John and Elizabeth Fowles, Rodney Legg, John Percival, Richard Mabey, and Charles Levison and Peter Rees from FoE became its first Trustees.

Betty became the principal fundraiser, even managing to extract a modest donation from some Rio Tinto Zinc executives. Andrew Lloyd-Webber pledged half his share of the proceeds from the charity preview of the film of *Jesus Christ Superstar*. John and Elizabeth Fowles generously donated £1,500. Friends of the Earth continued to subsidise the Trust with various office, postage and printing costs, including sending out 6,000 leaflets with pre-paid envelopes to potential donors.

On the other hand, neither the Nature Conservancy, the World Wildlife Fund, nor the new Avon County Council within whose boundaries Steep Holm lay, were prepared to make a donation. Even the BBC refused to give the Trust a slot on *The Week's Good Cause* - on the grounds that this would only lead to appeals for 'every old church in the land'. The memory of Allsop's confrontations with these and other organisations had not died with him - and the link with Friends of the Earth doubtless also alienated a number of potential donors.

The most generous donation came from Baroness Wharton's daughter, 'Ziki' Robertson. Baroness Wharton died in the spring of 1974 before the sale of Steep

Holm to the Trust had been completed. Her title and estates passed to her eldest daughter, Myrtle Olive Felix Robertson ('Ziki'), an actress, photographer and animal lover who was to become Vice President of the RSPCA. She was aware of the Trust's struggle to raise the £25,000 asking price, and of its outstanding debts to Friends of the Earth, and so agreed new terms including a substantial reduction in the selling price to £10,000. This was agreed on 8 April 1975 - five years almost to the day since the Allsops had first moved to Dorset. The formal completion of the sale took place on 25 March 1976, with the exchange of documents in John Fowles' house in Lyme Regis.

Rodney Legg recalled Mrs Robertson asking whether the Trust proposed to rename Steep Holm 'Allsop Island'. 'I hesitated and said no, adding that Steep Holm had been its identity for centuries,' he wrote later. 'That was, in retrospect, a mistake. Though it would always have caused a tussle for ascendancy between the two names, this would have acted as a reminder of the person who had indirectly made our work possible, and whose ideas we were committed to promoting.'[5] As it subsequently turned out, such a public reminder would indeed have been useful (see p.173).

Later in 1976, a commemorative plaque of heavy, black Welsh slate carved by a Bridport mason was fixed to the rocky cliff, looking east towards Allsop's Dorset home. It reads:

> This island of Steep Holm was bought by public subscription in the year 1976 to preserve the memory of the writer and naturalist Kenneth Allsop, 1920-1973.

Above the inscription is carved the image of a peregrine in flight - Allsop's favourite bird. Peregrines had bred regularly on the island until the arrival of the Army garrison during the Second World War drove them away. Pesticides then did the rest.

But on 27 September 1974 a pair of peregrines returned to Steep Holm, as if in celebration of its future new owners. They had not been seen on the island for almost twenty years.

1. Allsop, K., *In the Country*, Introduction by Brian Jackman, Little Toller Books, 2011, p.11
2. 'The threatened eggs of Wales', *The Sunday Times*, 10 June 1973, p.11
3. Fowles, John, 'The Man and the Island', in *Steep Holm: A Case History in the Study of Evolution*, Kenneth Allsop Memorial Trust

and John Fowles, Dorset Publishing Company, 1978, p.16

4. Legg, Rodney, *Steep Holm: Allsop Island,* Wincanton Press, 1992, p 18

5. Legg, Rodney, ibid., p.33

EPILOGUE

The island of Steep Holm in the Bristol Channel, purchased in 1976 as a nature reserve and living memorial to Kenneth Allsop. (©Rob Newman)

THE FAMILIAR FACE DISAPPEARED from the nation's TV screens. Gone from the pages of the national and local press were the regular by-lines, pictures and letters. The throaty growl of the E-Type was finally stilled and peace returned to the lanes of West Dorset. The Mill was put on the market after a few months, and Betty - unable on her own to keep up the mortgage - moved to a smaller house in Powerstock. The Defenders of West Dorset lost their sense of direction without their charismatic President, and eventually disbanded. Quite a few of the local residents seemed pleased that life could now revert to how it was three years before, when Allsop had first arrived on the scene. The waters seemed to be closing over.

So was Allsop an important figure? What, if anything, was his permanent contribution to saving Britain's threatened environment?

In March 1972, at the height of the campaign against Berkley Petroleums, the classically-schooled television presenter Peter Snow wrote to Allsop: 'I'll remember you on your balcony, a reincarnation of some Roman chronicler waiting for the Saxons to desecrate, reminiscent of Cavafy's poem '*On Waiting for the Barbarians*'.[1] Allsop had borrowed the metaphor in his last letter to Betty.

There were certainly some concrete achievements. On Powerstock Common, Allsop's interventions saved most of the ancient oak woodland from the chainsaws of the Forestry Commission - with the help of Brian Jackman and Rodney Legg, if not of the official and voluntary nature conservation 'guardians'.

He had also scented victory in the battle to save the face of Britain's second largest Area of Outstanding Natural Beauty from being pock-marked by oil rigs, gas pipelines and storage tanks. It was certainly a major achievement to set up a new local pressure group, the Defenders of West Dorset, and to orchestrate an effective local and national press campaign highlighting the vulnerability of a supposedly nationally-protected area. The campaign undoubtedly contributed to the pressures on Berkley Petroleums to withdraw. But probably more significant were the company's own geological surveys showing that the pay-off for drilling in the area would not be worth it, given the available technology (which, however, would inevitably advance in the future). In the meantime, there were new sites for the company to explore just across the county boundary in Somerset.

Allsop was a pessimistic environmentalist: he realised that the 'barbarians' could not be kept in check indefinitely. Even if the Defenders were right in claiming that the first skirmish with the oilmen had been won, the war was set to continue long into the future. Today, forty years on, the demand for new resources, energy and space has accelerated alongside the UK's population, which has grown by almost eight million compared with 1970 - almost the size of a new Greater London. Dorset is again under threat, this time from the exploitation of shale gas through 'fracking', that is, the fracturing of underground rock strata by injecting high pressure water and chemicals to release the gas. The process has already triggered a minor earthquake near Blackpool and could lead to the contamination of groundwater, as well as a rash of ugly surface infrastructure.

Meanwhile, Dorset's Jurassic coastline faces disfigurement by the Navitus Bay 'windpark' eight miles offshore. Over three hundred wind turbines covering 76 square miles of the English Channel will be fully visible from the cliffs above Swanage. And further afield, a hundred miles to the north-east, the proposed high-speed rail from London to the North (HS2) is set to scythe through Britain's largest Area of Outstanding Natural Beauty, the Chiltern Hills, in order to shave a few minutes off the journey time for busy executives.

Examples like these now seem to vindicate Allsop's pessimistic view that 'money talks; beauty is voiceless'. But there has been one shaft of optimism - that is, the greatly increased level of awareness and engagement by the public in today's environmental conflicts. For example, membership of the Royal Society for the Protection of Birds (RSPB) has increased almost tenfold since the early 1970s to around one million, while the National Trust has grown by a factor of twelve, to just under four million. In April 2011 the thirteen national and local environmental groups which signed up to the 'Right Lines' Charter together represent several million people determined to protect the Chilterns and oppose the government's approach to HS2.

And although Allsop could not foresee this, Britain has been obliged to introduce tougher environmental legislation as a consequence of joining the European Community in January 1973. Higher air and water quality standards; measures to protect wildlife (in the form of the Habitats and Birds Directives); and requirements for developers to assess and make public the likely impacts on the environment of their plans and projects together represent one form of 'interference' from Brussels that has had the beneficial effect of strengthening the hand of green campaigners against governments which fail to fulfil the legal obligations they have signed up to.

But this was not the picture Allsop saw in 1970 when he moved to Dorset. Britain had 'never had it so good,' Conservative Prime Minister Harold Macmillan had told the voters a decade earlier. But the post-war economic growth that boosted living standards also produced unprecedented environmental degradation in the form of pollution to air and water, declines in biodiversity and threats to historic landscapes. And while the challenges were huge, there was nothing like the range of environmental government departments, agencies and pressure groups we have today. The establishment of a dedicated Department of the Environment was still several months away. Britain's land-use planning system was only just over twenty years old, with council planning committees still dominated by the local squirearchy and retired service officers. There were few constraints on what landowners and farmers could do with their land, and whether or not environmental regulations were effectively enforced was often left to the discretion of government and council officials. Above all, especially in the countryside, there was a pervading culture of deference which meant that most decisions of the local Establishment went unchallenged.

'I've always thought of ex-Colonels etc as being strongly on the preservationist side,' wrote the writer, broadcaster and environmentalist Elspeth Huxley to Allsop in June 1972. 'The Wilts Trust for instance is full of ex-Majors chasing butterflies on bicycles. Now here they are, going on about Soviet submarines and oil rigs in Dorset, on the side of all the robber barons of Houston and RTZ. One feels almost the last bastion has fallen.'[2]

But despite the odds stacked against him, he could not simply give in. 'How can you sit back and let the bastards run things without interference?' he asked. In complete contrast to the ex-Colonels, Allsop was an outsider infused with the irreverent, post-imperialist culture of the 1960s - the spirit of *That Was the Week That Was*, of *Private Eye* and the fearless investigative journalism of *The Sunday Times'* Insight Team. His only weapons were the burgeoning power of the media, his national popularity and the access to people in high places that came with his status as one of Britain's first TV 'celebrities'.

Allsop happened to be the right man, in the right place, at the right time. But it was lonely and exposed out there in the amphitheatre, surrounded by lions. He was accused by some local farmers of adopting his corner of Dorset just so he could write about it and make money from it, regardless of the feelings of his neighbours. Others simply resented the meddling of a townie incomer in their local affairs, which they considered it was their birthright to control. Trade unionists continued to accuse him of jeopardising the creation of local jobs, even though the President of Berkley Petroleums himself had predicted there would be only fifteen of them. 'Everyone in Dorset now hates me,' Allsop told John Fowles, in distress and sorrow rather than pride.[3] Meanwhile, nationally, he made enemies in government departments and big corporations, who in turn put pressure on his employers at the BBC and *The Sunday Times*. Battling for the environment came at considerable personal cost, magnified in his case by poor physical health and regular bouts of deep depression.

Allsop's main contribution to Britain's fledgling environment movement was not so much what he achieved on the ground in Dorset, but rather the steady shift in public attitudes to the protection of wildlife and the countryside that he helped start through his campaigning national journalism. His fortnightly column in *The Sunday Times* educated a weekend readership of millions - far more than the combined membership at that time of all Britain's environmental pressure groups - with details of how illegal snares and hawk nets were still on sale to farmers and gamekeepers; or how the Shell oil company was seeking to stave off extended bans on the use of its pesticide products, deadly to birds of prey. He revealed how the government's Department of Trade was selling off licences to explore for oil and gas in every part of the country, regardless of the environmental consequences of possible future exploitation - and that even Buckingham Palace was not safe. And he showed how the 'paper garlands' bestowed by the Department of the Environment and its agencies - designations as National Parks, Areas of Outstanding Natural Beauty, Sites of Special Scientific Interest, or Heritage Coasts - were no protection against the Ministry of Agriculture's forty per cent subsidies to farmers for ripping out hedgerows, nor the cratering of the Dorset downs and heathlands by the Ministry of Defence.

Several of Allsop's articles warned of the imminent extinction of the peregrine. This was his favourite bird, and his bookplate, a woodcut of a peregrine hovering over its prey and clutching a quill pen, suggests why. In May 1973, when Allsop spent an idyllic birdwatching weekend in mid-Wales, there were only six pairs of peregrines successfully breeding across the whole of Wales, and they had all but disappeared in southern England. Now, forty years later, peregrines are thriving in Britain as never before, with 1,500 breeding pairs. Allsop exposed the devastating impact of poisoning, persecution and nest robbing by - or on behalf of - egg collectors and falconers. It helped rally public opinion, boosting the membership of the RSPB and indirectly contributing to this remarkable turnaround. No longer is it necessary for metropolitan birdwatchers to drive the 250 miles to Powys, for the peregrines themselves have come to town. Twenty-four pairs now nest in London, and every summer hundreds of tourists visit the RSPB's stand on the South Bank to watch a pair circling and tumbling from their roost high up on Tate Modern.

Once again, however, success in this particular battle did not win the war, for birds of prey continue to be illegally shot and deliberately poisoned or trapped, particularly by gamekeepers on northern shooting estates.[4] While peregrines are thriving, and in southern England red kites are a common sight, there is now only one pair of breeding hen harriers left in England.

As well as contributing to the public's understanding of what was happening to the world around them, Allsop also taught them an important political lesson. Time and again he hammered home this message: that those who had been given formal stewardship on the public's behalf for Britain's landscapes and wildlife could not be trusted to do the job - either through their incompetence, lack of resources, complacency or corruption. '*Quis custodiet ipsos custodes*' (Who will guard the guards themselves?) he asked of government departments like the Department of the Environment, agencies like the Nature Conservancy, and non-governmental organisations like the CPRE and National Trust. It was, he warned, ultimately our responsibility to do something about it. So when Dorset county councillors granted planning permission for exploratory drilling for oil and gas in the AONB which they themselves had created, he urged all local voters to take a careful note of their names and summarily eject them at the next available election.

More subtly, as a country and nature writer, Allsop's work helped change the way people perceived and valued the countryside. Week by week his *Daily Mail* column instilled delight in the small-scale, through drawing attention to the often unnoticed, local particularities of his corner of Dorset - an example of what the poet Gerard Manley Hopkins had earlier described as the 'Sweet especial rural scene'.

Allsop wrote in one of his 'In the Country' pieces that 'to earn the right to love a place you have to learn about it bit by bit', as he had done in relation to his 'Dear Wessex'. He described a routine walk along the by-ways of his parish:

> What did I see as the light dulled and I made my way back to more beaten tracks? Nothing remarkable, just immense space and quietness. Gorse spitting yellow sparks. Rooks blowing like charred scraps across great fields. The sun threw up thin white arms as it drowned in cloud. Bullfinches shot ahead down the hedge. A pheasant crossed the road, neck thrust forward from white collar like an overworked curate on his rounds.
>
> The light had become peculiar, mysterious. The land form dissolved and solidified again in a ruddy haze, and wind-crippled thorns with knobbly joints seemed to move like Ents, Tolkien's tree spirits, through the opalescent mist. And when, as I descended the ridge, I came upon a human being, an old man in a brown overcoat, shuffling up a woody lane, at first I thought, in a pulse of fright, that he was a wayside oak - advancing on roots!
>
> I was feeling vaguely uneasy on the exposed heights, in such solitude, with darkness lapping against the Iron Age camps and the beacon peak... I hurried back to the clattering warmth of the house, where dinner was cooking and the windows shone.
>
> Absolutely nothing had happened.[5]

And yet, that evening, so much had happened to the landscape, wildlife, weather and light - and it had had a profound impact on *him*.

Later British nature writers were to take over the baton and continue to explore the value and meaning of local distinctiveness - that a place need not be conventionally picturesque, rare or spectacular to be special. It was a message that reinforced Allsop's environmentalism. Local landscapes were important to ordinary people, and no-one - neither landowners, farmers, corporations, politicians nor bureaucrats - should presume they had an incontestable right to take them away.

Allsop is well remembered by the generation old enough to have seen him on their black and white television screens. But he is not universally remembered as an environmentalist nor as a nature writer, despite his pioneering contributions in these fields. In this respect he was not a Peter Scott or a David Attenborough, with whom the words 'birds' and 'wildlife' are instantly associated. One of the reasons for this was Allsop's amazing versatility - as a jazz critic, book reviewer, newspaper columnist, novelist, expert on the history and society of the United States, TV reporter and anchorman, University Rector, naturalist and environmental campaigner. By the time of his death, he had not succeeded in defining a clear trajectory for his life, so that his considerable achievements in each of his activities tended to distract attention from his attainments elsewhere.

There is another reason. With hindsight, the choice of Steep Holm as a memorial has not proved the most effective means of keeping alive Allsop's memory. As Brian Jackman and others had warned, the island is remote and difficult of access, so that no more than about a thousand visitors a year can read the carved slate plaque set in the rock face above the landing stage declaring that the island was bought 'to preserve the memory of the writer and naturalist Kenneth Allsop...' Moreover, in drawing up their original mission statement, the owners of the island, The Kenneth Allsop Memorial Trust, somehow lost sight of the commitment that had been made in a 1974 fundraising leaflet issued by FoE's charitable arm, Earth Resources Research. This had declared: 'Steep Holm will be more than a nature reserve. It will be a living memorial to a remarkable man. If you share Kenneth Allsop's and our belief that conservation is not a luxury but an essential adjunct to a civilised society, will you help us build it?' The exclusive purpose of the Trust as set out in its articles is to manage Steep Holm as a nature reserve and bird sanctuary 'and to advance the education of the public in the natural sciences'. This is without doubt a difficult and costly task which the Trustees and volunteers have discharged with energy and dedication—but it has left little scope and few resources to raise the public's awareness of the wider causes that Allsop fought for.

But now, after forty years, the island at last seems set to play a key role in reviving Allsop's reputation as a pioneer conservationist. In 2012 the construction of an eleven-mile barrage across the Severn Estuary from Lavernock Point in South Wales to Brean in Somerset came several steps closer with the submission of formal proposals to the government by a private limited company, Hafren Power. According to the developers, the £25 billion tidal power project could eventually produce enough cheap, green energy to provide five per cent of Britain's electricity needs - the output of four nuclear power stations - while saving over seven million tonnes annually of carbon emissions. At the same time, it holds out the promise of regenerating the economies of South Wales and south-west England by creating 20,000 new construction jobs and an additional 30,000 jobs in associated businesses.

But the predicted damage to the wildlife and ecosystem of the Severn Estuary would be immense - bigger than the impact of any previous development project in the UK. Reductions in inter-tidal habitats could reduce by around fifty per cent the populations of widgeon, teal, pintail, shoveler, knot, dunlin, ruff, curlew and redshank, on both sides of the estuary. Adverse impacts are expected on 25 Special Areas of Conservation, 231 Sites of Special Scientific Interest, 5 Ramsar Sites, 22 National Nature Reserves and 44 local nature reserves - while a further 302 rare plant species and 20 mammals are also likely to be affected. Moreover, adjacent landscapes could be devastated by the huge scale of quarrying to provide the millions of tons of rock and aggregate necessary to construct the barrage, as well as by the interlacing network of pylons and power lines required to feed the electricity into the national grid.

Although Britain's environmental NGOs support (most forms) of renewable energy, most of them, including the National Trust, the RSPB, Friends of the Earth and the Wildfowl and Wetlands Trust, have formally opposed the construction of a Severn Barrage along the lines proposed by Hafren Power. They argue that the potential of the Severn Estuary to produce green energy can and should be exploited, but smaller-scale technologies would minimise the huge damage to wildlife and habitats the construction and use of a solid barrage would inflict.

The role of renewable energy sources in tackling climate change poses acute dilemmas for conservationists that had not yet emerged in the early 1970s. However, it is fairly certain that despite the promise of long-term, cheap green energy, Allsop would have campaigned against the barrage. One can imagine him addressing a crowd of wind-blown protesters on Brean Down, hammering home the message that an eleven-mile concrete dam and its associated developments would not only destroy the estuary's wildlife but also a unique land- and seascape. He would have homed in on the diversion of huge sums of money that could be far better employed in cutting the demand for energy through mass programmes of home insulation, or a major boost to communications technology to cut out senseless daily commuting.

As regards Steep Holm itself, the impact of a Lavernock-Brean barrage would be profound - and very possibly terminal. In 1981 a government-appointed Severn Barrage Committee chaired by Sir Hermann Bondi, the Chairman and Chief Executive of the Natural Environment Research Council, proposed that the dam should physically incorporate most of Steep Holm, while using what remained of it as a quarry.[6] Eight years later, new plans from the Severn Tidal Power Group of major engineering companies placed the island just outside the barrage, by a few hundred metres.[7] The latest proposal by Hafren Power is imprecise as to the exact location of the dam, but its illustrative map shows the island inside the dam, about 2.5 kilometres from it.[8]

Even if Steep Holm were not to disappear entirely, its close proximity to the dam would almost certainly destroy its potential as a nature reserve. Disturbance during construction, followed by the continuous noise of road and/or rail traffic along the top of the barrage, combined with alterations in tidal flows and changes to the island's microclimate, would all have a profound impact on its biodiversity.

So the island of Steep Holm, still with its Victorian cannons, seems set to be at the centre of a future Severn 'barrage' (the word is used here in both its senses). It is fitting that after forty years, Kenneth Allsop will once again be in the vanguard - at least in spirit - of Britain's biggest battle for the environment so far this century.

1. Letter to Allsop from Peter Snow, 2 March 1972 (Constantine Cavafy, 1863-1933, was a Greek poet who lived in Alexandria, Egypt)

2. Letter to Allsop from Elspeth Huxley, 9 June 1972

3. Fowles, John, *The Journals* Charles Drazin (ed.), vol. 2, Vintage Books, 2007, p.90

4. 'Hawks in danger of extinction in illegal hunting campaign', *The Observer*, 6 January 2013, p.10

5. Allsop, K., *In the Country*, Hamish Hamilton, 1972, pp.144-45

6. *Tidal Power from the Severn Estuary*, Vol. 1, Energy paper 46, HMSO, 1981

7. *The Severn Barrage Project: General Report*. Energy Paper 57, HMSO, 1989

8. www.data.parliament.uk/writtenevidence/WrittenEvidence.svc/EvidencePdf/110

BIBLIOGRAPHY

Books by Kenneth Allsop

Adventure Lit Their Star, Latimer House, 1949
The Sun Himself Must Die, Latimer House, 1949
Pobbles Are Happier, 1949 (Privately Printed 2010)
Silver Flame, Percival Marshall, 1951
The Daybreak Edition, Percival Marshall, 1951
The Leopard Paw Orchid, Quality Press, 1954
Last Voyages of the Mayflower: A Story of the Pilgrims' Ship, John C. Winston Co., 1955 (USA only)
The Angry Decade, Peter Owen, 1958
Rare Bird, Jarrolds, 1958
The Bootlegger: The Story of Chicago's Prohibition Era, Hutchinson, 1961
Scan, Hodder & Stoughton, 1965
Hard Travellin': The Hobo and his History, Hodder & Stoughton, 1967
Fit to Live In? The Future of Britain's Countryside, Penguin Education, 1970
Harriet Beecher Stowe, Heron Books, 1971
In The Country, Hamish Hamilton, 1972
Letters to His Daughter (ed. Amanda Allsop), Hamish Hamilton, 1974
One and All: Two Years in the Chilterns, Alan Sutton Publishing, 1991
In the Country (Introduction by Brian Jackman), Little Toller Books, 2011

Books about Kenneth Allsop

Andresen, Mark, *Field of Vision: The Broadcast Life of Kenneth Allsop*, Trafford, 2004
Letters from My Father (ed. Amanda Allsop), Alan Sutton Publishing, 1992

Steep Holm

Kenneth Allsop Memorial Trust: www.steepholm.org.uk
Kenneth Allsop Memorial Trust and John Fowles, *Steep Holm: A Case History in the Study of Evolution,* Dorset Publishing Company, 1978
Legg, Rodney, *Steep Holm: Allsop Island*, Wincanton Press 1992

The Political Context

Johnson, Stanley, *The Politics of Environment: The British Experience,* Tom Stacey Ltd., 1973

MacEwen, Ann & MacEwen, Malcolm, *Greenprints for the Countryside: The Story of Britain's National Parks,* Allen & Unwin, 1987

McCormick, John, *The Global Environmental Movement: Reclaiming Paradise,* Belhaven Press, 1989

Moore, Norman, *The Bird of Time: The Science and Politics of Nature Conservation – A Personal Account,* Cambridge University Press, 1987

Nicholson, Max, *The New Environmental Age,* Cambridge University Press, 1987

Report of the Mining, Minerals and Sustainable Development Project, *Breaking New Ground,* Earthscan, 2002

Smith, Peter J., *The Politics of Physical Resources,* Penguin Education and Open University, 1975

INDEX

Abel, K. A. 72, 78, 89
Alkali Inspectorate 103
Allsop, Amanda 12, 150, 152, 159, 160
Allsop, Betty 5, 14, 32, 58, 71, 150, 155
Allsop, Kenneth
  appearance 2, 8
  artificial leg 2, 13, 71
  books 9,12, 99, 113, 114
  cars 8, 129
  early life 10-11
  environmentalism 27, 29, 168-69
  Fellow of Merton College, Oxford 12, 19,
    109, 113
  finances 23, 137
  houses 18-22
  depression 14, 71, 128, 131, 153
  relations with Friends of the Earth 81, 113
  journalism 9, 11, 26
  leaves *24 Hours* 98, 105, 108
  London 'scene' 26-27
  NIMBY-ism 73
  political views 11
  Rector, University of Edinburgh 5, 12, 26
  women 15
  kidney complaint 129
  suicide letter 152-54
  inquest 151-52
  funeral 159-61
Allsop, Fabian 12, 32, 159
Allsop, Tristan 5, 12, 159
Areas of Outstanding Natural Beauty (AONB)
  22, 31, 67, 74, 76, 85, 87, 168
Arnold, Edwin 93
Ashby, Sir Eric 30
Aspinall, John 12
Attenborough, David 98, 114, 115, 116

BBC
  BBC Enterprises 94, 125
  'grey men' 116
  Natural History Unit 23, 98, 113-19
  24 Hours 14, 23, 98, 99, 107, 115
  A Question of Ulster 105
  Conversations 4, 159
  Desert Island Discs 119
  Do You Dig National Parks? 93
  Doomwatch 98
  Down to Earth 24, 98-109
  Edition 129, 150, 151
  Living in the Past 109
  My Kind of Music 119

Nationwide 161
Save Our Suffolk 115
That Was the Week That Was 55, 102, 118,
  170
Week by Week 129, 130
The Wildlife of New York City 115-19
Zoo Quest 114
Ballantine Books 81
Barnes, Mike 127, 128
Barr, John 27, 81
Barratt, Michael 161
Barwythe Hall 17-18
Berkley Petroleums (UK) Ltd 33, 58
  planning application 72, 89-90
  'abandons' exploration in West Dorset 90
  returns 124, 131
birds
  at Milton Mill 26
  buzzard 144, 145
  chough 143
  golden eagle 141
  hen harrier 171
  hobby 37, 160
  kestrel 146, 160
  little ringed plover 10
  Montagu's harrier 37, 160
  peregrine 139, 141, 145, 165, 171
  red kite 142, 145, 171
  impact of Severn Barrage on 174
  nest robbers 142-144
  pesticides 141
Bondi, Sir Hermann 175
Brasher, Chris 99, 103
Brierley, Betty 62
Briggs, Prof. Asa 4
British Herpetological Society 52
Brittenden, Arthur 23
Brock, Richard 141
Brower, David 80, 92
Brotherton, Helen 46, 52
Brown, Gordon 12
Bugler, Jeremy 102
Byers, Lord 94

Carleton Greene, Sir Hugh 105, 108
Carr, Robert 133
Central Electricity Generating Board (CEGB)
  103, 122
Centre for Alternative Technology 140
Chadd, Paul, QC 82-84, 86-87
Christ Church Meadow, Oxford 19

178